INTRA! INTR
Towards an
INTRA SPACE

Publication Series of the Academy of Fine Arts Vienna
Volume 25

INTRA! INTRA!
Towards an
INTRA SPACE

Christina Jauernik
Wolfgang Tschapeller
(Eds.)

Sternberg Press

On the Publication Series

We are pleased to present the latest volume in the Academy of Fine Arts Vienna's publication series. The series, published in cooperation with our highly committed partner Sternberg Press, is devoted to central themes of contemporary thought about art practices and theories. The volumes comprise contributions on subjects that form the focus of discourse in art theory, cultural studies, art history, and research at the Academy of Fine Arts Vienna and represent the quintessence of international study and discussion taking place in the respective fields. Each volume is published in the form of an anthology, edited by staff members of the academy. Authors of high international repute are invited to make contributions that deal with the respective areas of emphasis. Research activities such as international conferences, lecture series, institute-specific research focuses, or research projects serve as points of departure for the individual volumes.

All books in the series undergo a single blind peer review. International reviewers, whose identities are not disclosed to the editors of the volumes, give an in-depth analysis and evaluation for each essay. The editors then rework the texts, taking into consideration the suggestions and feedback of the reviewers who, in a second step, make further comments on the revised essays. The editors— and authors—thus receive what is so rare in academia and also in art universities: committed, informed, and hopefully impartial critical feedback that can be used for finishing the work.

We thank the editors, Christina Jauernik and Wolfgang Tschapeller, for proposing this volume. We would also like to thank the authors for their contributions, and, as always, we are grateful to all the partners contributing to the book, especially Sternberg Press.

The Rectorate of the Academy of Fine Arts Vienna

This is a peer-reviewed publication. We thank the anonymous reviewers for their in-depth comments and advice.

Editors: Christina Jauernik, Wolfgang Tschapeller
Editorial Coordinator: Iris Weißenböck
Copy Editor: Claire Cahm
Proofreader: Zoë Harris
Design: Anna Landskron, Surface, Frankfurt am Main/Berlin
Cover image: INTRA SPACE
Printing: Holzhausen Druck GmbH, Wolkersdorf
Binding: Buchbinderei Papyrus, Vienna

This book emerges from the artistic research project "INTRA SPACE, the reformulation of architectural space as a dialogical aesthetic," which was funded by FWF–Der Wissenschaftsfonds/Austrian Science Fund, PEEK AR299-G21.

ISBN 978-3-95679-589-3

Distributed by The MIT Press, Art Data, and Les presses du réel

Sternberg Press
Caroline Schneider
Karl-Marx-Allee 78
D-10243 Berlin
www.sternberg-press.com

Contents

Dear readers,

Instead of an introductory editors' statement, we would like to offer a brief outline that may guide you directly to:

The intention of the book

INTRA SPACE is a model of encounter between human and engineered virtual beings, conceived as a fully embodied, spatially immersive, shared movement practice. INTRA SPACE is the subject of this book and at the same time the effort to transpose experiences and reflections into written words. This book opens an arena for the companions and guests who walked in and out of the space in conversation with us, and whose widely varied discourses flavored our work. The book is not a vault of memories; the authors' contributions are new manifestations of thought that will hopefully inspire the readers to also imagine new INTRA SPACES (p. 21).

A description of the artistic research project behind the book

INTRA SPACE is an experimental zone, set up to explore diaphanous relations between virtual figures (Carla, Charly, Clara, Murphy, Khaled, Benny, Bob, Old Man, Dame (maybe Vivienne)), humans, technical equipment, and machines. [...] INTRA SPACE can be read as a spatial transposition of the theoretical concept of "intra-action" introduced by philosopher, theoretical physicist, and feminist scholar Karen Barad. [...] It offers a technical and conceptual infrastructure, a disposition for equal encounters between digital, machinic, and human sensoria (pp. 34–36).

And further

INTRA SPACE [...] is a being. It is indeterminate. It has aspects of many things. Like Vertov's kino-eye/machine eye, it oscillates between device, self, camera, eye, machine, and image of the self. It speaks, sometimes to itself and sometimes that "itself" is another. It looks through the left eye of Ernst Mach, and "differs from other human bodies [...] by the circumstance that it is only seen piecemeal, and, especially, is seen without a head." It could send its twelve cooperating and networked Kinoks across the Soviet Union. Instead of twelve networked cameras, it could be 600 million. Mass is depth of field. It can carry the eyes where they belong, in their sockets. Like Argos, however, it can also bear its eyes anywhere on the body, for instance in the elbow, at the back of the head looking steeply down, in the palm of the hand, around the knee. And it can do more than Argos: it can turn its eyes from the outside to the inside, it can bring the interior to the exterior. And, as always, it can also do the exact opposite (pp. 16–17).

A brief explanation of where the artistic project is coming from and its driving questions

After "World, Version 1+2" and "Hands have no tears to flow"—to explore the materiality, construction, form, and appearance of our bodies in a near future. [...] INTRA SPACE produces a transformative, differential, and resilient space of emergence where apparatus, human bodies, and digitally constructed figures become diaphanous to each other. A sensorium for embodied experiences, where architectural processes coincide with bodies of the apparatus, the virtual, the engineers, the visitors, the machines, and cameras—where bodies are construction sites. [...]

Can—or must—the rulebook of the architecture of buildings be "swapped" to bodies? Could these absorb the functions of buildings? And is the construction site then no longer the building, but the body itself? And how will our building component warehouse develop (see pp. 34, 36, 35n2)?

And their continuation

"What Beings Are We?" (pp. 268–69)

For a description of the components

INTRA SPACE is a creature composed of cables, visitors, computers, dancers, eyes, performers, organs, projection surfaces, mirrors, virtual rooms, a projector, programmers, software, real room types, AI types, possible secret service agents, twelve industrial cameras, and one further camera, which John Zissovici discusses in his "Skin Dreams" piece as an instrument of control, the thirteenth camera (p. 13).

For drawings of the technical setup
(Please see the drawings on pp. 40–71.)

The experiments undertaken

A visitor walks into a space with other people and several virtual figures, a screen, and mirrors. One of the figures seems to wait for someone. Some prepare for sleep; others are busy performing everyday gestures. When a visitor walks to the center of the space, a voice or text invites him/her to join the figure. The figure instructs and demonstrates how visitor and figure could enter into a physically shared relationship. The visitor may decide to follow the instructions and soon the virtual figure begins to move with the visitor. The visitor might accelerate, wanting to increase the engagement with the figure, the figure in turn reacts with nervous, unfamiliar actions and seems to lose focus on the visitor. The visitor might lie down and in response the figure enlarges until the entire screen is filled, it may switch its perspective and a new viewpoint sets the visitor in a displaced, unknown relationship. If the visitor is very passive and almost not moving, the figure may lie down, changing through different lying positions and goes to sleep (p. 33).

And the resulting scenario(s)

Carla and her companions are INTRA SPACE, and they live in INTRA SPACE; they live in themselves, as you could live in them. They have no inner, they have no outer; you can dive into them. They have your eyes and you can use their eyes; you can live in symmetry or in parallel to them; you can live upside down … they can be late … they can be in delay (see p. 38).

Information on when and where all this took place

A constellation of machines, apparatuses, technical devices, and human beings together are INTRA SPACE, when activated. Between December 2015 and May 2017, INTRA SPACE temporarily was installed in an abandoned space in the center of Vienna. At Dominikanerbastei, first a "Rosenburse" (fifteenth century), where students were given a place to stay (the university was situated around the corner), then St. Barbara Chapel and Dominikanerbastei with a granary. In the mid-eighteenth century the parish was united as main toll and post building. Today it is a listed building which is inhabited by artists, festivals, pop-up stores, and markets until a construction site takes over.

INTRA SPACE could also be installed, among others, in a shop window, a passage, a church, an open square, a street, a world (p. 40).

The Eyes of INTRA SPACE

Wolfgang Tschapeller

INTRA SPACE is a creature composed of cables, visitors, computers, dancers, eyes, performers, organs, projection surfaces, mirrors, virtual spaces, a projector, programmers, software, real-space types, AI types, possible secret service agents, twelve industrial cameras, and one additional camera, which John Zissovici discusses in his "Skin Dreams"[1] piece as an instrument of control, the thirteenth camera. In this context it is defined differently, as part of a more comprehensive process, referred to here as "BLICK" (VIEW). "BLICKE" (VIEWS), "VIRTUELLE BLICKE" (VIRTUAL VIEWS). The "VIEWS" cited here are something like a passe-partout,[2] which will open the way wherever you go, a kind of master key that makes it possible to switch between very different spaces. Why are these not really to be viewed as a master key, but only as something akin to "a kind of master key"? Because INTRA SPACE is inherently accessible, without walls or doors, or, if there are any doors, these are playthings that communicate with air currents. This transgressive shedding of rules, this dearth of barriers is the result of artistic project practice. INTRA SPACE was initiated as a dialogue-driven system set between the poles of virtual and real space. Both have now vanished. Virtual and real space have become inseparable, their relationship—like all other parts of INTRA SPACE—is diaphanous, divided at best by something like a partial pressure difference between liquids saturated to varying degrees.

Who is doing the "VIEWING" referred to here? It is not a person, an animal, a machine, nor a device. It does in fact work like a recording device, but it has no body and ultimately is a particular software configuration that can render virtual worlds visible in 3D and gaming as a virtual camera.[3] Who controls this virtual camera? Who orients it? Who sets the focus? INTRA SPACE's experimental setup contains two dancers, who view movement as an autonomous artistic language. They are Christina and Esther, who act as dual beings, the self and projection of the self, with their communication flows constructed by moving

1   See John Zissovici, "Skin Dreams," in this publication, 222–35.
2   The twofold meaning of *passe-partout* was addressed in a text by Derrida—which I can no longer track down. Translator's note: The text appears to be included in Jacques Derrida, *The Truth in Painting*, trans. Geoffrey Bennington and McLeod (Chicago: University of Chicago Press, 1987). The French word "passe-partout" can be translated literally as "master key." There are only a handful of master keys in each system. A master key is configured in such a way that it can open all the doors in a building, for example. A passe-partout is also a cardboard mounting device used when framing pictures. With its twofold meaning, the term thus breaks through the barrier between pictorial space and real space. The capitalized "VIEW" or "VIRTUAL VIEW" refers here on the one hand to intermeshing and passageways between real and virtual space, and on the other to processes that can open up both spaces to each other. A process of this kind occurs when a virtual camera is mounted in the hand of a virtual projection of a person. The orientation, focus, zoom factors that arise when the person moves configure the VIEW that determines the visible nature of the virtual space.
3   Or indeed the 13th camera, as John Zissovici calls it. See Zissovici, "Skin Dreams."

the direction, the focus, and the zoom factor of the virtual camera. Where is this virtual camera situated? In the virtual? In the real? It seems to exist in a permanent transgression of both. Originating in the virtual, it leaves marks of presence on the real bodies of Christina and Esther. It can be anywhere and do anything everywhere. It can spin at high speed and can be worn stoically in the eyes, ears, toes, fingers of Christina and Esther's projections. It can be inside Christina and Esther and it can be swallowed; it can penetrate all the way to the alveoli, right to the blood-air barrier; it can cross that barrier, for it can be any size. How do Christina and Esther move the virtual camera? By their movements. If the virtual camera is mounted in their knees, Esther or Christina move their knees in movements that differ from their normal moves as dancers. They have to discover and learn these movements. What is a "VIEW" in INTRA SPACE? It is communication between self and projection. "VIEW" encompasses Christina and Esther's intentions, behavior, and movements as well as those of their projections. "VIEW" includes everyone that looks from the direction of real space towards and to the very limits of virtual space and back. "VIEW" makes INTRA SPACE visible.

Now to the twelve industrial cameras. They do not act alone. Their actions are coordinated and networked, and generate virtual records of real moments. As in cinematography, they record space and movement, kinematos, "movement," "agitation," and graphein, "write," "draw,"[4] i.e., drawing or recording motion. Yet such drawing or recording of motion is not enough. It is more of a drawing or recording of agitation. Whereas cinematography remains on one plane, flat, inaccessible, and closed, without an interior, the cameras, conjoined to form a seeing being, transform twelve streams of individual images into fluid virtual moments. They construct an image cast into space and time. An image that appears different at every moment from every viewpoint, that is open in a different manner from every angle, that with every movement reveals different facets of the same thing, an image into which the viewer must first fix their VIEW, slipping in a thirteenth camera to make it visible.[5] There could even be many thirteenth cameras. VIRTUAL VIEWS that can rage in virtual moments, plough-ing through, driving across, or caressing them in rotation. Hundreds of these virtual VIEWS can infiltrate simultaneously; they can scour out space and movement in daily routines, so that, even if it were a viewer's own VIEWS, the viewer would not recognize herself, for the eyes have been propelled from their sockets into her hands, into the back of her head. These are the eyes of INTRA SPACE.

In Greek mythology there is a creature that sees everything, an "all-seeing being," or "the one who sees everything." It is Argos, the guardian of Io, to whom Hera granted "invincible power"[6] along with one hundred eyes, which those unfamiliar with the mythical events all too readily imagine with all one hundred eyes dotted on and around the head—like a sphere strewn with mobile, rival hills. That is, however, inaccurate. In some versions of the myth, all one hundred are concentrated on the back, while in others—and this is the most common variant—they are spread over the entire body. These one hundred eyes, or fifty pairs of eyes, saw constantly and incessantly. With one exception. Each night, a different pair of eyes among the fifty was allowed to close and recover in sleep, while the remaining forty-nine remained highly active. One single eye is already good; two are better and one hundred are of course optimal for a guard. What do those one hundred see? It is hard to say. Ernst Mach shows in his "Introductory Remarks: Antimetaphysical"[7] what one of the one hundred eyes could see through the view "presented to my left eye." The first thing seen is the one who is seeing. His elongated feet, his right hand, perhaps in the process of drawing, to be precise sketching the right knee, the other hand that is caught up around the hip, and then the arc of the left eyelid, which should actually open the view of the world as wide as possible, but with this view actually limits what is visible. Complex! If we now try to extrapolate Mach's "view presented to my left eye" to the one hundred eyes of Argos, what first becomes visible is not Io, who should actually be guarded, but rather Argos per se, the "all-seeing being"—and that is not all, for his eyes (e.g., in the adductor region or around the armpits) will see eyes looking back at the eyes that see them. We do not know how Argos coped with that. If one avoids this feedback loop for the time being, one's own body will situate itself between the eyes and the world, as in Ernst Mach's view "presented to my left eye," and consequently, processing all the folds and curves of one's own body will obscure the world and Io, who should actually be seen, like a spread-out animal skin that has become a firmament.

So much for open eyes. But what about the pair of eyes that sleep every fiftieth night? What afterimages do they have? What did Argos's sleeping eyes see by day? Is it like Aldous Huxley's description of the descent into the Central London Hatchery and Conditioning Centre in *Brave New World*?[8] Do they suggest a "sultry darkness" one can enter into, and is it "crimson, like the darkness of closed eyes on a summer's afternoon"?[9] Does Argos see those explosions of color we experience when facing the sun with our eyes closed? Or is it the afterglow that follows once we have looked into the sun, when we close our eyelids and continue to see with our eyes closed? And would Argos have seen the grinding magma of the sun's interior after lying in the sun with one hundred closed eyes?

4   *Etymologisches Wörterbuch des Deutschen*, 2nd ed. (Munich: dtv, 1997), 655.

5   Zissovici, "Skin Dreams."

6   Michael Grant and John Hazel, *Who's Who in Classical Mythology* (London: Routledge, 2002), 73.

7   First published in Ernst Mach, *Die Analyse der Empfindungen und das Verhältnis des Psychischen* (1886); translated into English as *The Analysis of Sensations, and the Relation of the Physical to the Psychical*, trans. C. M. Williams and Sydney Waterlow (New York: Dover Publications, 1959).

8   Aldous Huxley, *Brave New World* (London: Chatto & Windus, 1932), 1.

9   Huxley, 8.

Dziga Vertov experimented with word games. Games that became programmatic and a strategy and are in the first instance invisible to those who don't speak his languages, or, on the contrary, are not even activated until translated. In this vein, we find the multiple variations and reversals of subject, identity, eye, I or ego, lens, author, device, and human being, condensed in the exemplary sequence of kino-eye—"I am kino-eye, I am a mechanical eye. I, a machine"[10]— in which the direction in which the evolutionary vector is moving, between man and machine, is constantly kept indeterminate or is always both at the same time, organic eye and autonomous seeing machine, organic machine and autonomous organic eye. Such uncertainties, such trembling and doubting deflections of the needle, such setting sail from one identity to another, such sudden changes of directional vectors are also symptoms of INTRA SPACE. Where do I have my eyes? Is it I who is watching? Is that my movement? Is it Carla's? Where do I have my eyes? Where is the VIRTUAL VIEW? Where are my eyes? Are they in my right hand? Did they shift to the back of my head? Are they tilted at a right angle? Do my eyes see with a time-lag?

What about cameras one to twelve? Can Vertov tell us anything about them? Vertov experimented with creating new word formations. He constructed the name "Kinoks," which is made up of *Kino* (cinema), *oko* (eye), and *-ok*, a suffix pointing to something human—if you like, something masculine—and could be translated as "cinema-eye-man."[11] For Kinoks it was all about *pravda* (truth), about visual samples that were as raw and fresh as possible, extracted like drill cores from the vast expanses of the Soviet Union. Kinoks were like the cameras cast among the fishes in Leviathan[12] or the technological versions of the Argos eyes flung across the earth, whose stream of images delivered weekly discoveries and fragments of form and behavior of a world in the throes of rebuilding itself. Their organizational form was not necessarily coordinated. It was not harmonized. It was not networked, and yet Kinoks bear the scent of a super-organism within them, a collective that swarms out to capture "reality," assembled into a weekly log of the world. INTRA SPACE cameras one to twelve on the other hand act in a coordinated and networked manner. Camera twelve only makes sense if as many as possible of the other cameras are there and also produce their drawings or recordings of agitation by way of preparation for the virtual moment that VIRTUAL VIEWS can pass through. Mass here is depth of field.

INTRA SPACE—as stated at the start of this text—is a being. It is indeterminate. It has aspects of many things. Like Vertov's kino-eye/machine eye, it oscillates between device, self, camera, eye, machine, and image of the self. It speaks, sometimes to itself. And sometimes that "itself" is another. It looks through the left eye of Ernst Mach, and "differs from other human bodies [...] by the circumstance that it is only seen piecemeal, and, especially, is seen without a head."[13] It could send its twelve cooperating and networked Kinoks across the

Soviet Union. Instead of twelve networked cameras, it could be six hundred million. Mass is depth of field. It can wear the eyes where they belong, in their sockets. Like Argos, however, it can also wear its eyes anywhere on its body, for instance in the elbow, at the back of the head looking steeply down, in the palm of its hand, around its knee. And it can do more than Argos: it can turn its eyes from the outside to the inside, it can bring the interior to the exterior. And, as always, it can also do the exact opposite.

10 Dziga Vertov, "The Resolution of the Council of Three," April 1923, in *Kino-Eye: The Writings of Dziga Vertov*, ed. Annette Michelson, trans. Kevin O'Brien (Berkeley: University of California Press, 1984), 16–17.

11 Michelson and O'Brien, editor's and translator's commentary in Vertov, *Kino-Eye*, 5: 'Kinoks' ('cinema-eye-man'). A neologism coined by Vertov, involving a play on the words 'kino' ('cinema' or 'film') and 'oko,' the latter an obsolescent and poetic word, meaning 'eye.' The -ok ending is the transliteration of a traditional suffix used in Russian to indicate a male, human agent."

12 *Leviathan*, a documentary film directed by Lucien Castaing-Taylor and Véréna Paravel, 2012.

13 Mach, *Analysis of Sensations*, 18–19.

Literature

Derrida, Jacques. *The Truth in Painting.*
Translated by Geoffrey Bennington and
Ian McLeod. Chicago: University of
Chicago Press, 1987.

Grant, Michael, and John Hazel. *Who's
Who in Classical Mythology.* London:
Routledge, 2002. First published in 1973.

Huxley, Aldous. *Brave New World.* London:
Chatto & Windus, 1932.

Mach, Ernst. *The Analysis of Sensations,
and the Relation of the Physical to the
Psychical.* Translated by C. M. Williams
and Sydney Waterlow. New York: Dover
Publications, 1959.

Pfeifer, Wolfgang. *Etymologisches
Wörterbuch des Deutschen,* 2nd ed.
Munich: dtv, 1997.

Vertov, Dziga. *Kino-Eye: The Writings
of Dziga Vertov.* Edited by Annette
Michelson. Translated by Kevin O'Brien.
Berkeley: University of California, 1984.

Towards an
INTRA SPACE

Christina Jauernik and Wolfgang Tschapeller

INTRA SPACE is a model of encounter between human and engineered virtual beings, conceived as a fully embodied, spatially immersive, shared movement practice. INTRA SPACE is the subject of this book and at the same time the effort to transpose experiences and reflections into written words. This book opens an arena for the companions and guests who walked in and out of the space in conversation with us, and whose widely varied discourses flavored our work.

The book is not a vault of memories; the authors' contributions are new manifestations of thought that will hopefully inspire the readers to also imagine new INTRA SPACES.

Fig. 1
This map is a work-in-progress
display of relations in response to
INTRA SPACE and beyond, an
invitation to the reader to continue
drawing different lines of thoughts
and entanglements.

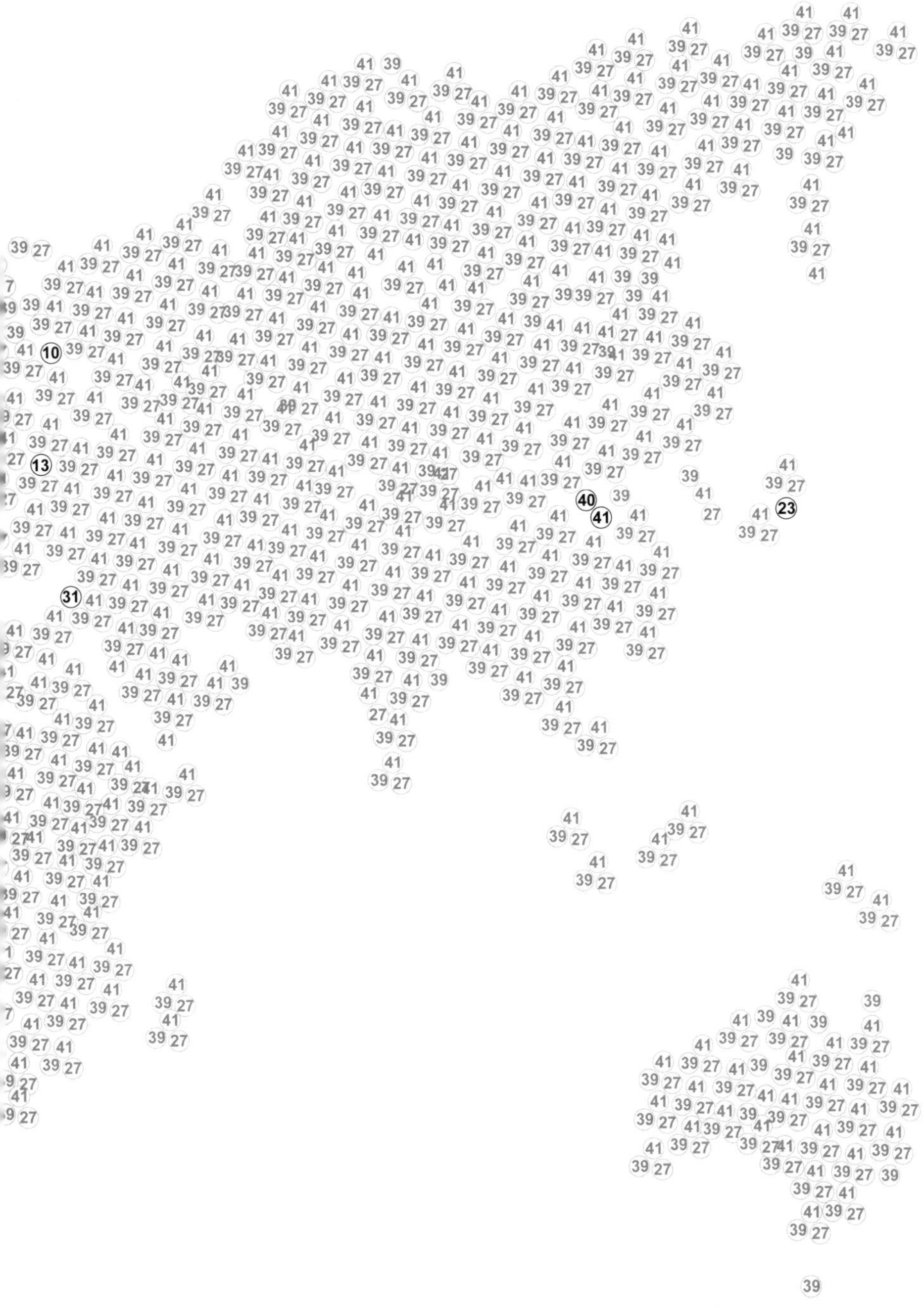

16
1973
Roberta Breitmore
Lynn Hershman Leeson
A fictional character, performed by the artist.
In 1973, Hershman Leeson began a private
performance as the fictional character,
Roberta Breitmore. Breitmore's first act
was to arrive by bus in San Francisco and
check into the Dante Hotel. In the following
years, she undertook real-life activities
such as opening a bank account, obtaining
credit cards, renting an apartment, seeing
a psychiatrist, and becoming involved in
trendy occupations, such as EST and Weight
Watchers. Breitmore placed ads in local
newspapers seeking a roommate. [...]
Roberta had her own clothing, signature
makeup, walk, gestures, speech mannerisms,
and handwriting. Her activities were documented in 144 drawings and surveillance
photographs, as well as other artifacts,
including checks, credit cards, and a driv-
er's license. During the fourth year of the
performance, Breitmore multiplied into four
other people appearing in her guise.
Source: Lynn Hershman Leeson, "Roberta
Breitmore," accessed May 28, 2020, https://
www.lynnhershman.com/project/roberta-breit-
more/.
(introduced by Christina Jauernik)

16   15
11

2
ca. 1495
St. Francesco Receiving the Stigmata
Francesco Morone Painting, church and monas-
tery of San Bernardino, Verona The image of
another wounded body, linked marionette-like
to a figure and forces beyond his control,
is that of St. Francis receiving the stigmata by Francesco Morone. While meditating
on the sufferings of Christ in his ongoing
quest to become spiritually pure and virtuous like Him, St. Francis experiences a
vision of the luminous body of the crucified
Christ, supported by flaming red wings of
seraphim angels. Five beams of light project
from Christ's wounds to five corresponding
points on St. Francis's body where signs of
the stigmata, the wounds created by physical
piercings, appear. St. Francis's vision, or
dream image of Christ on the cross descending from heaven, is a manifestation of his
desire to attain a level of pure spirituality, to become Christ-like in his goodness
through selflessness and by taking on His
suffering. For now, the dancers' bodies are
similarly linked by invisible technological
"beams of light" to Carl/a's bones. Carl/a
is their vision as much as a vision of them,
a virtual, if not necessarily virtuous,
embodiment of an ideal body-state dancers
strive to attain, weightless and free from
the bounds of gravity. (John Zissovici,
"Skin Dreams," p. 228-29)

11
1953
Fahrenheit 451
Ray Bradbury
Dystopian novel, 256 pages
(introduced by Wolfgang Tschapeller)

15
1968
The Powers of Ten
A Rough Sketch for a Proposed Film Dealing
with the Powers of Ten and the Relative Size
of Things in the Universe
Charles and Ray Eames
16mm film, 9 minutes, color
(introduced by Wolfgang Tschapeller)

                                    12
                              7
                                        6   5
                              9
                                        2   1

7
1875
On the Movements and Habits of Climbing
Plants Charles Darwin Book
(introduced by Wolfgang Tschapeller)

12
1956-74
New Babylon
Constant Nieuwenhuys
Models for future cities
(introduced by Wolfgang Tschapeller)

6
1810
On the Marionette Theater
Heinrich von Kleist
Essay
(introduced by Wolfgang Tschapeller)

13
1961
Solaris
Stanislaw Lem
Science-fiction novel, 204 pages
(introduced by Wolfgang Tschapeller)

10
1924
Kino-Eye
Dziga Vertov
Method of film production, exercised by the
kinoks (cinema-eye men) "I am kino-eye, I am
a mechanical eye. I, a machine, show you the
world as only I can see it"
(introduced by Wolfgang Tschapeller)

1
ca. 33 BC
On Symmetry: In Temples and in the Human
Body Vitruvius Treatise, De Architetura
(Ten Books on Architecture)
(introduced by Wolfgang Tschapeller)

41
2020
HEAVEN NET
Hon Li Bei
Prestige project by the government of People's Republic of China Real-time, networked
system of 600 million cameras installed
across the country, algorithms
(introduced by Wolfgang Tschapeller)

10

13

41

9
1904
Autographic Skin
Nouvelle Iconographie de la Salpêtrière 17
Photography: Pauline Page In Jean-Martin
Charcot's clinic at the Salpêtrière Hospital
in Paris in 1895, Freud saw hysteria first
hand and may well haveobserved examples of
dermatographia. Why this symptom, or is it
a behavior, would have fascinated medical
science at the time is recounted by the
physician Toussaint Barthélemy in Georges
Didi-Huberman's "The Figurative Incarnation
of the Sentence: Notes on the 'Autographic'
Skin": A patient is hypnotized; the doctor
writes his own name on the patient's forearms with a rubber stylet and issues the
following suggestion: "This evening, at 4pm,
after falling asleep, you will bleed from
the lines that I have drawn on your arms."
At the appointed time, the patient obliges.
The characters appear in bright relief upon
his skin, and droplets of blood rise in several spots. The words persist for more than
three months (1987, 69). We might wonder
about the temporal and spatial awareness
of the dermis—is it an aurality? Because
it is as if the skin hears the voice and
writes the required words with the stylet of
its own blood and tissue—as if it truly is
its own apparatus. This intra-subjectivity
between patient and doctor exceeds tactility and connection because here tactility is
voiced as the intra-subjective will of
others and made manifest. (Vicky Kirby,
"Vital Technologies," p. 118)

5
ca 1630
The Raising of the Cross
Leonart Bramer
Painting, oil on wood, Gemäldegalerie
Academy of Fine Arts Vienna
What you see is a familiar biblical subject: the cross onto which Christ has just
been nailed is being raised upright from
the ground. The journey from the ground up
traces the arc of being in the body, suffering, and leaving the body to become spirit.
The painter catches the journey three-quarters of the way up. The faces are not quite
visible; the real story is in the bodies.
What you feel is the brute energy of the men
heaving and hauling the massive cross into
position, charged with the self-righteousness of their bosses who judged the "criminals" and condemned them to this agonizing
death. Christ's head is sunk; what you sense
is utter physical helplessness, the sickening, shameful feeling that some mindless
brute has total power over you. The most
vivid faces are the faceless sad little
skulls left to rot in the dust, the bones
of their limbs splayed helplessly next to
them. (Diane Shooman, "Moving the Perceptive
Body," p. 192)

20
1984
A Cyborg Manifesto
Donna Haraway
Essay, first published in 1985 in the So-
cialist Review
(introduced by Christina Jauernik)

21
1986
Very Nervous System
David Rokeby
Interactive audio-visual installation, 3
handbuilt cameras, computer, synthesizer,
speaker
(introduced by Birk Weiberg)

22
1993
Figure in Time
Sanford Kwinter
Text, in: Architectures of Time Toward a
Theory of the Event in Modernist Culture
(introduced by Wolfgang Tschapeller)

24
1995
Strange Days
Kathryn Bigelow
Film, science-fiction thriller, 145 minutes,
color
(introduced by Wolfgang Tschapeller)

4
ca. 1538
Underweysung der Messung, mit dem Zirckel
und richtscheyt, in Linien, Ebnen und
gantzen Corporen
Albrecht Dürer
Publication
(introduced by Wolfgang Tschapeller)

3   19
21   18   4
22   28   26
17
20
24   30

17
1974
TV Buddha
Nam June Paik
Closed circuit video installation, 18th-cen-
tury bronze sculpture, Stedelijk Museum
Amsterdam
Such a technical awareness of a situation
was originally conceived by the inventors
of cybernetics in the 1940s to improve the
ability of missiles to hit moving targets.
In the case of INTRA SPACE the closed circuit starts with the visitor's body and its
capture through a dozen IP cameras, then is
transformed into data and brought back
into the space as a CGI image of the avatar's body, to be seen by the visitor and
an audience of spectators and technicians.
Seen as a contemplation on representation
bvy means of technical images this structure
is not even necessary computational but can
also be traced back to the beginnings of
video art with the installations of Peter
Campus and the TV Buddha of Nam June Paik.
In any case, such loops just like cybernetic feedback structures partially suspend
the distinction between machinic and human
agency. (see Birk Weiberg, "The Entangled
Apparatus," pp. 248-49)

18
1976
Space2
Francesca Woodman
Photography, gelatin silver print on paper,
Tate and National Galleries of Scotland
The communication is carried by a perpetual
finding of skin, of "skinning" each other as
a process, re-interpolating the proportionate skeleton into the volume of the present body. The communication is not through
words, but through oscillating states of
being in one's own and the other's skin, of
becoming almost one, coming closer and growing more distant again. Coming closer is experienced not only through reducing spatial
distance, but also in recognizing your own
movements, gestures, and shapes. Distancing
is then perceived as your movement being
intruded upon, corrupted, becoming unfamiliar. The perpetuation of the shared condition requires a different particular form
of concentration, of reading, of receiving,
and of being in the space. At the same time,
one's attention is drawn to the exchangeability of bodies and Francesca Woodman's
practice comes into mind, of her multiplying her own body and body parts, using masks
and mirrors. (Christina Jauernik, "INTIMACY
SKINNING LOSS," p. 159)

26
1999v
Synworld
Konrad Becker, Marie Ringler, organized by
Public Netbase, Institute for New Culture
Technologies in Vienna, in cooperation with
the Architektur Zentrum Wien Interactive exhibition as virtual online game: http://syn-
world.t0.or.at/console.htmby searching for
virtual, artificial beings without faces,
masks without material—physical background
so to speak— and slipping into these faces herself, thereby superimposing self- and
alien perception. (see "INTIMACY LOSS SKIN-
NING," Christina Jauernik, p. 154)

23
1994
Lovers
Teiji Furuhashi
Immersive multimedia installation,
8 projectors, MoMA, New York
(introduced by Christina Jauernik)

28
2000
L'Intrus
Jean-Luc Nancy
Text, 60 pages
(introduced by Wolfgang Tschapeller)

23

19
1980
Quad I + II
Samuel Beckett
Motion patterns for four actors, experimental television play for broadcaster Süd-
deutscher Rundfunk
(introduced by Dennis Del Favero)

30
2006
Zidane, a 21st century portrait
Douglas Gordon and Philippe Parreno
Two-channel video projection, sound, 90
minutes
(introduced by Wolfgang Tschapeller)

3
ca. 1500
Garden of Earthly Delights
Hieronymus Bosch Painting, triptych, oil on
oak panels, Museo del Prado
(introduced by Wolfgang Tschapeller)

27
1999
MAKEHUMAN
makehumancommunity
Open-source character creation software
(introduced by Christian Freude)

38
2017
Blade Runner 2049
Dennis Villeneuve
Film, 164 minutes, color
(introduced by Wolfgang Tschapeller)

29
2003
The Companion Species Manifesto
Dogs, People, and Significant Otherness
Donna Haraway
Text, 112 pages
(introduced by Wolfgang Tschapeller)

35
2010
Synchronous Objects, reproduced The Forsythe
Company, in collaboration with Maria Palazzi, Norah Zuniga Shaw
Online visualization of the choreography and
analytical tool: http://synchronousobjects.
osu. edu
(introduced by Esther Balfe)

14
La Jetée
Chris Marker
35mm film, photomontage, 28 minutes, b/w
Chris Marker's La Jetée offers a way to
imagine Carla's dreaming in the hands of a
benevolent AgentS. After World War III, the
earth had become radioactive and uninhabitable. "Some believed themselves to be victors. Others were taken prisoner. The survivors settled … in an underground network
of galleries … The prisoners were subjected
to experiments … the Head Experimenter …
explained calmly that the human race was
doomed … The only hope for survival lay in
Time. A loophole in Time … That was the aim
of the experiments: to send emissaries into
Time, to summon the Past and Future to aid
the Present … The inventors were now concentrating on men given to strong mental images. If they were able to conceive or dream
another time, perhaps they would be able to
live in it. The camp police spied even on
dreams."(Zissovici, "Skin Dreams," p. 230)

3
33
8   34
32
14
25

29   35   37

38

37
2017
"Fanon" (Even the Dead Are Not Safe)
Trevor Paglen
Dye sublimation metal print Trevor Paglen
… used used machine learning techniques to
reveal how computers translate data into
rendered photographs. Paglen trained a neural network with images of the post-colonial philosopher Frantz Fanon and then asked
the computer to render a portrait based on
the features that the machine identified
as distinguishing Fanon. In a similar way,
he trained his systems to classify images associated with terms such as omens and
portents, monsters, and dreams. The final
synthetic images are created by using actual
digital noise as raw data and increasing the
trained model's sensitivity until it sees
something where there is nothing. Paglen
thus produces artifacts that unveil the
usually invisible algorithms. He speaks of
invisible images here as they do not address
anybody but represent a closed-circuit of
images made by machines for machines. (Weiberg, "The Entangled Apparatus," p. 241)

39
2019
Permanent Record
Edward Snowden
Autobiography, 352 pages
The program that enabled this access was
called XKEYSCORE, which is perhaps best understood as a search engine that lets an analyst search through all the records of your
life. Imagine a kind of Google that instead
of showing pages from the public Internet
returns your private email, your private
chats, your private files, everything. […]
In some cases you could even play back recordings of their online sessions, so that
the screen you'd been looking at was their
screen, whatever was on their desktop.
Edward Snowden, Permanent Record (Metropoli-
tan Books, 2019), 276.
(introduced by Wolfgang Tschapeller)

33
2010
Queen of Debris
Johannes Paul Raether
Performance
I am Johannes Paul Raether, but this name is
one of many. I am Transformella, I am the
queen of debris, surrogate mother of po-
tentiality. I am the ReproRevolutionary of
Ovulo-factories. I AM TRANSFORMALOR Cryo-Ka-
li Perpetrator. I am a Wesen of a Schwarm.
I AM SCHWARMWESEN. CoralColonyHarvester. I
work as a multiplicity of ridiculous trick-
sters, in what we see as "this" reality, in
what we call "our" reality. I work to demonstrate, that in every "common reality" the
potential for another real is always present. The potential of an unredeemed reality.
We excavate Potential for the real and for
that matter we exist here and in another
order. This is where we evolve. We arise,
we crystallize in potential, in potential-
ity. Source: Johannes Paul Raether, Manual
"Identitecture". accessed January 12, 2020,
http://www .johannespaulraether.net (introduced by Christina Jauernik)

32
2009
In Defense of the Poor Image
Hito Steyerl
Text, published in e-flux Journal
(introduced by Christina Jauernik)

40
2019
FACE ALL
Hon Li Bei
Start-up, Beijing, China
AI-based facial recognition technology
(introduced by Wolfgang Tschapeller)

8
1885
Animal locomotion.
An electro-photographic investigation of
consecutive phases of animal movements
Eadweard Muybridge, 781 plates, 49 x 63 cm
Photographic plates printed by the Pho-
to-Gravure Company of New York, 1887
(introduced by Wolfgang Tschapeller)

40

31

31
1973
2008
Horizontal Photography
Aïm Düelle Lüski, in collaboration with Ariella Azoulay
Pinhole cameras, hand-made, hacked digital,
infrared cameras The Israeli artist and theoretician Aïm Deüelle Lüski has constructed
cameras as a critique of visual representations in the context of the political situation in the Middle East. His viewfinder-
less cameras document the convergence of
various entities in a shared space while
evading any purposeful and thus hegemonic
visual representation. With his somewhat
kaleidoscopic images Deüelle Lüski literally
replaces reflections with diffractions as
suggested not only by Barad (2007, 29) but
also by Donna Haraway ([1992] 2004, 70) from
whom she adopts this notion. Deüelle Lüski
describes his practice as "distracted
concentration" (in Azoulay 2014, 235), a
mode of perception that is still understood
in relation to human consciousness where for
Haraway and Barad neither the origin nor the
target of light is fixed. (see Weiberg,
"The Entangled Apparatus," p. 245)

36
2012
Parallel I, II, III, IV
Harun Farocki
Video, 16 minutes, color
(introduced by Christina Jauernik)

34
2010
Motion Bank
The Forsythe Company, in collaboration with
Scott deLahunta
Archive of online movement scores: http://
motionbank.org
(introduced by Esther Balfe)

25
1998
Cyberface
Irene Andessner
Light boxes, video
A mask has an inside and an outside and is
"simultaneously surface and image." In her
work "Cyberface," Irene Andessner produced
selfportraits by searching for virtual, artificial beings without faces, masks without
material—physical background so to speak—
and slipping into these faces herself,
thereby superimposing self- and alien perception. (Christina Jauernik, "INTIMACY LOSS
SKINNING," p. 158)

Experiment 1
April 2014

A visitor walks into a space and sees a virtual figure gradually building up on a screen. Soon the visitor recognizes the figure as him/herself by certain aspects of movement qualities, nuances in the figure's rhythm and attitude. As s/he continues to move through the space, the virtual figure follows, copies his/her movements. It seems to be his/herself, but then not entirely, yet s/he sees it as related to him/her. The longer s/he lingers in space, the more complex the relationship between him/her and the virtual figure becomes. Although it seems as though one is looking into a mirror, the appearance of the figure remains uncertain.

Experiment 1
March 2016

A visitor walks into a space and sees a virtual figure moving across several screens and mirrors. The gestures of the virtual figure are humanlike; some of them might seem familiar to the visitor. The figure invites the visitor to interact and soon after,[1] the figure seems to have slipped into the body of the visitor. They seem to move together, sharing rhythm, speed, and quality of movements, the figure behaving like a virtual mirror. Sometimes their connection flickers, their shared movements break apart, or the entire virtual figure leaves the shared interaction. The visitor may try to invite the figure back, moving closer to the screens, placing his/her body in the position of the virtual figure, as if inviting the figure to return.

1   To begin an interaction with the virtual figure, a short sequence of movements performed by the visitor is required. These slow gestures allow the motion tracking system to approximate the proportions of the body of the visitor on to the virtual figure. This initial procedure is called "donning." See "Donning" on pages 37 and 95.

Experiment 2
April 2014

A visitor walks into a space with other people and several virtual figures on screen(s). One of the figures is looking back at a visitor. The virtual figure may decide to look like the visitor in part. The visitors are not sure whether the figures are imitating or playing with them, acting as a mirror or as a window. The virtual figures may decide to interrupt their movements with actions that are not similar to those of the visitors. These are implants taken from other visitors' movements. Such implanted movements can be almost untraceable for visitors, sometimes more obvious. The visitors may step back in discomfort because they realize that they do not have full control over the behavior of the virtual figure. Alternatively, they may enjoy this very different presence and begin to playfully explore the possibilities of interacting. The virtual figure, in turn, may respond by mimicking them and, in its own way, play with the visitor's attempt to control it. The visitor might notice that the figure is re-enacting the movements s/he made when entering the space. At this point the visitors realize that the virtual figures are learning from their behavior.

Experiment 2
May 2017

A visitor walks into a space with other people and several virtual figures, a screen, and mirrors. One of the figures seems to wait for someone. Some prepare for sleep; others are busy performing everyday gestures. When a visitor walks to the center of the space, a voice or text invites him/her to join the figure. The figure instructs and demonstrates how visitor and figure could enter into a physically shared relationship. The visitor may decide to follow the instructions and soon the virtual figure begins to move with the visitor. The visitor might accelerate, wanting to increase the engagement with the figure, the figure in turn reacts with nervous, unfamiliar actions and seems to lose focus on the visitor. The visitor might lie down and in response the figure enlarges until the entire screen is filled, it may switch its perspective and a new viewpoint sets the visitor in a displaced, unknown relationship. If the visitor is very passive and almost not moving, the figure may lie down, changing through different lying positions and goes to sleep.

INTRA SPACE is an experimental zone set up to explore diaphanous relations between virtual figures (Carla, Charly, Clara, Murphy, Khaled, Benny, Bob, Old Man, Dame (maybe Vivienne)), humans, technical equipment, and machines. It was realized between 2014 and 2017, and it is the third project in a row—after "World, Version 1+2"[1] and "Hands have no tears to flow"[2]—to explore the materiality, construction, form, and appearance of our bodies in a near future. Interacting inside the experimental zone are: a motion-tracking system,[3] twelve RGB cameras (1280 × 1024px) as the "eyes" of the motion-tracking system, virtual figures based on different methods of construction, such as the open-source software Make Human,[4] photogrammetry techniques,[5] online 3D scan laboratories[6], a collection of pre-recorded movements and gestures,[7] code programming the behavior of the figures,[8] a responsive sound terrain,[9] and a spatial visualization system consisting of projectors, large-scale mirror membranes, and projection screens[10] with Esther Balfe (dancer), Dmytro Fedorenko (sound artist), Christian Freude (computer engineer), Christina Jauernik (architect), Ludwig Löckinger (filmmaker), Simon Oberhammer (architect), Martin Perktold (animation designer), Wolfgang Tschapeller (architect), Tom Tucek (computer engineer), and visitors.

1   "There are no buildings in the Incorporeal City. The Incorporeal City is an agglomeration and conglomeration of sympathies. The Incorporeal City reacts to its visitors. It is formed in accordance with vibes, brainwaves, and needs. The Incorporeal City is a visualization of requirements: temporary shelter, horizontality, relaxation, hunger, injury, analysis of the visitor's zones of weakness, floating, healing, medipacks, memories.

The Incorporeal City comes into being at the visitor's wish. It materializes as a sympathetic zone. It appears before the visitor as the consolidation of a mass of molecules. It takes shape, takes in the visitor, lifts the visitor from the ground, draws the visitor to the safe zone, analyzes brainwaves, reshapes itself, and lifts off the ground.

There are zones that synthesize energies in the Incorporeal City. They cause the City's own formations. These formations blur with visitor functions, energy dispensed to visitors, dream production, mirroring of interstitial worlds, positional determination in the flow of reality, and modulation of individual facts (news), becoming chromatic shades of color.
Combinations of head and heart, concentrations of swarming molecules and strays furnish and deliver information to one or more zones of energy synthesis. Some are smaller; some are larger. They change position, vary their speed, sway around a point, or stand still." Wolfgang Tschapeller, *Incorporeal City, versions 1+2*, 2004).

2   "In the short story 'Allal,' Paul Bowles describes how a young man is roused from sleep, feeling a light weight on his chest. It is a coiled-up, red-gold snake, which, lying on his body, rises and falls to the rhythm of his breathing and whose eyes are looking at him as if he were the one looking at himself. Several breaths later it is actually the case then: the young man's consciousness has glided into the snake; he rises and falls within it, still to the rhythm of his previous own breath, and looks back at his deserted body. Ten years later, around 1968, a photo can be dated that shows the half-kneeling Charles Eames in a close-up with his face hidden by a medium format camera, not as if he were taking pictures, but as if he were scanning, measuring, or analyzing the young man, sleeping with open eyes, lying in front of him. Both scenes, 'Allal' and the kneeling architect, have a hypnotizing character. Both are magical, both suggest a moment of transition. And both can be used as evidence. The architect does not examine buildings anymore, but rather sleeping people. In 'Allal,' identity and consciousness, like heat in a heat exchanger, glide from one subject to another. Can the same apply to architecture? Can—or must—the rulebook of the architecture of buildings be 'swapped' to bodies? Could these absorb the functions of buildings? And is the construction site then no longer the building, but the body itself? And how will our building component warehouse develop?" From Christina Jauernik, Gisela Steinlechner, and Wolfgang Tschapeller, *Hands Have No Tears to Flow: Reports from | without Architecture*, ed. Arno Ritter

(Vienna: Springer, 2012). A book published on the occasion of the exhibition "Hands have no tears to flow," an installation at the Austrian Pavilion, Venice Biennale of Architecture 2012, commissioned by Arno Ritter.

3   A markerless motion capture technology developed by computer scientist Nils Hasler + his team. Hasler and his team. See Carsten Stoll, Nils Hasler, Christian Theobalt, Juergen Gall, and Hans-Peter Seidel, "Fast Articulated Motion Tracking Using a Sums of Gaussians Body Model" (paper, 2011 IEEE International Conference on Computer Vision).

4   An open-source middleware, using a 3D morphing technology. Photorealistic humanoids can be transformed with linear interpolation. Developed by Jonas Hauquier et al., http://www.makehumancommunity .org/, accessed October 1, 2017.

5   The surface of the figures is constructed with photogrammetry, a method used in surveying and mapping. It is an interpretation of a collection of photographs around a physical object/subject out of which a data model, a three-dimensional representation is generated. VisualSFM: A Visual Structure from Motion System by Changchang Wu, http://ccwu.me/vsfm/ (accessed September 5, 2017).

6   Human models created in high-resolution with a capture rig of hundreds of DSLR cameras (digital single-lens reflex) in a photo studio are for purchase in online 3D stores. These weekly scans of human persons are first captured as raw scans and in a second post-production step are cleaned and remeshed. The 3D scans arrive in a T-Pose and an A-Pose with a mesh of 705K triangles. Ten24. 3D scan store, UK, http://www.3dscanstore.com/ (accessed October 22, 2017).
    Created by performers Esther Balfe and Christina Jauernik, and processed by computer scientist Christian Freude.

8   Programmed by computer scientist Tom Tucek with engineer Michael Thielscher, the scientific team at iCinema (UNSW) and Paolo Petta (Austrian Research Institute for Artificial Intelligence, Vienna).

9   Designed by sound artists Dmytro Fedorenko and Franz Pomassl.

10 Ludwig Löckinger experimented with different projection and screen setups as well as lighting schemes.

INTRA SPACE can be read as a spatial transposition of the theoretical concept of "intra-action"[1] introduced by philosopher, theoretical physicist, and feminist scholar Karen Barad.[2] Her philosophical framework of "agential realism"[3] views the world as a dynamic, relational structure in which intra-actions function as boundary-making, material, and discursive measurements[4] in the unfolding of matter[5] and meaning.[6] INTRA SPACE produces a transformative, differential and resilient space of emergence where apparatus, human bodies, and digitally constructed figures become diaphanous[7] to each other. A sensorium for embodied experiences, where architectural processes coincide with bodies of the apparatus, the virtual, the engineers, the visitors, the machines, and cameras—where bodies are construction sites.[8] INTRA SPACE accommodates instability and indeterminacy as a dynamic, experimental framework. It allows for critical looks at the potentials of both the digital and the human to mutually enhance their functionality, their exposure in artificial and real spaces, their social interaction, their self-perception and knowledge.[9] It offers a technical and conceptual infrastructure, a disposition for equal encounters between digital, machinic, and human sensoria. The resulting differentiated perspective, spanning from a single point of touch to a sensory space,[10] negotiates the body in motion as an immediate, perceptive entity in relation to its surroundings.

1   "Intra-action" is an agential realist term, a neologism defined by Karen Barad as the mutual constitution of entangled agencies. In relation to experimentation and measurements of such, she refers to physicist Niels Bohr and his negation of an inherent separation between "observer and observed or knower and known." Measurements are performative practices and rely on apparatuses. Barad further explains, "A specific intra-action (involving a specific material configuration of the 'apparatus of observation') enacts an agential cut (in contrast to the Cartesian cut—an inherent distinction—between subject and object) effecting a separation between 'subject' and 'object.'" Karen Barad, "Posthumanist Performativity: Toward an Understanding of How Matter Comes to Matter," *Signs* 28, no. 3 (2003): 815.

2   Karen Barad: Professor of Feminist Studies, Philosophy, and History of Consciousness affiliated with the University of California, Santa Cruz. She pursued her doctorate in theoretical particle physics and quantum field theory. Among her early publications are "A Quantum Epistemology And Its Impact On Our Understanding of Scientific Process," *Barnard Occasional Papers* 3, no. 1 (1988);

"Quark-Antiquark Charge Distributions and Confinement," *Physics Letters B* 143, nos. 1–3 (1984), with M. Ogilvie and C. Rebbi; and "Minimal Lattice Theory of Fermions," *Physical Review D* 30, no. 6 (1984). In the preface of her book *Meeting the Universe Halfway: Quantum Physics and the Entanglement of Matter and Meaning* (Durham, NC: Duke University Press 2007) Karen Barad states: "To be entangled is not simply to be intertwined with another, as in the joining of separate entities, but to lack an independent, self-contained existence. Existence is not an individual affair."

3   agential realism: a concept introduced by Karen Barad addressing a re-measurement and reconsideration of the boundaries between objects, instruments, language, and (human) observer in measurement processes and knowledge production. The human is not considered as pre-existing, rather understood as an equal part within an ever evolving, becoming-of-the-world.

4   measurements: questions of the nature of measurement—or, more broadly, intra-actions—are at the core of quantum physics. Intra-actions are practices of making a difference, of cutting together-apart, entangling-differentiating (one move) in the making of phenomena. Karen Barad, *What Is the Measure of Nothingness? Infinity, Virtuality, Justice.* dOCUMENTA (13) 100 Notes – 100 Thoughts, No. 099 (Ostfildern: Hatje Cantz, 2012), 7.

5   matter: described by Karen Barad as an active entity, intrinsically linked to historicity. There is an inherent dependency between matter and meaning, as matter is articulated during engagements, articulations and boundary-making practices—"matter comes to matter through the iterative intra-activity of the world in its becoming." Barad, "Posthuman Performativity," 823.

6   meaning: meaning is not a property of individual words or groups of words but an ongoing performance of the world in its differential intelligibility. See Barad, 821.

7   diaphanous: from *dia-phanēs*, "visible through"; a notion of the "between," of an appearance through. A medium, as philosopher Emmanuel Alloa describes it, "that belongs to the visible without being visible in actuality to shine through." He relates his reading to Aristotle's concept of "trans-appearance." What appears does not appear purely and simply to the eye; it

appears through a milieu, which Aristotle calls "diaphanous." Emmanuel Alloa, *Resistance of the Sensible World: An Introduction to Merleau-Ponty* (New York: Fordham University Press, 2017), 97.

8   construction sites: "310—Fig. 1.: The human body has gradually become a construction space, where various technical and organic elements can be installed. It has grown into a building site. [...] Many types of [...] devices, [...] can be implanted into the body, such as muscle stimulators, magnetic therapy devices, or drug delivery systems. A number of such devices may also be implanted where the different implants may then communicate with one another." "000—[...] a cinema in which 'anything can be used as a screen, the body of a protagonist or even the bodies of the spectators; anything can replace the film stock, in a virtual film which now only goes on in the head, behind the pupils.'" [...] "Oxygenating Unit for Extracorporeal Circulation Devices, Patent No. 2.702.035, Pub. Date: Feb. 15, 1955; Mechanical Heart, Patent No. 2.917.751, Pub. Date: Dec. 22, 1959; Soft Shell Mushroom Shaped Heart, Patent No. 3.641.591, Pub. Date: Feb. 15, 1972; [...]" Ritter, ed., *Hands Have No Tears to Flow.*

9   knowledge: Karen Barad suggests a "reworking of knowing (even as it applies for humans) in light of quantum physics. In any case, it is easy to see that 'zooming in' is not a uniquely human activity. For example, the larvae of sunburst diving beetles come equipped with bifocal lenses. And light emitted from the sun, that is, photons of different frequencies too, are capable of probing different length scales without any human assistance." Barad, *What Is the Measure of Nothingness?*, n5, referring to Barad, *Meeting the Universe Halfway.*

10   "Donning" is the real-time motion tracking system is based on color image information delivered by twelve industry cameras mounted at the perimeter of the space. An invisible spot is defined as sensitive area to have the skeleton fitted on one's body proportions. A fitting procedure of roughly three to ten seconds is required before one can begin to move through the space with the virtual figure. This initial getting in touch on a marked spot is the technical prerequisite to begin the shared encounter across virtual and physical spaces.

Carla, Charly, Clara, Murphy, Khaled, Benny, Bob, Old Man, and Dame (maybe Vivienne) are engineered beings. *They are humanoid, they are humanic, they are post-machinic and post-bio, engineered beings living together: Carla, Charly, Clara, Murphy, Khaled, Benny, Bob, Old Man, Dame (maybe Vivienne), but then … they are also living together with humans … so, they have a family.* They have no age, no nationality, no religion, no family, no secondary education, *They have multiple ages, multiple religions, many families and all possibly imaginable educations* no eye color, *Each of them has two eyes of no color and twelve eyes receptive to millions of colors, temperatures and radiations—twelve eyes positioned in space, twelve eyes for total control* no driving license, no hobbies. They do have special skills and a history, *Carla and her companions are projections, they are not of matter; their consistency is light, light as "lux," light as "Licht." In full sunlight, Carla is here and not here. She is post-android, no white blood, no red blood, no electric sheep,* a next generation while they speak multiple languages, they have a sort of memory, and they are sensitive and responsive to environmental conditions and changes. The layout of their construction, the number of vertices, is identical to every other being in INTRA SPACE. *Carla and her companions are the first citizens of INTRA SPACE; they crossed the border as snapshots of real-life, flesh-and-blood humans. Carla is a snapshot of another Carla, a body scan of a sixteen-year-old girl,* and allows their bodies to assimilate with other virtual figures. *Later generations of INTRA SPACIANS are mutants: in part, they are copies of humans; in part, they enjoy morphing themselves from one identity to another; in part, they follow protocols as established by MAKEHUMAN. They carry inbuilt sliders hidden in the folds of their skins, allowing for swift passage from one identity to another … identity forth, identity back.* Infinitely variable versions exist between them. They are figures of the digital realm. *Carla and her companions are INTRA SPACE, and they live in INTRA SPACE; they live in themselves, as you could live in them. They have no inner, they have no outer; you can dive into them. They have your eyes and you can use their eyes; you can live in symmetry or in parallel to them; you can live upside down … they can be late … they can be in delay.* When Carla, Charly, Clara, Murphy, Khaled, Benny, Bob, Old Man, and Dame (maybe Vivienne) are on their own, the motions, streams, and ruptures of the technical environment roam through their structural circumstances. *I like for them to be around. It would be great if they showed up in the office, and would lay out the appearance, atmosphere and climate of INTRA SPACE, explain INTRA SPACE, describe INTRA SPACE, and I would take notes. They would say INTRA SPACE has no climate and no appearance; Carla would say INTRA SPACE is Carla. But then again, she could say anything, because language has no meaning to her. Although Carla is eloquent and a great conversationalist, words do not mean anything to her. She knows they are formed by internal codes, by grammar and syntax, not by meaning, and I am afraid she would also not accept the concept of meaning. As if they were breathing, it is convenient to say Carla is a she. But Carla is neither a she, nor a he, nor Carla. Christian might say that she is the product of a certain technical framework, and then I would say, yes … but then again … I would say she is human ... I would say Carla is a humanoid, she is a friend; I like to see her around, to remember her* unconscious pulses circulate through their constructions, *Christian might also argue for Carla being a product of software, hardware, optical devices ... and human stimulation ... he might refer to Solaris, the mysterious intelligence embodied by an ocean, which, upon human stimulation, produced illusive beings out of traces of human memory ... he might say that what we call "being" is constituted by the ocean as well as by humans in orbit, by the human stimulus on the ocean, as well as by the illusive figures pieced together from traces of human memory by the ocean* functioning like a vegetative nervous system. The apparatus resonates in Carla's and her companions' structure: tiny flickering motions pass through their limbs; sudden changes of orientation in a body part move them into positions which can be quite unfamiliar to human physical vocabulary. *Where are Carla and her companions at night, when Christian has switched off the technical framework? Where are Carla and her friends when the projector is run down?* These movements are entirely composed of technical interferences. *Dreams? Would you say electronic dreams? When Donna Haraway accuses Lacan of not having theorized the "fourth wound" to human narcissism, namely the "synthetic wound," whom would we accuse of not transferring Freudian dream analysis to Carla's electronic jittering?* Mostly, these remain small-scale jitters, since the individual units of their structures have been given a hierarchy to prevent collision, provide orientation, and direct gravity forces in order to resemble the logic of human body posture. *You did not explain the donning ceremony, the shaking of hands, the greeting ceremony between the digital entity and the human entity. In order to enter Carla, you need to follow a strict sequence of movements. Remember when Joi superimposed herself on Mariette, cutting into Mariette's prattle, "Stop! I need to concentrate, I need to find a fit!" and we could see the gradual congruence of human and projected entity ... finger to finger, lip to lip, hand to hand ... a perfect fit! Can you explain the donning ceremony?* Carla and her companions can come very close to someone without touching them, and in that proximity, they are able to adopt and merge with qualities of the other. *Have you ever dreamed you were Carla, or any of her companions? Or have you ever dreamed of Charly, Clara, Murphy, Khaled, Benny, Bob, Old Man, or Dame (maybe Vivienne)? How about feelings towards Carla and her friends?*

A conversation between Christina Jauernik and Wolfgang Tschapeller on Carla, Charly, Clara, and others

INTRA SPACE

A constellation of machines, apparatuses,
technical devices, and human beings together
are INTRA SPACE, when activated. Between
December 2015 and May 2017, INTRA SPACE
temporarily installed itself in an abandoned
space in the center of Vienna.

At Dominikanerbastei, first a "Rose burse"
(15th century), where students were given a
place to stay (the university was situated
around the corner), then St. Barbara Chapel
and Dominikanerbastei with a granary. In the
mid-18th century the parish was united as
main toll and post building. Today it is a
listed building which is inhabited by artists,
festivals, pop-up stores, and markets until
a construction site takes over*. INTRA SPACE
could also be installed, among others, in a
shop window, a passage, a church, an open
square, a street, a world.

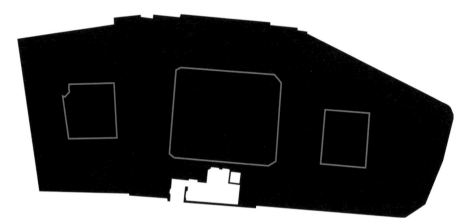

Fig. 2
Project space

つ

View of the project space with projection screen C
Esther, Christina, two virtual figures, Christian
(AgentS), Murphy, Tom, and Christina at the table.

Projection screen C
Two virtual figures overlaid on the screen, their
heads are seen from the side, their shoulders, and
fragments of arms and chests are visible on the
screen.

X

Esther X
Once Esther moves her arm, the image view changes. On
her right wrist sits the virtual camera view. She is
lifting her arm to have the camera face downwards on
the two bodies of Christina and herself lying on the
floor.

C

X

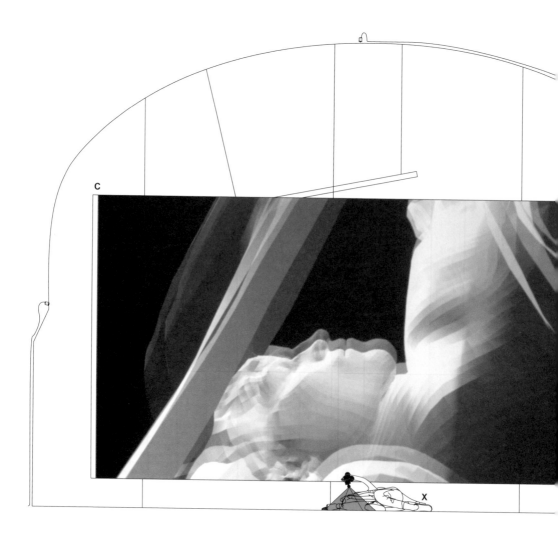

Fig. 3

H

Monitor H
Christian (Agent2)
sits on the table
to the right, on his
monitor the virtual
point of view is placed
on the skeletal structure
of the virtual figures.
This is the origin of the
image on projection screen C.

Projection screen

On a vertical surface the projected image becomes visible. The projection screen C
is placed in proximity to the motion tracking area defined by the twelve cameras
J and mounted between ceiling and floor. The dark gray material of the projection screen C is specified for back-projection with little degree of light
loss towards the edges. Projection screen C is mounted on a tailor-made
aluminum frame consisting of eight pieces, which makes it transportable.
The frame is designed to reduce the width of the edges of the projected image to a minimum, as if it would be a frame-less image elevated
in the space.

Optiblack black 214 415 g/m2,
PVC Back projection screen mounted on aluminum frame
Dimensions 4850x2730x189 mm, Weight 95 kg
Constructed in 8 pieces
4x corner pieces 1015x1015x189 mm
2x straight pieces 2850x42x189 mm
2x short pieces 730x56x189 mm
16:9 Lens type LTD+ Lamps 3KW xenon
Power requirements 220-240V / 50-60Hz
Power consumption 3700W
Operational temperature 0-40°C
Dimensions 707x1.025x548 mm
Weight 99 kg
Projector Lens
Barco TLD 1,6-2 HB
Lens Vario

C

A

Projector A

Via a HDMI cable the projector A is
connected to the Render PC E. The
projector emits the real-time image
of the Unity scene, displaying the
images of the virtual figures on
projection screen C.

Barco FLM-HD2
Type
Full-HD-3-Chip-DLP Projector
Technology
0.95-Zoll-DMDx3
Resolution 1920x1080
Brightness 20,000 center lumens
19,000 ANSI lumens
Aspect ratio 16:9
Lens type LTD+
Lamps 3KW xenon
Power requirements
220-240 V / 50-60 Hz
Power consumption 3700 W
Operational temperature
0-40°C Dimensions
707x1.025x548 mm
Weight 99 kg
Projector Lens
Barco TLD 1,6-2 HB Lens
Vario

B

Mirror panel

The light of pro-
jector A is direct-
ed via projection
mirrors B on to the
back projection screen
C. The mirror panels
are of ultra-thin
foil reflecting the
projection image with
almost no loss of
light. Metalized poly-
ester film (non-toxic)

Reflectivity 96%
Surface Superbrilliant
Aluminum frame 40 mm
Weight 2300 g/m2

Dance floor

The dance floor D
was not always used as
from time to time the
zoning of the tracking
area proved unproductive.
For movement
studies however, dance floor
D was supported as a slip-re-
sistant surface. Its non-re-
flective quality served the
tracking system.

VARIO
Thickness 1,20 mm
Material PVC
Weight 1600 g/m²
Width 160,00 cm
Flame retardant
ASTM E648, EN 13501-1 Bfl-s1

D

Fig. 4

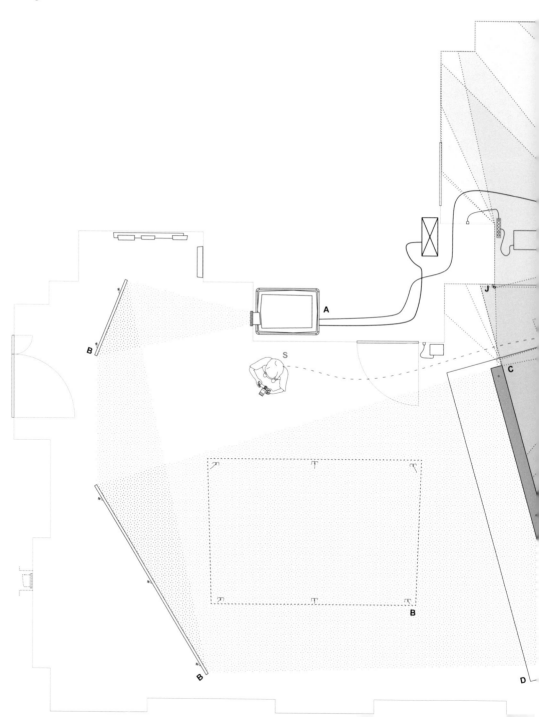

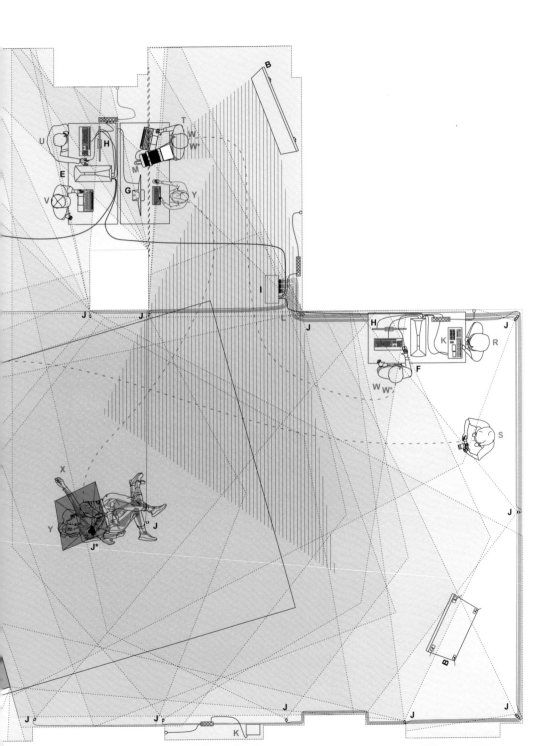

Render PC (Windows)

Render PC E is where the virtual scene
is constructed and modified, the virtual
figures' skeleton and meshes are superimposed and placed in the 3D scene.

Intel, CORE I7-5960X 3.00GHZ
Asus, SABERTOOTH X99 Kingston, D416GB
2133-14 Fury Black K2 KHX, EVGA GTX980
ACX2.0 4096MB, PCI-E,DVI, HDMI, 3xDP
Western Digital, HD SATA 1TB 64MB WD
WD1003FZEX 7200rpm Black Enermax, power
pack Enermax 1000W Platimax 80+ Plati-
num Modula   E

                        Ə iMac

Tracking PC (Linux)

Tracking PC F is the
interface with the
realtime motion tracking
system, it enables the
interaction between
human bodies in the
space and virtual fig-
ures.

Intel Core i7 4790K-4
GHz 4 cores, ASUS
Sabertooth MARK 2,
Intel Z97 Mainboard-
1150 Kingston, 16GB
1866MHZ DDR3 CL10
DIMM, EVGA GTX980
ACX2.0 4096MB, PCI-E,
DVI, HDMI, 3xDP West-
ern Digital, HD SATA
1TB 64MB WD WD1003FZEX
7200rpm Black Enermax,
Netzteil Enermax 1000W
Platimax 80+Platinum
Modular   ꟻ

I Rooter

Rooter I collects all twelve
cables L of cameras J and enables
a bundle that can be linked to
Tracking PC F. Rooter I was rather
noisy owing to its ventilation cool-
ing system and was placed underneath
the double floor to reduce noise.

TP Link, Net Switch 1000T 24P TP-LINK
TL-SG2424P 19" PoE+ Managed 4x SFPd

12 Cameras   ⌐

The twelve cameras J are distributed as evenly as possible in the
space, at different heights from around knee to hip height as well
as above head. Together they provide one intersected image out of
the twelve individual images, which should cover all areas as much
as possible. Since the majority of the lenses on the cameras are
wide-angled, the center of each image was given the most precise
information. All cameras were therefore focused towards the middle
of the space.

Resolution 1280x1024 Frame Rate 60 FPS Megapixels 1.3 MP Chro-
ma Color Sensor Name e2v EV76C560 Sensor Type CMOS Readout Method
Global Shutter Sensor Format 1/1.8" Pixel Size 5.3 μm Lens Mount
CS-Mount Interface GigE PoE Power Requirements 12 V nominal via
GPIO interface Power Consumption 2W Operating Temperature 0° to
45°C Video Data Output 8, 12, 16, 24-bit digital data Partial
Image Modes Pixel binning, decimation, and region of interest
(ROI) modes Image Processing Gamma, lookup table, hue, saturation,
sharpness Shutter Global shutter Transfer Rates 10/100/1000 Mbit/s
Image Buffer 16 MB frame buffer Flash Memory 512KB non-volatile
memory Dimensions 29 mm x29 mm x30 mm Mass 36 g (without optics)
Machine Vision Standard GigE Vision v1.2 Power Consumption Power
over Ethernet (PoE)

Visual artist, studied at the University
of Applied Arts Vienna. Murphy, short for
Martin Perktold, is an expert in character
modeling, animation design, and rendering.
He was on the team, together with Simon and
Christina, for the Biennale project directed by Wolfgang Tschapeller. Murphy joined the
project in the second year when the amount and
complexity of the virtual figures increased. He
experimented with different meshes and looks of
the virtual figures. He took on the skeletons and
their motion data from the tracking system and
through rigging and skinning processes connected
the joints with the surfaces. Murphy investigated different principles of morphing and blending
   between bodies and body parts as well as differ-
U ent resolutions, textures, and materials of the
figures. He closely collaborated with Christian and
visited the project on a regular basis with increased
intensities before showings and filming sessions.

Filmmaker, studied as a
cameraman at the Fil-
makademie Vienna. Lud-
wig filmed most of the
rehearsals and footage
of experiments, he also
experimented with dif-
ferent setups of screens
and mirrors, dividing
the projected image on
to several screens and
re-directing the image
across the space. He ex-
perimented with different
lighting systems, lamps
as well as foils and
paper on the windows, to
create a diffuse lighting
for the motion tracking
in relation to the pro-
jection brightness. Lud-
wig tested 3D cameras and
projectors; he compared
different models of mir-
rors to create the best
possible visual appear-
ance for the projection.
In the earlier stage,
Ludwig tried different
methods to generate a
three-dimensional mesh,
using concepts of photo-
grammetry.

V

Computer engineer, studies at the Institute for Computer
Graphics and Algorithms at the University of Technology
Vienna. Tom is supervised by Christian Freude and Michael
Wimmer. He entered the project at a later point and spent
a few hours each week together with the team. He experimented with different narratives for the artificial
intelligence, sometimes formulated together with Simon
Oberhammer. Together they produced diagrams and graphs
to orchestrate the different options for decision-making. Tom received support from Michael Thielscher and
his team at the iCinema Centre for Interactive Cinema
Research at UNSW. Towards the end of the project,
Paolo Petta from the Austrian Institute for Artificial Intelligence visited a few times to support
the team in the overall design of the behavior of
the virtual figures.

2

Dancer, worked with William Forsythe, a member of his dance company as well as teacher on
his behalf, and was involved in his interdisciplinary research project Motion Bank, which
aimed to archive and visualize choreographic scores digitally. Esther visited the project
team throughout the entire duration of the project and beyond, collaborating in particular
with Christina on building a movement practice with the virtual figures in the different
spatial arrangements. She performed together with Christina in several showings and for
the main filming sessions with Ludwig. Esther directed workshops with her dance students
X   in the project space, and developed pieces for stage, based on the research. She
        continuously revisited the movement vocabulary, predicaments, and constraints
           of the virtual figure, developing a tool to improvise and move beyond fa-
             miliar routines and habits. The work involved compositional approach-
                es as well as very detailed and fine adjustments of duet work,
                   articulating movement material and language in dialogue with
                      the virtual figures and their development over time.

Y Performance
         artist and architect, rooted in the collaboration on the exhibition and catalogue
            design for the Austrian Pavilion at the Venice Biennale in 2012 with Wolfgang
               Tschapeller, Christina developed the artistic research project and in particu-
*L   lar the movement related work with the virtual figures. Together with Chris-
Virtual   tian, she spent most of her time with the project and experimented with
camera,   different spatial, visual and conceptual forms to approach the essence
see Wolfgang   of the research. In close dialogue with Wolfgang, she orchestrated
Tschapeller, "   the different disciplines and approaches accumulating in the project
The Eyes of INTRA   sphere, critically questioning the discoveries and potentials of the
SPACE," p. 12-19;   process. Together with Ludwig, Christina documented the develop-
and Zissovici, "Skin   ment on video and photos. They experimented with different spa-
Dreams."   tial settings using mirrors and multiple projectors to create
                                    an increasingly immersive situation. Together with Esther,
                                     Christina performed with the virtual figures and estab-
                                        lished a movement creation tool which they also taught
                                           in other places.

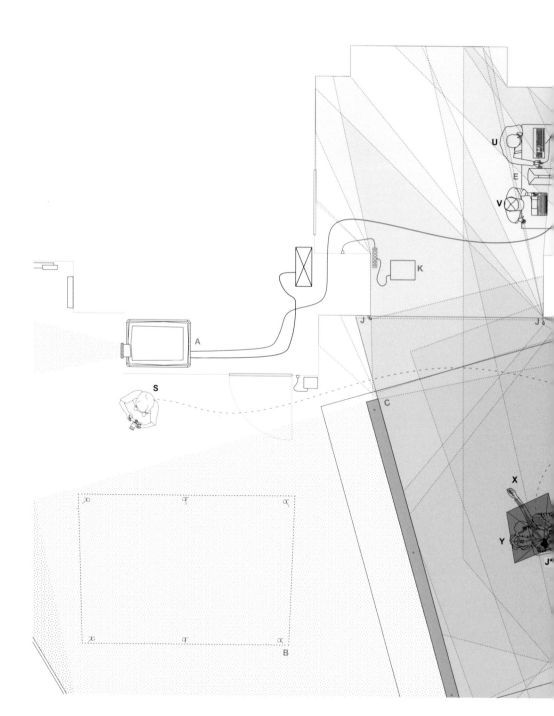

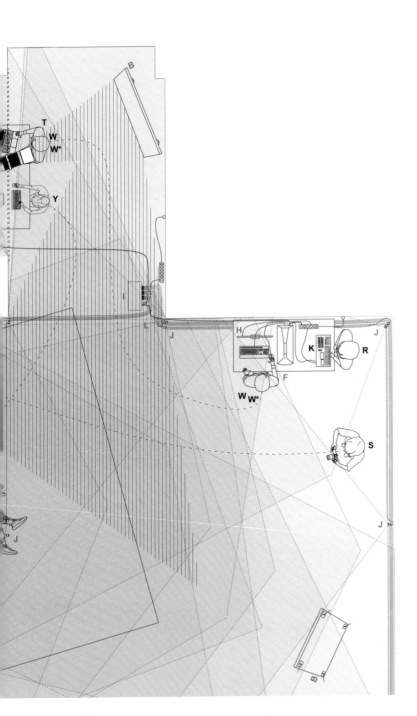

Fig. 5

Architect, worked at Wolfgang Tschapeller's architectural office, where he led the exhibition design for the Austrian Pavilion at the 2012 Venice Biennale of Architecture, which is the predecessor of INTRA SPACE. Simon participated in the early conceptual experiments, had an eye on the administrative and organizational aspects of the project, and coordinated orders and purchases. He also designed the aluminum frame for the projection screen and built furniture for the tracking space, which was used in correspondence with the artificial intelligence narratives for which he worked together with Tom to sketch different scenarios.

T

Light
A 2KW fresnel lamp, light M, was directed into the arches of the ceiling to create indirect, even lighting for the tracking space.

Sound system K
consists of two
passivespeakers,
an amplifier,
and a subwoofer.

Ʞ

⅃ 12 Cables Network
cables using power
over Eternet connected
each camera J with
Rooter I.

Sound artist, engineer, and ℞ music publisher exploring his own and audiences perception limits, experimenting how music can affect body and mind at the most extreme points. Dmytro runs his own music label Kvitnu, releasing experimental electronic music from around the world. In collaboration with Christian, he developed real-time sound responses between virtual figures and moving bodies in space, in relation to speed, position and proximities to devices and bodies in space. Together with Esther, Diane, and Christina, he experimented with transpositions of motion tracking data,frequencies, and voice work as sound layers for performative showings as well as sampling recordings attributing voices to the virtual figures.

AgentS, see
Zissovici,
"Skin Dreams." *W

W Computer engineer, studies at the Institute for Computer Graphics and Algorithms at the Vienna University of Technology. H specialized in photo-realistic real-time rendering of human skin, supervised by Michael Wimmer (expert in real-time renderin of shadows). Christian communicated with Nils Hasler (TheCaptury, former Max Planck Institute for Informatics in Saarbrücken), who developed the markerless, real-time motion tracking system. With Nils's help Christian calibrated and adapted the tracking system to the demands of the research and experimented with different setups of camera arrangements. Christian designed the system architecture, linking the motion tracking system with the rendered virtual figures, improving their appearance, movement qualities, modes of interaction, definition o the different virtual points of views of the cameras, including any particular conditions or parameters in the virtual space. He also su pervised the artificial intelligence design for the virtual figures, supported by Tom Tucek, who entered the project in the last phase. Christian also closely worked together with Mar tin Perktold, Murphy, as the visual appearance, textures, and lighting was closely linked with the motion and behavior of the figures. Christia and Christina spent almost every day in the space together with the technical equipment and formulated the project together, looking at the work while developing it further.

Fig. 5a
Body model, skeleton, and spheres;
drawn based on the concept
developed by Nils Hasler, 2017

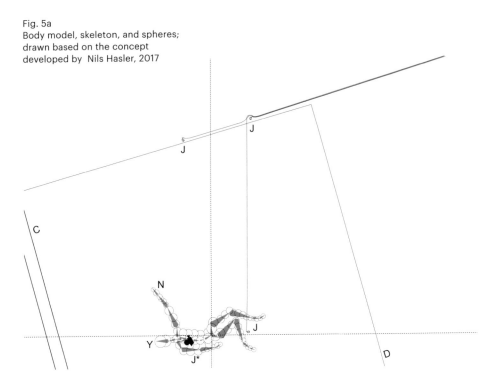

и

The virtual model of the human body is an approximation constructed through the twelve multiple views J. The geometrical
model is defined by Sums of spatial Gaussians (SoG), described
by computer engineer Nils Hasler and his team at the Max Planck
Institute for Computer Science[2].2 With this model they created
a kinematic skeleton of 58 joints with 63 Gaussians attached
to it[3]; each Gaussian is then assigned a color value based on
the clothing of the person who is tracked in the space. The
virtual model is a composite system of spheres and joints,
enabling it to adapt to the proportions of the human body.

2 see C. Stoll and N. Hassler et al., "Fast
Articulated Motion Tracking Using a Sums of
Gaussians Body Model." (paper, 2011 IEEE
International Conference on Computer Vision).

3 see Stoll et al., 3.Vision).

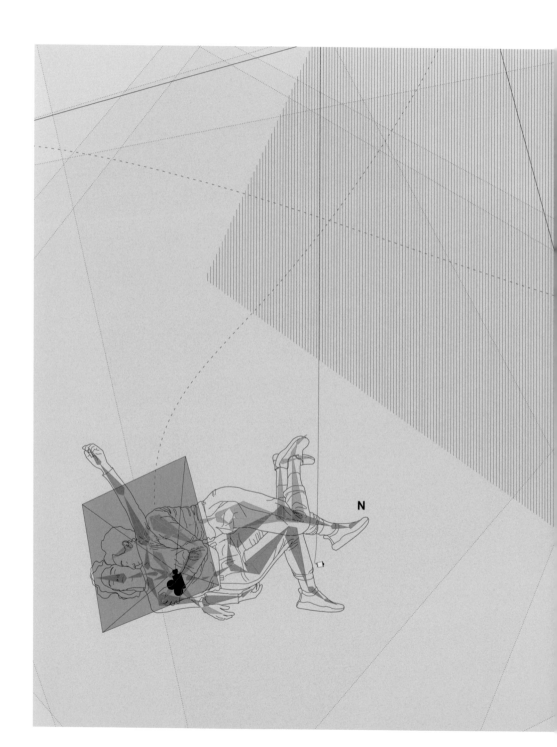

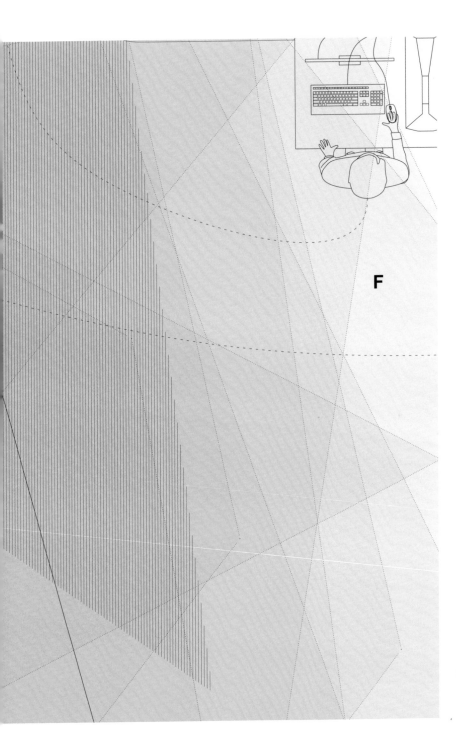

F

Fig. 6

J

Fig. 6a
Industry camera
installed in the
tracking area,
2017

Fig. 6b
Virtual camera
positioned in the
Unity scene

J*

⅂ Tracking PC

Virtual cameras J* are
positioned in the virtual
scene (Unity software) by
Christian W (AgentS W*). In
this scene, cameras J* can
be rotated three-
dimensionally, their focal
length can be adjusted, and
attributes can be assigned.
For example, the camera
J* can be bound to always
center on the head; a path
can be created on to which
the camera J* is linked to
create an orbiting camera
J* around a figure; zoom
functions can be added or
a light can be attached.
Experiments included placing a camera J* between
the eyes, on the right
wrist, on the inside of the
arm, between the shoulder
blades, on the left knee,
in extension of the left
finger, on the sternum. All
twelve industrial camer-
as J are interlinked via
PoE (Power over Ethernet)
cables through rooter I to
tracking PC F. The indus-
trial cameras J provide RGB
information in real-time
for the tracking system.

N Skeleton

Fragments for a History of Other Bodies. The position of the two intertwined
bodies of Esther and Christina lying on the floor in the project space can be
read as a reference to Agnolo Bronzino's allegorical painting Venus, Cupid,
Folly and Time (1546), used on the cover of Michel Feher, Ramona Naddaff, and
Nadia Tazi's book, "Fragments for a History of the Human Body, part 2" (Zone
Books, 1989). In the case of INTRA SPACE, on each of the two lying bodies a
colored skeleton is fitted onto their bodily proportions. These skeletons are
placed virtually in Esther and Christina's bodies, visible only on monitor H.
The skeletons will stay with them as long as Esther and Christina remain
within the sight of the twelve cameras J. The more of these twelve camera
views overlap*, the greater the coverage of their body volumes and therefore
the higher precision of how the skeleton sits on their physical bodies.

* The darker the gray, the more camera views overlap. See the map on pp. 46-47

Fig. 7a
Photograph, reenacting *Venus Cupid
Folly Time*, Esther and Christina

Fig. 7b
View from the tracking camera,
screenshot of software interface.
Esther and Christina with two
skeletons (unknown-2;
snapPoseSkeleton-6)

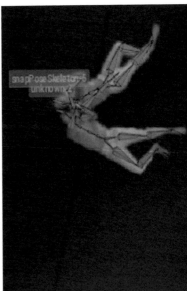

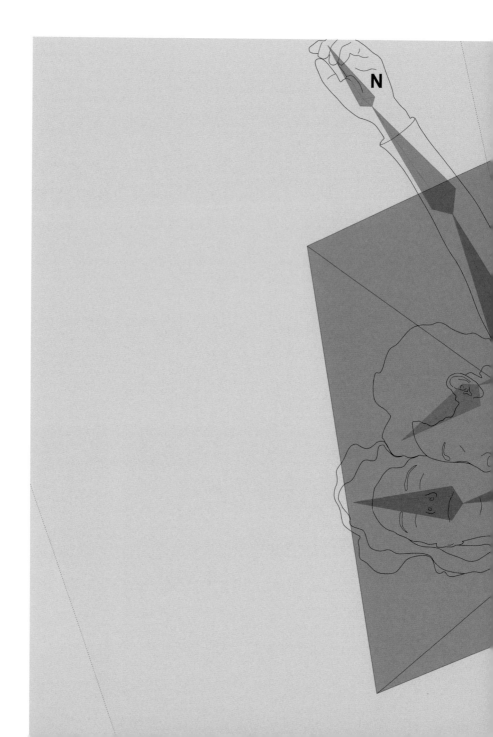

Fig. 7

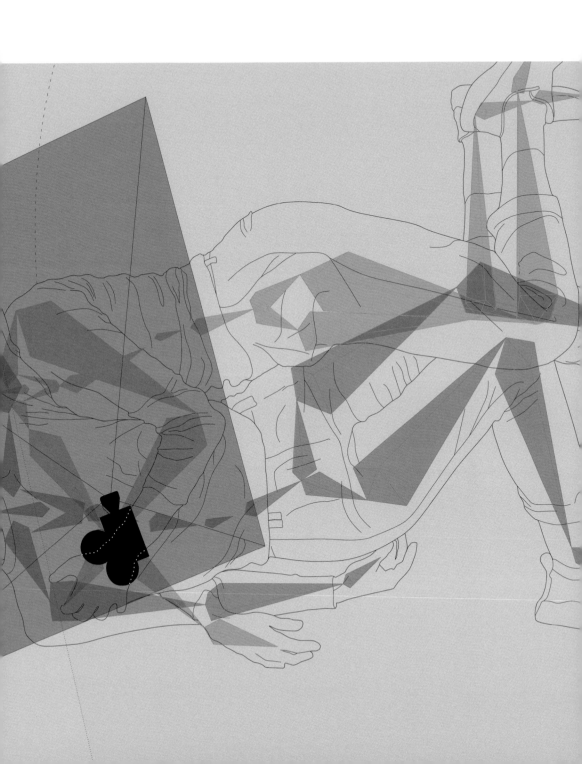

N Skeleton

The tracking system uses a skeleton-like structure modeled
after a human body to trace the movements in the space. It
is a simplified skeleton with 27 bones, approximating the
human posture (an adult human skeleton counts at least 206
bones). If other-than-human shapes are introduced to the
tracking system, the 27 bones arrange themselves on the
unknown form as much as possible without changing the order
or joint positions. The reduced amount of bones is necessary
to allow for a real-time processing of complex movement.
Consequently, the quality of detailed gestures can sometimes get lost, simply because the articulation of smaller
bones is not represented in this skeleton. For example, the
hand is represented with a single bone. As a result, fine
finger movements cannot be described. The template skeleton
is modeled after Nils's body. Nils is the inventor of the
motion-tracking system; he is tall, slim, adult, and male.
Nils's skeleton is then adapted to each unknown body entering the tracking area by scaling the proportions of each
bone. The capacity of this template skeleton to adjust to
bodies in wheelchairs, small children, or animals is limited.
In order to achieve a more accurate tracking, a set of different template skeletons would be necessary.

2 see Carsten Stoll + et al., "Fast
Articulated Motion Tracking Using a Sums of
Gaussians Body Model" (paper, 2011 IEEE
International Conference on Computer Vision).

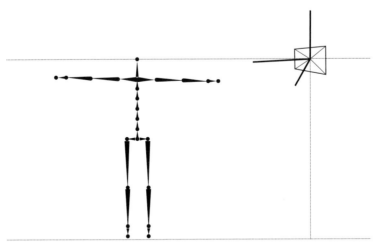

Experiment 1
Placement of virtual camera
opposite eye level / orthogonal

Fig. 6c
Figure shown
with virtually
placed camera
positions,
experiments 2017

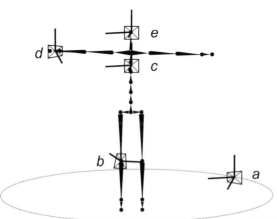

Experiment 2
Placements of virtual camera
a orbit around body / perspective
b knee / perspective
c heart / perspective
d wrist / perspective
e eyes / perspective

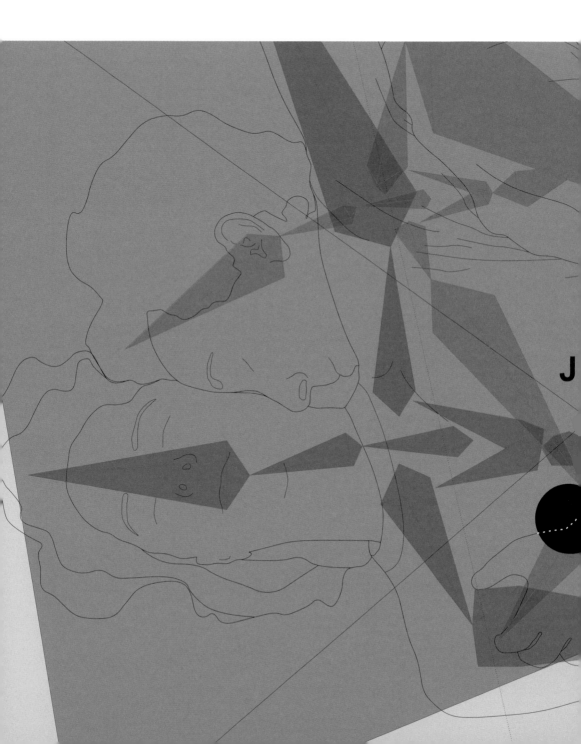

Fig. 8

Fig. 8a
Four of the twelve cameras, motion-tracking
screen (monitor H), 2017

*⌡ The Virtual Camera

The virtually placed camera defines a point
of view. This view is visible on the projection screen C, it is geometrically placed
in the 3D scene on monitor H by Christian
(AgentS). The experiments began with placing
a virtual camera orthogonal, opposite to the
virtual figure in the 3D scene. The appearance
of the virtual figure on the screen C seemed
mirror-like, without depth and perspective
distortion. The immediate and familiar perspective
of this orthogonal view allowed perceiving and
comprehending the entirety of the projected body.
Sizes, orientation, and positioning of body parts
in relation to each other remain recognizable.
Once the virtual cameras started to be placed virtually on the skeleton of the virtual figure and
changing the camera properties to perspective view,
the experience changed dramatically. Magnified,
angled, displaced viewpoints, detached from the pair
of eyes in the head, yet linked to the body. This
shift complicated the relationship between movement,
body position, and orientation in space, posture,
and speed of movements. As much as the human body is
trained to unde stand oneself and others as upright
standing, frontal constellations, this capacity disap-
pears once the visual sense is shifted from the eyes to
other places on the body and in the space.

* Or the thirteenth camera (see Zissovici, "Skin Dreams")

Fig. 9

J*

```
+actorstate(ACTOR, STATE) : my_actor(ACTOR) & not animating
& phase(3) & STATE == handstogether & onGround
     <- +animating;          // currently mid-animation
     -onGround;              // not on ground level
     switchToIdle;          // stop moving, go idle
     !waitForIdle(250,0);
     switchToCeiling;       // agent figure to ceiling
     !waitForIdle(2000,0);
     switchToLive;          // mirror visitor movements
     -animating.            // no longer mid-animation


+sympathy(S) : max_negative_sympathy(MNS) & S <= MNS
     <- !!switchToPhase(11);
     .drop_desire(adjust_sympathy).

+!phase(11) : true
     <- environment(narcotic);
     setTimedZoom(0,1);
     setXRotation(0, 10);
     playanimation(narcotic_sleep_loop, 1, 1, 1);
     ?my_actor(ACTOR);
     ?actorposition(ACTOR,X,Y,Z);
     -+narcotic_position(X, Y, Z).


@react_fast_go_live
+activity_level(AL) & AL > 2 & auto & not sleeping
     <- -auto;
        switchToLive.
```

Fig. 10
Screenshot excerpt of Jason, the
programming language for the
virtual figures' behavior, 2017

4 Tom Tucek, "INTRA SPACE Agent: An Agent-
Based Architecture for an Artistic Real-Time Installation" (BSc thesis, Faculty
of Informatics, TU Vienna, 2018).

5 Felix Kistler, "FUBI - Full Body Interaction Network," accessed November 28, 2018,
https://www.informatik.uni-augsburg.de/en/
chairs/hcm/projects/tools/fubi/.

O Jason

Some aspects of the interaction between human and virtual figures
have been processed through artificial intelligence. This implementation was closely linked with the experiments on perspective, virtually
displaced cameras. Already this procedure of displaced views created
scenarios that no longer could be understood as mere mirroring of the
virtual. On the contrary, it turned out to have qualities of alienation
and unexpected turns. In contrast to these studies on shifting the sense
of body and place and thereby triggering unfamiliar perceptions, the work
with artificial intelligence tried to introduce reactions of the virtual
figures based on spatial or physical parameters leaving the mirroring behavior behind. The agent system implemented uses Jason, a Java-based interpreter
of the agent-programming language AgentSpeak.[4] This open-source system is based
on a belief-desire-intention (BDI) model, which allows agents in Jason to interpret different requirements. In order to provide the information of actions,
body positions, and spatial placement, it was required to recognize and categorize the actions in the space in real-time. Software developed by Felix Kistler,
registering information on human movement and positions called FUBI (Full Body
Interaction Framework)[5] enabled this intermediate, but important step. FUBI, being
a full body interaction framework, allowed to read and interpret the movements. This
information was then forwarded to AgentSpeak. The artificial intelligence of Agent-
Speak links the virtual figures to a library of pre-recorded movements by Esther and
Christina, and with this reservoir of gestures, the virtual figures were given scenarios to leave their mirroring behavior and respond in other ways. We scripted different
angle points of decisions, of reactions to given parameters, including chance. Each figure in AgentSpeak was defined by its initial belief and its plan. Even though narratives
were formulated and transferred into AgentSpeak, the communication between virtual figure
and moving body remained difficult. No comparison to the intuitive and immanent responses
arising from the displaced body cameras of perspective view. The increased, alienated yet
narrated relationship contributed less to the mutual engagement, rather remained stagnant
and confusing. Many times, a loss of contact led to the end of the encounter, whereas in the
meetings without artificial intelligence, contact could be re-established through a shared body
knowledge that remained intact beyond the complete mirroring. Whereas once artificial intelligence was introduced, it seemed intuition ceased to function. As if one would need to learn anew.

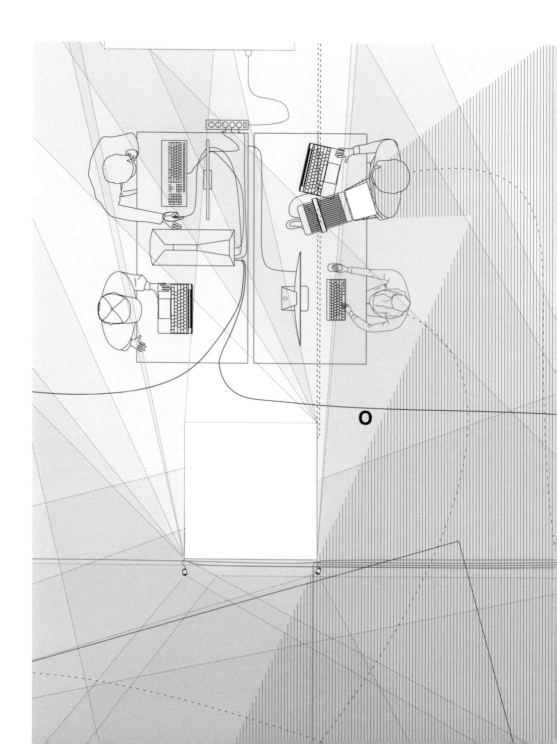

Fig. 10a

Fig. 11
Experiment 1: Orthogonal camera
as mirror with Carla and Esther,
January 2016

Fig. 12
Experiment 1: Orthogonal camera
as mirror with Carla and Esther,
January 2016

Fig. 13
Experiment 2: Perspective camera attached to
Christina's right hand, working with Carla, April 2016

Fig. 14
Experiment 2: Perspective camera attached to
Christina's right hand, working with Old Man, May 2017

Fig. 15
Experiment 2: Perspective camera attached to
Christina's right hand, working with Old Man, May 2017

Fig. 16
Experiment 2: Perspective camera attached to
Christina's right hand, working with Old Man, May 2017

Fig. 17
Experiment 2: Perspective
camera attached to Christina's
right hand, working with Old
Man, May 2017

Fig. 18
Experiment 2: Perspective
camera attached to
Christina's right hand,
working with Old Man,
May 2017

Fig. 19
Experiment 2: Rehearsal Esther, Christina, and two figures, Bob and Bob, perspective
camera attached to Esther's inner-right wrist, May 2017

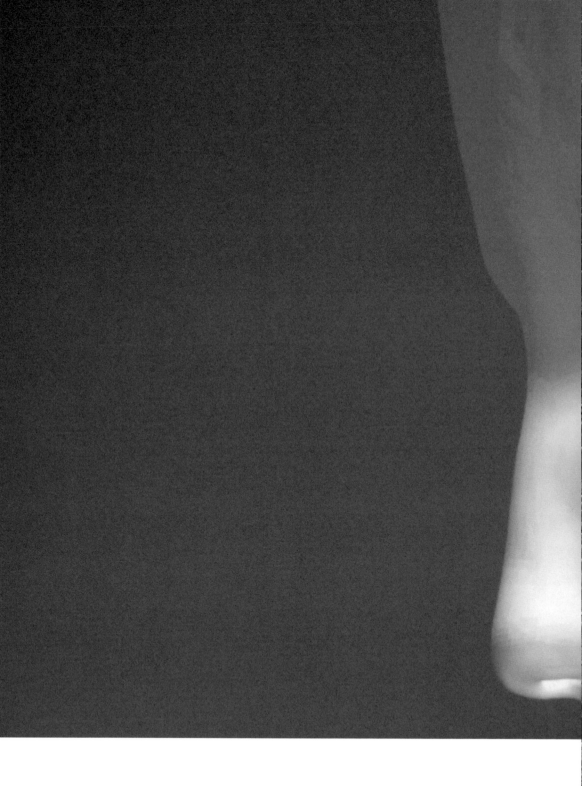

Fig. 20
Experiment 2: Rehearsal Esther and Bob, perspective camera attached to Esther's inner-right wrist, May 2017

Exercises for Re/doing INTRA SPACE

Christina Jauernik

The following exercises have been developed for the reader of this volume, and are based on the physical practice with the virtual figures. A brief preface serves as a "boarding aid" or entrance to each of the eight exercises. As the reader is practicing in absence of the spatial setting of the project and without the virtual figures, these prefaces are thought to allow a subjective, personal exploration with one's own body, inspired by the work with the virtual figures.

Each is accompanied by a description of the exercises practiced in the project by Esther Balfe, Christina Jauernik, and visitors. These could be used as impulses to initiate a movement improvisation, to play with the particular constraints or unfamiliarity of the described scenario, or as an imaginary exercise, a journey for the mind.

Ideally, the exercises are practiced in pairs, which allows one person to read while the other person moves. Practicing with another person also enables each to assume different positions and perspectives. When swapping roles, the knowledge of the observed and of the doing may affect the re/doing and seeing for both the mover and the reader/observer of the translation of the text onto the other body. It is a bodily reconstruction of INTRA SPACE, enabling explorations of physical and attentional forms in other spaces, without the technical equipment. A speculation about the material substance of INTRA SPACE, as a form of perception that can be practiced, shared and communicated and in the practice of re/doing becomes translatable to other spaces, bodies, and sites.

Lerp[1]

Stand upright and close your eyes. Take a moment in stillness. Gradually shift your awareness to the points of touch between your body and the supporting surface, the floor. Sense how the soles of your feet rest on the floor; sense the skin touching the material of the floor. Are your toes touching each other? Feel the contact between skin and skin, skin and material. Change your focus to the in-between spaces, the voids around your feet. Sense the little air pillows underneath each toe, the void space created by the curvature of the large arch between the ball of your foot and your heel. Maybe you can sense an air cushion underneath the anklebone. Notice how the weight is organized within each foot. Is there more pressure towards the front, are you leaning to one side more than the other? In what way is there more pressure towards the front? Are you leaning more to one side than to the other? How is the weight distributed between your two feet? Just observe without changing anything. Sense the small changes, adaptions, and shifts of weight that maintain your upright position. Notice how body parts compensate for tiny, almost imperceptible movements of other body parts. Observe your breathing and its relationship to the balancing acts. Just witness; don't make adjustments.

Note: Try practicing barefoot, in socks, and in shoes.

The virtual figure lifts off the floor and rotates around its own axis until its feet reach the ceiling, only to continue to orbit spiraling back down to the floor. The rotating movement never stops; there is no moment of arrival. All points on the path between floor and ceiling are equal. Neither gravity nor weight exists. Consequently, verticality, and other kinds of orientation are dissolved. Every movement is also a continuous rotation. There is no floor anymore, and there is no ceiling. Turning movements accelerate junctures with the radius of an invisible, inclined orbit. Even resting positions still revolve and remain on the circular path. The weightless journey is suspended between two points in space that once were ceiling and floor.

---

1   Lerp is a term borrowed from computing and mathematics, describing a method of linear interpolation. In computer graphics jargon a lerp is understood as a basic operation of linear interpolation between two values.

Donning[2]

Close your eyes and turn the focus of your vision inward. Consider your
structural setup, the skeletal framework holding your body in the position you
are in now. Bring your attention to your feet. Imagine the tiny bones of your
toes, their joint structure and their possible movement range. Envision them
first in stillness, without moving. Then start to move the little toe joints; test
their abilities to bend, to stretch. Pause. Continue to the ankle joints, and with
your inner eye, picture the possibilities of rotation in the ankles and the degrees of freedom of motion, and then test them. Continue to your knee joints;
picture the planes of rotation and the directions of bending before activating
them. Apply this method to your hip joints. Then move on to the spine, imagin-
ing the complex range of motion of each vertebra before exploring their
actual movement possibilities. Repeat with your shoulder, elbow, wrists, hand,
and finger joints. Finish with your head. Open your eyes and direct your gaze
out into the room. Keep the sense of the witnessed structural components of
your body while seeing the spatial compositions of objects and bodies
around you.

The virtual figure begins donning in a so-called T-pose, which is also the
starting position for this exercise. Standing with the legs hip-width apart and
the arms extended out to the side, a little lower than shoulder level, and
bent at the elbows to the front. The figure looks straight ahead. This position
is held for a moment. Then the structural elements, the bones and joints of
the virtual figure are bent and stretched again, one after the other. It is a first
recognition of the movement premises of the virtual. The articulation and
flexion of each joint introduces the relations and proportions of the virtual,
other body. The movements are performed slowly, as if presenting every body
part to the space. It is a three-dimensional reading of gestures, rather than a
mere demonstration to the front. It is similar to a greeting, conducted, however,
in all directions simultaneously, one joint after the other, bending at the ankles,
knees, hips, shoulders, elbows, wrists, and head.

2   To don: from the late Middle English
    contraction of "do on."

Hand Camera[3]

Begin in a standing position. Look at the space around you. Then pick a body part, for example your left elbow. While still standing, put your eyes in your elbow and start seeing from your elbow. What does this change of perspective reveal, what do you see of your own body? Can you see your back? Can you see underneath your armpit? What does a chair look like from the perspective of your elbow? Then begin to move, leading from the elbow outwards as if reading the space through these new eyes. Explore its range of vision, its relation to other body parts, new proximities and distances. After some experimentation, let the elbow begin to travel through space. Initiate the movement from the point of view of the elbow, the rest of the body following. Allow the elbow to take on different speeds as your guide through the space. Do this for a while. Then pause for a moment and relocate the point of view, your eyes, to another body part. Repeat.

The virtual figure's vision can be placed anywhere in the space or on the figure's body. There is no hierarchy given to the head, or to a pair of frontward-facing eyes in the head. Eyes can be moved, and their focal length and field of vision adjusted, or zoomed in and out. They can be rotated three-dimensionally like an insect eye. For example, a camera, the virtual point of view, can be placed on the wrist of the figure's and/or your right hand, on the inner side with the lens parallel to the lower arm, facing away. From this new perspective, one looks at oneself from the point of view of the wrist. The wrist being at the outer limit of the body, allows for a very mobile eye, extending into a tentacular type of vision, with the ability to look between your shoulders and down your back, to peek behind your neck or your ear, looking upwards from the knee towards the head. The scale, the proportions of the body seem unfamiliar, the contours seem unknown, and the occlusions seen from these new viewpoints create mysterious constellations of body parts intersecting and melding in new ways. Movements slow down dramatically in an effort to re-orientate and recalibrate the sense of the body in space. Proprioceptive sensors are challenged; the positioning is detached from coordinates such as horizons, verticality, or floor-eye level relationships, and a careful contingency of relational three-dimensionality emerges.

3   The hand camera is one example of a series of body cameras. A body camera is a virtually placed point of view, which can be attached to the skeleton of the virtual figure. In some versions, the camera was given constraints, e.g., a fixed direction on a body part, like the head, or the possibility to dynamically zoom in and out, to act as a mirroring or distortion surface.

Interiors[4]

This exercise is based on the hand camera. You can start with the hand camera exercise and continue with interiors. Choose a body part and establish vision from this perspective. Rather than looking outward, this time imagine that the camera is placed on your body part of choice, facing into the body. Imagine your body interior as empty, the skin forming a shell like a cast. The interior of the entire body, the negative, can be seen. Then, for example, place your eyes into your left heel with the point of view orientating up the legs towards the left shoulder. What do these eyes see? What is the interior landscape like? Slowly begin to move to explore this interior vision. Try different body parts. To complicate this exercise, practice it in pairs, with one person guiding the other person as eye/camera, and vice versa.

The virtual figure's eyes are placed on the inside of its right palm. The position of the eyes, the lens, is slightly offset from the actual surface of the hand. The offset is unnoticeable during movements of the hand distant from the body's skin, but once the hand moves closer, the offset becomes apparent. The view of the invisibly installed eye seems infinite; its sight moves through the skin into the interior of the virtual figure. The margin between exterior and interior space is very thin, and minute, careful adjustments of the hand close to the skin shift between the two. As if there were no threshold, the skin is permeated with the ease of a gesture. As immediate as the entry, the stay is never secured. A sudden flicker may catapult the eyes outward. Once again, they carefully feel their way back towards the interiors, aiming for example to enter through the chin. The hand has not yet touched the chin; the eyes have already passed the skin's surface to the inside of the figure. The interior space is lit, and shadows along the curves and bulges of the negative surface of the figure's body support orientation in the unknown landscape inverted to the usual view of the body. The ear with its prominent shape may be recognized and the view of the distant fingertips could set the coordinates for a positioning. It is complicated. With every movement the interior landscape changes, while at the same time the slightest movement of the palm influences the view. The hand slowly traces along the skin, searching, adjusting, and pausing. It is a slow and concentrated scan, a cognitive exhaustion, and a practice of a different form of attention. The "interiors" exercise is extendable to more than one camera and more than one person. The multiplication of eyes creates an even more complex relation-ship of perspectives, relationships, and permeations.

4   The virtual figures are constructed as meshes, a virtual skin that has no thickness and leaves the interior of the figures as empty space. The only interior elements that have been modeled are two spheres for two eyeballs, and the tongue.

Morphing[5]

This exercise is based on the idea of unstable bodies and identities. You will use your imagination, memories of encounters and observations, or video footage and photographs. If there are other people in the room, their bodies can be used as material as well. Take a moment in stillness to arrive. Imagine or watch another body, read the other's posture, its proportions, its tensions, the expression of its gestures, its rhythms while moving. What is particular about this body, what is similar to yours, what is unfamiliar? Continue watching/imagining this other body, and begin to observe any changes in your body, in your posture, in your breathing, in your body tension. After watching the other for a while, and switching back and forth between seeing the other and registering the effect on your own body, look away or stop studying in your imagination. Start moving from what you remember. Translate into your body what you have studied; try to gradually leave your body knowledge behind and move with the other. You can continue this exercise exploring a series of different bodies, either in the space, or from memories/images/footage.

There are several virtual figures; they all share the exact same number of points in their construction. One could say that construction-wise they are related. This particular attribute that they all have in common, also manifests their in-stability. Between Carla and Bob, there are infinite in-between states of Carla and Bob: more Carla, less Bob, more Bob, less Carla. The speed of change can be obvious and rather explicit, but most often it is a gradual and almost im-perceptible transformation from one to the other. The virtual figures not only look different to each other; they have different proportions, sizes, postures, and references to gender and age, even though these cross-fade with layers of post-production and processing. The figures move and simultaneously change bodies. How does such gradual change from one body to the next influence movement qualities and rhythms? Ultimately, how does the proximity of other-ness affect oneself?

5   Morphing is a term used in film industry to blend from one character to another. In order to do this with the virtual figures, the typology, the number of vertices, of each virtual figure exactly matches the other. This prerequisite allows a seamless and continuous change from one figure to the next. The procedure described as morphing links every point of the one figure with a point on the other figure.

Mirroring[6]

This exercise is practiced with another person. Start standing, facing each other. One person begins to move, while the other person tries to mirror the movements in real-time. Begin with slow movements, and increase tempo and complexity over time. After a while, begin to move through space, change your direction, turn away from the mirroring person, change the distance between the bodies. Notice how your focus shifts between your choices of movements, and seeing the other move as you do. Observe how it influences your decision-making when you return to yourself and your intuition, and when you actually begin to respond to what you see. Sense whether with increased tempo, who is mirroring whom becomes more and more ambivalent. The person following you as a mirror notices your gaze. How do you look at the other body in order to grasp its entirety and the details? What strategies do you use to immediately transpose it onto your body, and what do you leave out once the tempo accelerates? Are you anticipating movements? As a variation of this exercise, the mover can begin with eyes closed and the other person following.

The virtual figure performs movements that are not its own. It is a real-time data stream that feeds the virtual body. This body is modeled after a human, adult male body, but composed of fewer components. The points of articulation are placed in reference to the human template, however, their degrees of freedom and rotation are not restricted.[7] The movement feed informing the virtual figure may be interrupted by a sudden connection error, a network breakdown, or simply by a cloud traveling across the sun. The mirror is inconsistent, only partially resembling what you think is reality. Owing to the virtual figure's different construction, a loss of information is compensated for through the figure's inherent logic. What does the figure do when no information arrives, where does it return to? How is information loss or breakdown translated into the figure's movement vocabulary? What are the transition movements between the human's, the figure's, and the system's vocabulary? In the moment when connection is lost, do we reach into each other's spaces?

6   Mirroring refers to Experiment 1 of the research and aims to establish a virtual mirror. This is achieved with a real-time motion tracking system, which captures the movements of a person in space and maps them on to the virtual body.

7   After a series of experiments, collision capsules were introduced. These spherical cushions were placed on the virtual figure to prevent body parts intersecting.

Swapping Skeletons

This exercise is practiced with another person. It can follow the donning exercise, as it builds upon principles studied there. Both of you begin standing, and take a moment to arrive. Feel the weight pouring down into the floor; feel how your feet ground your body. Breathe. Then bring your attention to your body center, the area below your bellybutton. Breathe in and out. Step close to the other person and try to match the other skeleton as close as possible. Keep adjusting to the other proportions, as if embracing a new body composition. Once both have accommodated to the new contours, very slowly detach from each other. Leave the other first at the outer most parts of the bodies, and gradually peel off each other, remaining together at the center. The connection between the hips is the strongest and remains until the very last moment. Depart.

The figure's skeletal structure is most stable in the hip area. The farther away a body part is from the hip, the more likely the figure is to lose it. Lower arms and lower legs are easily lost to other bodies, surfaces, and objects, or even to the system itself. When one virtual figure passes another, chances are high that the hips retain their original figure, whereas a lower leg might swap to and continue with the other figure. The figures are very relaxed about borrowing each other body parts, sharing a foot for a while. This principle of sharing each other's bodies can also be used to swap skeletons entirely. As the skeleton's strongest connection is with its hips, the swapping activity concentrates on the right moment to peel off from the other's center. Once with the new skeleton, a skeleton that has been fitted to another body, movements are less precise. The system has a stronger voice, as the poorly fitted skeleton calls on it to compensate for the missing information.

Hooking Up

This exercise is practiced with another person and can be seen as a continuation of mirroring. One person takes a position; the other person first looks at the position, registering the points in space, the composition of body parts, and their orientation. Then this person tries to take this position with his/her own body, like a fitting piece molding into an invisible given shape. Hold it for a moment, remembering the position, then let go. Try to arrive in this position again dynamically, out of a movement, "take" it and leave it. Repeat this action a few times, as if "catching" the position with momentum. Switch roles, and offer a new position to the other person.

The virtual figure is sometimes attracted to other bodies, objects, and surfaces in the space. If this is the case, the virtual figure huddles against that other structure. Depending on the size of the structure, the figure spreads out, or folds and collapses into a heap. Sometimes it is just body parts that are lost to something else present in the space. By fetching the virtual figure at that spot, and with approximately the same body position, the figure may return to the body.

Vital Technologies
The Involvements of "the Intra"

Vicki Kirby

When I first heard about the INTRA SPACE project at the Institute of Art and Architecture, Academy of Fine Arts Vienna,[1] I was intrigued. The prefix "INTRA" in the title makes deliberate reference to the work of feminist theorist and particle physicist Karen Barad. In *Meeting the Universe Halfway: Quantum Physics and the Entanglement of Matter and Meaning*,[2] Barad introduces the reader to notions of space/time that are so disorienting and counter-intuitive that they test credulity. Indeed, her assault on common sense and our shared perceptions about the nature of reality requires careful unpacking if we are to appreciate the implications of this radical shake-up. The detail of Barad's argument is woven through the arcane complexities of mathematical formulae and science diagrams, laboratory tests and *Gedankenexperimenten*, or thought experiments, and the associated difficulties can be daunting for a reader outside the discipline of physics. However, Barad allows that there are different pathways into this space/time riddle as its uncanny implications are ubiquitous. In other words, wherever we begin our investigation, whether in literature, art practice, biological research, or through an interrogation of plain old common sense, the paradoxes that exercise Barad's attentions in physics are arguably hiding in plain sight, albeit in a different guise.

This is a sweeping assertion and one that seems difficult to excavate easily and persuasively. However, if we concede that the familiar and straightforward may very well conceal unrecognized complexities, then the common conviction that the truth of reality is more or less apparent and verifiable will provide a provisional departure point for our discussion. To begin with this assumption, it seems fair to say that the adjudicating power of observation—"seeing is believing"—is widely accepted as both a felt and rational truth. It grounds empiricism, provides the touchstone for the scientific method, and allows individual perception its pragmatic leverage as something communicable and shared. However, our reliance on the equation of observation with common experience requires further unpacking as this umbrella term can include more than vision when other sensory modalities and forms of attention are involved. And yet even here, in the simple statement that "observation" might involve more than one sensory modality, what seems unarguable becomes surprisingly complicated if this "more" is not a matter of addition. To explain this, we tend to think of perception as a combination of modalities such as vision, touch, smell, and so on, where each "awareness" involves a unique sensory technology, entirely separate and distinct from other channels of experience. However, as we go about the daily business of "being ourselves" we do not give too much thought to how this assemblage of distinct technologies is trans-

1   "INTRA SPACE: PRACTICING–VIRTUAL–
     CONDITIONS," Institute of Art and
     Architecture, Academy of Fine Arts
     Vienna, April 5–8, 2017.

2   Karen Barad, *Meeting the Universe
    Halfway: Quantum Physics and the
    Entanglement of Matter and Meaning*
    (Durham, NC: Duke University Press, 2007).

lated into a seamless unity. And importantly, we cannot petition consciousness as the agential ghost in this particular translating machine because, although a constitutive ingredient in the very possibility of self-awareness, "the how" of these physical operations is largely subliminal.

It seems inescapable that even the most preliminary consideration of corporeal being will evoke quandaries as we are left to wonder what overarching technology has the capacity to translate very distinct perceptions into the inter-modal accord that we live as "self." The question is even more curious if we consider the detail of its implications because the efficacy of this "technology" and its capacity to "translate" must inhere *within* biology, which is an unfamiliar way to explain who and how we are in the world. We will explore the suggestion that the creative abilities we ascribe to human culture and deliberative intelligence are also evident in biological competences, but at this initial stage we need only note the descriptive crossovers that usually go unremarked. If we suggest, for example, that biology behaves like culture, is this comparative likeness mere metaphor, a similarity that is strictly literary with no actual relevance or purchase for an extra-linguistic reality such as corporeal being? Or can this confusion between one thing and another, a sort of reversal or blurring of what comes first and what makes the difference legible or meaningful indicate something unexpected and questionable about all our terms of reference?

These types of question appear even more intricately interwoven as further difficulties emerge. For example, the word I have used to anchor the previous question—"inter-modal"—posits an aggregation of perceptual modalities that are *somehow* in communication, their different capacities translated into a common, unified experience. However, the term "intra" challenges this notion of separate modalities by evoking a sense of overlap and coincidence. It is as if each component in the process is already involved with what is other and elsewhere, as if there is no pure and coherent starting point that is not fundamentally compromised in some way. Karen Barad outlines the challenge and affront that the term "intra" anticipates:

> The usual notion of interaction assumes that there are individual inde-pendently existing entities or agents that preexist their acting upon one another. By contrast, the notion of "intra-action" queers the familiar sense of causality (where one or more causal agents precede and produce an effect), and more generally unsettles the metaphysics of individualism (the belief that there are individually constituted agents or entities, as well as times and places). [...] "Individuals" do not preexist as such but rather materialize in intra-action. That is, intra-action goes to the question of the making of differences, of "individuals," rather than assuming their inde-pendent or prior existence.[3]

With this interventionary caution in mind we can build on the earlier discussion of perception to better understand why Barad is averse to a communication model of causal *intera*ction, and why "appearance," or what seems to be so, can conceal unexpected mysteries.

Until relatively recently it was assumed that the brain was divided into fixed regions of specialization. Just as common sense tells us that sensory modalities are distinct and separate, brain science was also of the view that different regions of brain function were largely independent of each other. Although it was well known that the impairment of a particular sensory competence owing to brain trauma or disease could result in the compensatory enhancement of other senses—a sort of sensory substitution—how an isolated region could remain alert to the health of another and modulate its capacity accordingly inspired little curiosity. It was not until brain imaging technologies were able to refute the assumption that perceptual modalities are localized and fixed that the page was refreshed under a new conceptual model—brain plasticity. However, well before such technological advancements, the early work of scientist and rehabilitation physician Paul Bach-y-Rita makes surprising reading. In anticipation of this argument's discussion of what "the intra" might evoke and why this "concept" exceeds any sense of joining, or gathering together—because this sense of connection or relation between different entities already assumes their prior existence—we note that this maverick researcher into perception had an unusual understanding of sensory differences. He asks, for example, "Are eyes necessary for vision, or ears for hearing, tongues for tasting, noses for smelling?"[4] For Bach-y-Rita, it seems that the specifics of a particular sensory modality are unimportant. As he comments:

> When a blind man uses a cane, he sweeps it back and forth, and has only one point, the tip, feeding him information through the skin receptors in the hand. Yet this sweeping allows him to sort out where the doorjamb is, or the chair, or distinguish a foot when he hits it, because it will give a little. Then he uses this information to guide himself to the chair to sit down. Though his hand sensors are where he gets the information and where the cane "interfaces" with him, what he *subjectively* perceives is not the cane's pressure on his hand but the layout of the room: chairs, walls, feet, the three-dimensional space. The actual receptor surface in the hand becomes merely a relay for information, a data port. The receptor surface loses its identity in the process.[5]

3 Karen Barad, "Intra-actions," interview by Adam Kleinmann, *Mousse Magazine,* Summer 2012, 77.
4 Bach-y-Rita, cited in Norman Doidge, *The Brain that Changes Itself: Stories of* *Personal Triumph from the Frontiers of Brain Science* (New York: Viking, 2007), 14.
5 Bach-y-Rita, in Doidge, 15–16.

Importantly, this is not evidence of sensory substitution where one receptor might hope to repair or enhance another for the process involves something more mangled that is inherently translative and synesthetic in nature, "something" where the specific characteristics of a particular receptor "lose their identity." If, in this example, tactility on the skin is an operative retina that sees the spatial dimension and content of a room, then as Bach-y-Rita suggests, the actual identity of a particular sensory modality can take unusual and unpredictable form.

Over thirty years ago when I was beginning to appreciate that sensory receptors could transpose in surprising ways, I learned of the celebrated musician Evelyn Glennie and mentioned her achievement in my first book, *Telling Flesh: The Substance of the Corporeal*[6]. Her considerable success as the world's premier solo percussionist is especially impressive as she has been profoundly deaf since the age of twelve. Although the label "deaf" is a medical fact, her TED Talk, "How to Truly Listen,"[7] troubles its understanding. Indeed, it is easy to forget that sound is vibration and that receptors for hearing can assume unlikely and surprising appearances—the feet, the jaw, skin, bone, floor, drumsticks, and so on. And yet, perhaps there is even more going on than "tactile audition" in this example, because sound can also be seen if "modes of attention" are practiced and attuned. Is it too far-fetched to consider perceptive technologies as diverse arrangements, a sort of musical score of inventive potentials where "visible audition" and other crossovers might be at play?[8] Because if audition can be tactile, if it escapes the localized parameters of a specific aural apparatus, if it can be found in places that are "not aural," then what exactly does "aural" involve? What remains specific to the identity and technology of hearing?

If the possibility of "visible audition" seems like too much of a stretch then Ben Underwood's story convincingly dispatches any lingering skepticism: remarkably, this teenager's blindness does not prevent him from seeing, and seeing with demonstrable accuracy. In the documentary *The Boy Who Can See without Eyes*,[9] we learn that Ben's surgeon attributes his special abilities to his mother, Acquanetta, and we soon understand why.[10] When her three-year-old son has his eyes removed after a cancer diagnosis, his post-operative anguish at being unable to see is met with a response that could reasonably be described as denial. His mother recalls: "I told him, I said, baby, yes you *can* see. I said you can see with your hands, and I put his little hands on my face, I said, 'See me?' And then I said you can see me with your nose, and I put my hand to his nose and I said, 'You smell me?' I said you can see me with your ears. I said, 'You hear me?' I said, baby, you can't use your eyes anymore, but you still have your hands and your nose and your ears. I said, baby, you can still see."

Acquanetta's heartfelt belief that her son would not be blind is later realized in Ben's practical talents; skateboarding and cycling in the street while negotiating obstacles such as garbage bins, running with pace up and down stairs, physically wrangling with his brother with an easy responsiveness, and taking his measure for a basketball throw that successfully lands in the hoop. His younger brother underlines what he perceived as the banality of Ben's achievement in a casual comment: "When I was a little kid, I didn't really know he was blind. I just knew he was my brother." It seems that Ben's "disability" is not at all obvious, because he learned to see through a process of echo-location similar to the spatial readings of dolphin sonar clicks. By generating his own form of clicking Ben translates the resulting soundscape that bounces back from street surfaces, people, and objects into three-dimensional, visual images that are registered in the visual cortex and therefore "seen."

What is interesting about these different examples of sensory crossover, whether tactile audition, or here, auditory vision, is that the resulting perception is not an aggregation of different modalities that mix together in a composite blend, even though the descriptive terms suggest this. Importantly, a localization model which understands different sensory modalities as separate and independent of each other is unable to explain "the how" of sensory transposition, where identity itself, the actual ontological specificity of what is involved in vision, audition, or tactility for example, proves *inherently* unstable and *intrinsically* transformative *from the beginning*. Although evidence of an originary synesthesia is arguably there from the start, that is, evidence of an *intra*-modal metaphoricity that requires no supplement—no addition of another sense to repair what appears to be missing—it is almost impossible to understand such sensory entanglements outside the logic of aggregation. This is not a mistake that is easily remedied because even when a hybrid sensorium is acknowledged and we self-consciously strive to appreciate its originary intra-implication, the very words we use to describe and explain its merged involvements will surreptitiously return us to the logic of identity and its supplement—one plus another one.

6   Vicky Kirby, *Telling Flesh: The Substance of the Corporeal* (London: Routledge, 1997).
7   Evelyn Glennie, "How to Truly Listen," TED Talk, 2003, accessed May 22, 2019, https://www.ted.com/talks/evelyn_glennie _shows_how_to_listen?language=en.
8   The work of Norman Doidge, mentioned above, together with fascinating examples of sensory adaptation and reinvention explored by the neurologist Oliver Sacks, provide provocative illustrations of such perceptual "crossovers." For the reader who is unfamiliar with Sacks's work a good place to start is *The Man Who Mistook His Wife for a Hat* (1998).
9   See "The Boy Who Can See without Eyes," Dailymotion video, https://www.dailymotion .com/video/x2mqebt.
10 For further discussion of why the status of "being blind" is less obvious than we might think, and how the expectations of others can affect visual ability, see the podcast "How to Become Batman," *Invisibilia*, NPR, January 23, 2015, https://www.npr.org /programs/invisibilia/378577902/how-to -become-batman.

We need to take a step back to examine why the notion of identity, a notion that is necessary to the very process of thinking and making sense, might nevertheless be more problematic than it seems. We could begin with a simple definition of identity—"the fact of being who or what a person or thing is"[11]—but already this dictionary explanation thwarts clarification with a tautological loop that returns us to our starting point. To define a particular entity as essentially and always itself, as if the haecceity of its particular "thisness" is self-evident, makes identity synonymous with enclosure and autonomy. As a consequence, any interrogation of process, or "the how" of "becoming entity," will make little sense. And yet it is a simple truism that the endurance of an entity over time involves constant transformation and this process of being othered will arise from both internal and external causes, as we see with aging. The relevance of this for our discussion of "the intra" is that perhaps identity/the entity is *inherently* undone and never simply "itself"—essentially incoherent *at its first appearing*.[12] Although this runs against the accepted belief that an identifiable point of departure must possess a stability and coherence that is only later subjected to change, "the intra" recognizes that the specific ontology or being of an entity is constitutively mysterious: it cannot be defined in negative terms as either present or absent—entirely itself or not itself.

As counter-intuitive as this may sound, "the intra" recognizes that the "something-ness" of entities, whether material or conceptual, is not generated through a negative economy of differentiation that assumes one thing is independent of another. If an interaction is considerably more involved than the notion of "coming together" might suggest, then terms such as addition, composite, amalgam, hybrid, combination, mixture, assemblage, and compound have effectively displaced a question about the actualization, or even the very possibility, of these processes. Similarly, when we deploy terms such as cause, effect, communicate, translate—that is, words whose different meanings evoke a sense of transit and relationality across a gap or interval that divides one thing from another—could these concepts be likened to band-aids, words that work to conceal the intricacies of an operation that remains invisible and poorly understood?

To try to anchor what might seem an especially abstract discussion with no physical grounding in real life I want to return to the previous examination of sensory plasticity. We have already witnessed examples of hearing and seeing that do not originate in organs considered appropriate and necessary to their respective functions.[13] In fact, evidence of such intra-active exchange challenges the what and where of a perceptual experience and how we identify what is specific to a modality's technological apparatus. If vision is aural, as Ben Underwood's experience suggests, and audition can be tactile, as Evelyn Glennie's achievements indicate, then perhaps perception involves modalities of attunement and interpretation that were always intra-actively operational: perhaps there never was just one modality among others, or one regional site of the brain whose function was specific and circumscribed before its augmentation, or repair, by another.[14] But how far can we take an argument that begins and ends in "originary intra-action"? Should we assume that this mangle of involvements can be *un*tangled to reach a first operation, capacity, or identity that had integrity at some point in the past? As the dilation on "the intra" so far has focused on biological, or material structures, can we reasonably conclude that the structuration of "the intra" only has particular relevance to questions of ontology, or the physical and material aspects of being? This suggestion requires further examination because its implications unsettle many of the referential coordinates that frame this discussion and drive its narrative development. For example, and in anticipation of where this line of thinking might lead, if we find similar evidence of the enfolded relationality of "the intra" within culture, should we assume that this entanglement is operational in *both* systems or that what secures the difference between nature and culture, ontology and epistemology, or what is strictly material from what is ephemeral and abstract, is no longer intact?

In pursuit of an answer to this difficult question we will again return to what seems obvious and undeniable. Our perceptions tell us that the world is a pretty stable place made up of independent things such as people, animals, buildings, plants, bicycles, and the like. These entities are commonly regarded as material because we can touch them and perceive the weight and resistance of their push-back, or presence in the world. Against this sense of matter and its substantive consequence we recognize a more ephemeral realm of words, images, and representations that can assume myriad appearance across different media platforms and in everyday communications. Indeed, it is in this arena of cultural endeavor and exchange that concepts and ideas, notional allegiances and commitments about how the world works and what matters most—or not at all—are forged and contested. And yet even here, in this simple description of the difference between substantive matter and a more ideological under-

11 See "Identity", https://en.oxforddictionaries.com/definition/identity (accessed May 22, 2019).
12 For an analysis of the problematic nature of identity from a very different perspective, one that considers the problem of auto-immunity, see Vicki Kirby, "Autoimmunity: The Political State of Nature," *Parallax* 23, no. 1 (2017): 46–60.
13 Learning to see through the tongue further complicates examples already noted; see "Blind Learn To See With Tongue," YouTube video, 3:06, posted by CBS, January 19, 2007, https://www.youtube.com/watch?v=OKd56D2mvNO (accessed May 22, 2019).
14 For a more detailed discussion of originary synesthesia, Florence Chiew, "Originary Synaesthesia," *Australian Feminist Studies.* Accessed November 24, 2016, https://doi.org/10.1080/08164649.2016.1254028 and Florence Chiew, "Sensory Substitution: The Plasticity of the Eye/I," in *What If Culture Was Nature All Along?*, edited V. Kirby (Edinburgh: Edinburgh University Press, 2017).

standing of matter as meaning, or "what matters," things get confusing. Considerable, even mortal consequence can attach to signification, as the tensions between competing regimes of cultural and political values, aesthetic appreciation, and ethical decision reside within our perceptions and what counts as truth. Despite the ability of information to "become" us, to provide directional modes of attention, orientation, and understanding, most of us will draw a line between these particular regimes of cultural agency and political consequence and what we assume are nature's relatively unchanging regimes of causal force. In other words, although language, images, and representations more generally can shape lives, experiences, and expectations in profound ways, these "economies" of signification are regarded as operationally different from substantive matter, the sort of "stuff" which is of an entirely different order. We have already seen that the biology of perceptual performance is intra-active and surprisingly plastic in its ability to mutate and reinvent itself. But are such expressions of creative aptitude and intra-action always internal to only one system or another, such that the sense of play and chiasmic possibility cannot transit and completely undo the mediating barrier between what belongs to nature and what we deem as culture?

The question of the nature/culture division has always exercised my interest, appearing again and again in associated guises that return us to the ground-versus-figure logic of -A/A: body/mind, woman/man, the other/the one, ignorance/enlightenment, absence/presence. The opposition anchors an evolutionary narrative that posits the primitive, programmatic, and primordial against what is complex, intentional, and more progressed—the definitional significance and value of their differences weighed and affirmed by the very structure of the opposition. The dark, ignorant, emotional menace of nature is pitted against the light, clarifying, and enlightened rationality of culture. However, these divisions can be tricky as they easily morph into their apparent opposites. For example, an original, Edenic, and wholesome nature can be valorized as good and certainly preferable in its lack of instrumental calculation, however, this state of comparative innocence becomes a site for nostalgic regret because it has invariably been contaminated and ruined by the menace of technological penetration, instrumental reason, and exploitation. A quite different story can also emerge where the implied ignorance, deficiency, and threat of what came before is repaired, transformed, and improved by technological innovation and creative insight. This flip-flop between narratives that privilege one side of the opposition as more valuable or worthy than the other suggests an equivalence, such that the politics of what counts can go either way. However, this is far from the case. What remains politically important in these reversals where the content of sexualized and racialized terms are flipped—in other words, where the subject that menaces or is considered good or better can be drawn from either side of the ledger—is that a progressivist narrative of time's arrow unfolds in only one possible direction, from past to present.

Consequently, whatever comes second (and it is always a synonym for culture, or being human) is perceived as more complex, powerful, and inevitably superior, whether for good or for bad, because it breaks with what is comparatively primitive, lacking, and defenseless (nature, the feminine).

Although when looked at closely these divisions are more like simple cartoons that we could easily reject, the power of their resonances and cross-infections resists easy correction. How often, for example, are we encouraged to galvanize our efforts into the "outing" of oppositional thinking, as if the corrective is not a reaffirmation of binary difference. Ironically, the triumphalism of a discourse that eschews binaries requires binaries to identify its improved value—binary versus non-binary, error versus correction—and these recuperated entanglements are pervasive and insistent, providing no escape from such metaphysical duplicities. And yet although we remain unwittingly mired in binary repetition this need not mean that we are doomed to repeat them. If the perversities and unexpected possibilities that *inhabit* metaphysics are as enabling as they are restrictive, then the very identity of metaphysics, how we determine freedom from restraint or indeed the identity of anything for that matter, might involve more than meets the eye.

To return to the importance of the nature/culture division for this discussion, the philosopher Jacques Derrida risks a foundational claim: "The opposition between nature and culture [...] is congenital to philosophy [...] even older than Plato [...] passed on to us by a whole historical chain which opposes 'nature' to the law, to education, to art, to technics—and also to liberty"[15]. Although we can certainly argue that the binary segregation of nature from culture is a mistake, its ubiquity and persistence continue to haunt and organize contemporary debate nevertheless, as we see in the apocalyptic overtones that attach to deliberations around the Anthropocene, the mooted name for the geological stratum of human profligacy and destruction.[16] But here again the tricky aspects of binary agonistics are revealed when what is rejected is quickly, albeit surreptitiously, recuperated. On the one hand, there is a noisy demand to condemn human exceptionalism (culture and its violations), diagnosing anthropocentrism's pomposity, myopia, and murderous self-absorption in the confession—*we are culpable*. On the other hand, however, the special role of responsible overseer, the one who can take reparative action and redeem previous sins is also understood in terms of human exceptionalism as it rein-

15 Jacques Derrida, "Structure, Sign, and Play in the Discourse of the Human Sciences," in *The Languages of Criticism and the Sciences of Man: The Structuralist Controversy*, ed. R. Macksey and E. Donato (Baltimore: Johns Hopkins University Press, 2007), 252.

16 For a detailed discussion of this term's contemporary relevance, see Timothy Clark, *Ecocriticism on the Edge: The Anthropocene as a Threshold Concept* (London: Bloomsbury, 2015).

stalls the human as intelligent and protective agent over the vulnerable, passive, inarticulate, and largely unintelligent body of nature. It seems that whether culpable or responsible the agent of change and control, the subject who can think, decide, and choose, is necessarily human according to this logic. But can we be satisfied with this familiar tale of good versus evil, knowledge and ignorance, passive and active, sinners and saviors? More to the point, can we continue to assume that the identity of human species being, with its specialist capacities and properties—we are the ones who choose the apparatus, who invent and use the technology, to good or bad ends—has persuasive weight? Can the appeal of "the intra" reroute this story by acknowledging its referential confusion and ambiguity, its inability to easily isolate a cause from an effect, nature from culture, a beginning from an end, or even human from nonhuman? Implicit within this series of questions is one about the nature of mediation, or what divides and secures differences of any sort.

Acknowledging the importance of this question, the arts and humanities disciplines have paid considerable attention to mediation as the space where politics happens. Mediation is regarded as that third, intervening "something" between culture (human practices) and an assumed order of things which science investigates. Indeed, there is a widely held conviction that politics is pretty much synonymous with how these cultural and social systems of representation/mediation actually work. For example, on the humanities side of research we are used to arguments whose aim has been to denaturalize received truths in order to contest any sense that they provide an accurate starting point with prescriptive leverage. A successful corrective will displace the rigidity of judgements, concepts, and truths that appear inevitable because naturally determined by proving them historically and culturally inflected. The clear message is that things can be otherwise because we humans are agents of change. However, these gestures entrench the sense that nature is, indeed, static, programmed, primitive, and certainly lacking in agency; and that to be human is, quite simply, to be un-natural because we are severed from our roots. Along these lines we should not be surprised that any mention of biology as an explanatory cause has been regarded warily until relatively recently, especially since previous manifestations of biologism, such as sociobiology, placed causal importance in biology as the unarguable and timeless determinant of what should happen in social life.[17] It was against this style of conservative agenda and its justification that the historical importance and contributions of such figures as Simone de Beauvoir can be read. Her simple assertion "One is not born, but rather becomes, a woman" anticipated the sweeping changes that were to follow: in sum, oppression and prejudice were explained by cultural and social forces, not biological ones.

In her influential book Bodies That Matter: On the Discursive Limits of "Sex,"[18] Judith Butler's title recapitulates Beauvoir's argument in more contemporary form by placing the word sex in inverted commas. In what operates as an effective qualification, the presumptive and enduring truth of sex is displaced, indeed, a pre-cultural, or extra-linguistic appeal to what we might term the reality of sex is not just impossible to grasp because access is denied; more profoundly, it is rendered unthinkable because it is only with/in language and discourse that the world appears sensible. As a consequence "sex" reappears, but as a specific historical and social artifact, and this more complicated understanding of what constitutes the thingness of an object, or what seems inherent to a particular experience, act, or behavior, must discount the stability, persistence, and facticity of a reality that science claims to measure. In short, what we observe and perceive as nature is really culture in disguise.

In an interview with Judith Butler which in part explores the argument that we cannot escape language and cultural representations, Butler explains that all data, regardless of their disciplinary provenance, are interpreted through a cultural lens. Following from this, my question concerns the routine assumption in social analysis that signs, or what we mean by language—representation, codes, ideation—are confined to the arena of cultural production even as certain breakthroughs in the sciences purport to discover languages in nature. An even more compelling question for cultural constructionism concerns the actual practice of science: how can the results of scientific research have any credibility and purchase if we are unable to escape the hermeticism of culture? With these quandaries in mind I asked Butler the following question: "There is a serious suggestion that 'life itself' *is* creative encryption. Does your understanding of language and discourse extend to the workings of biological codes and their apparent intelligence?"[19] What motivated my inquiry was evidence that bacteria have code-cracking capacities inasmuch as they decipher the chemical encryption of antibiotic data. The example has an extra fascination because what constitutes an apparent epistemological skill by bacteria is at the same time an ontological process of reinvention: in the act of reading and decipherment (knowing), bacteria re-engineer themselves and evolve accordingly (being). Given this remarkable collapse of epistemology with/in ontology, I wondered why such an achievement could not be regarded as a language skill. Or to put this another way, I wondered if the achievements of culture could be generalized. Butler's response is a cautionary warning that illuminates what is at stake in cultural constructionist commitments and why they are so fiercely defended:

17 For examples of sociobiology that tend to explain political injustice in terms of nature's operations, see Edward O. Wilson, *Sociobiology: The New Synthesis* (Cambridge, MA: Harvard University Press, 1975); and P. L. van den Berghe, "Race and Ethnicity: A Sociobiological Perspective," *Ethnic and Racial Studies* 1, no. 4 (1974): 401–11.

18 Butler, Judith, *Bodies that Matter: On the Discursive Limits of "Sex"* (New York: Routledge, 1993).

19 Vicky Kirby, *Quantum Anthropologies: Life at Large* (Durham, NC: Duke University Press, 2011), 73.

There are models according to which we might try to understand biology, and models by which we might try to understand how genes function. And in some cases, the models are taken to be inherent to the phenomena that are being explained. [...] I worry that a notion like "biological code," on the face of it, runs the risk of that sort of conflation. I am sure that encryption can be used as a metaphor or model by which to understand biological processes, especially cell reproduction, but do we then make the move to render what is useful as an explanatory model into the ontology of biology itself? This worries me, especially when it is mechanistic models which lay discursive claims on biological life. What of life exceeds the model? When does the discourse claim to become the very life it purports to explain? I am not sure it is possible to say "life itself" is creative encryption unless we make the mistake of thinking that the model is the ontology of life. Indeed, we might need to think first about the relation of any definition of life to life itself, and whether it must, by virtue of its very task, fail.[20]

A constructivist perspective such as Butler's emphasizes that the weight of reality is experienced through the force field of the political, where sociocultural grids of understanding are active in producing our most intimate sense of self, our dearest moral and ethical convictions, the rationale and felt compulsions for why we love or hate, or why we live our gender, race, and sexuality in ways that have historical and social significance. In other words, if pleasures, perceptions, and experiences resonate with political possibility and discrimination then these quite specific cultural forces are intrinsic to who we are, how we perceive ourselves, and what makes reality livable ... or not. Understandably, it is this sense that things can change, that "biology" is just a sign, a contestable representation and not a prescriptive fact, that explains the popularity of constructivism as a strategy that might encourage the possibility of a different future. But can we subscribe to constructivism's assumption that mutability and political contestation are the defining aspects of culture, as if whatever nature (under erasure) is made of is inherently otherwise? Or to put this in a very different way that is perhaps almost unthinkable, could the intra-actions of identity formation, those which encourage us to question what might appear prescribed and given, express nature's own propensity to change itself? Importantly, even if we stick with Butler's approach, it leaves one looking pretty silly in regard to the efficacy of science. Why do scientific models work at all if, by definition, they can have no access to what we regard as the substantive and insistent stuff of reality? Why trust the knowledge of aeronautical engineers, surgeons or chemists if their objects of study are mere representations, models which "by virtue of [their] very task" must "fail"?

As we are now getting closer to what is at stake in this meditation on "the intra" I want to emphasize the special contributions of two thinkers who hail from different sides of the research spectrum. We have already been introduced to Karen Barad, feminist theorist and particle physicist by training.[21] Indeed, it is her notion of intra-action and its unexpected assault on what we mean by identity that we are keen to engage. On the other side of "the two cultures"[22] divide we have Jacques Derrida, philosopher, literary critic: someone whose work has even found a home in certain art and architecture circles. Importantly for our discussion it can be argued that Derrida also explores this notion of "the intra" through what he terms the "non-concept" *différance*. The silent "a" that graphically marks a deviation from différence acknowledges that there is more going on with regard to identity than the oppositional logic of presence versus absence: this or not this. Although one might conventionally assume that différance is not différence, such an assertion is more misleading than clarifying because there are structural complicities *within* binarity that remain relatively hidden, complicities that can stretch identity formation into odd and contagious configurations that thwart definition and correction even as their entanglements are constitutive of them. In sum, Barad's intra-action and Derrida's différance, or "intra-textuality" as he calls it, evoke similar quandaries and provocations. And what is interesting and perhaps unsurprising about this particular difference, especially given what has already been said, is that the separation between the sciences and the humanities is strangely confounded in these examples that appear to draw on unrelated subject matter. Is this because, as Butler insists, we remain inside culture, that is, inside one hetero-geneous system of representational meaning-making regardless of the subject matter? Is it because similar structures of involvement are in operation across the divide, where one side concerns physical, or ontological matters (nature) and the other engages more ephemeral systems of representation and ideation (culture)? Or more profoundly, does evidence that an operational complexity might be held in common necessitate a radical reassessment of division, identity, and binarity itself? In other words, could culture be an expression of nature, not as a second-order, more complex by-product that evolves *from* nature as Butler's cultural hermeticism assumes, but as an expression *of* nature's "own" operational intricacies? That is to say, could fractures, rifts, and involvements be internal to "one" intra-textual system whose generative motor is the self-differentiation of all identity, including its "own"?

20 Judith Butler, cited in Kirby, 73–74.

21 There is an understandable belief that Barad is a feminist and cultural theorist before anything else, in other words, that she writes *about* physics. Given the reach of her work however, it is important to acknowledge that she earned her doctorate in theoretical physics at Stony Brook University and held a tenured teaching position in physics at Barnard College.

22 "The two cultures" refers to C. P. Snow's "The Two Cultures and the Scientific Revolution" (1959), a lecture that addressed the knowledge deficit of those in the sciences regarding the literary canon, and vice versa.

The discussion so far has focused on the problematic aspects of identity and difference, however, as mentioned earlier, a corollary without which identity *as such* is impossible is that of mediation, or the apparent "in-between" one thing and another. Is the limit, the border or barrier an entity, a this-ness, or does it fall prey to what we have already seen is the problematic nature of such a notion? Put simply, can we identify and segregate the boundary, or perimeter of each system, whether nature or culture, from what it either protects or defends against?

To consider this question I want to return to the two thinkers already mentioned, because with regard to this exact quandary their work proves especially pertinent. To take Jacques Derrida's intervention first, in 1975 he gave a series of seminars that addressed the nature/culture division—"La vie la mort." The context, which is not unrelated to the present discussion, involved an analysis of François Jacob's *The Logic of Life* (1993). Jacob, a geneticist, had been working with the linguist Roman Jakobson to understand if the language of the gene could be likened to a natural language, namely the language of cultural practices, instruction, and institutional logic. Derrida questions Jacob's need to assume there are two systems in the first place when he considers the gene's pedagogical achievement, or how it communicates, instructs, or reproduces itself. Does the gene's capacity compare with the reproducibility, or communicative structures, of social and cultural institutions, or what Derrida will gloss as "cerebral institutional—psychic, social, cultural, institutional, politico-economic etc."?[23]. In a meditation that quickly comes to rest on the status of language, a competence invariably interpreted as the essence of what can only be cultural, Derrida generalizes this operation to *include* biological processes. However, the very notion "language," is stretched into unfamiliarity if biology reads and writes, and consequently, it seems reasonable to wonder if Derrida is evoking something entirely different from what is usually implied by the term. Is this a return to Butler's understanding that culture has the capacity to masquerade as nature; in other words, is "biology" a mere representation that inevitably fails to capture what it names?

Although Derrida appears to enclose, or certainly to corral language in the now infamous assertion, "there is no outside text" (*il n'y a pas de hors-texte*)[24], this much cited aphorism can prove misleading if we commit to its commonplace, or restricted meaning. To explain this, Derrida's "language in the general sense" ("textuality") is not a catch-all for the variety of spoken, gestural, or written forms of human expression. Although linguistics is certainly included in what Derrida describes as the "non-concept" "textuality," it loses its pre-eminence as an identifiable, referential touchstone against which other forms of expression might be ranked. If linguistics is an instantiation of textuality's operational complexity rather than an object of analysis among others, the challenge is that what appeared as its unique intricacy and structure is compounded and rendered ubiquitous, its capacity to assume myriad form in clear evidence. Derrida's term is intended to conjure up the relational productivity, or economy, of systematicity *as such*, and systematicity's involvements "with itself" can't be understood, or defined against, anything external to these same processes. In other words, Derrida's "no outside text" does not install an extra-textual, or pre-textual outside that cannot be accessed or known, as Butler conceives it. Indeed, there is no suggestion that the "enclosure" that is "textuality" or "language" is demarcated by a sense of limit or border that divides the integrity of language, or what is proper to it, from what is other and exterior—what is "not language." And this means that the sense of the limit in Derrida's hands is not so much a fixed perimeter that binds interiority against an unknown exterior, but rather an ongoing process of identity formation that is intra-actively pervasive.

Implicit within Derrida's exegesis is another perspective on how we might explore and displace the conventions of scientific inquiry, or cultural constructivism for that matter, when he reads the graphematic structure, intra-textuality or différance, as already a vital *dispositif* whose object is itself. And this, because for Derrida the structure of an intervening model, representation, or medium that separates the knower from the known and epistemology from ontology is no difference at all:

> That which we, men, claim to accept in culture as model, that is to say discursive texts or calculators and all that we believe to understand familiarly under the name of text, that which we pretend then to accept as model, comparison, analogy with the view of understanding the basic living entity; this itself is a complex product of life, of the living, and the claimed model is exterior neither to the knowing subject nor to the known object. The text is not a third term in the relation between the biologist and the living, it is the very structure of the living as shared structure of the biologist—as living—of science as a production of life, and the living itself.[25]

And in a similar passage which again underlines the inseparability of cause and effect, and sender, message, and receiver Derrida notes: "The message does not emit something, it says nothing, it communicates nothing; what it emits has the same structure as it, i.e. it is a message, and it is this emitted message that is going to allow the decipherment or translation of the emitting

23 Jacques Derrida, *La vie la mort: Séminaire (1975–1976)*, 1975. Jacques Derrida Papers MS-CO1, Special Collections and Archives, UC Irvine Libraries, Irvine, CA. Private copy, trans. A. Pont, Seminar 4, 16.

24 Jacques Derrida, *Of Grammatology*, trans. Gayatri Spivak (Baltimore: Johns Hopkins University Press, 1997), 158.

25 Derrida, *La vie la mort: Sèminaire (1975–1976)*, 1975, 5.

message, which implies the absence of anything outside the message, the information, the communication. This is why we have to be clear here that the words communication, information, message, are intra-textual and operate on condition of text, contrary to what they ordinarily lead one to think, namely that they communicate, emit or inform something."[26]

As I have argued that Derrida's intra-textual is Barad's intra-action, we should not be surprised that Barad makes a very similar point about mediation/the model when she states: "Rather blasphemously, agential realism denies the suggestion that our access to the world is mediated, whether by consciousness, experience, language, or any other alleged medium [...] Rather like the special theory of relativity, agential realism calls into question the presumption that a medium—an 'ether'—is even necessary."[27]

If "entities," now in quotes, do not preexist relationality, then what *is* an entity, or for that matter, a relationship, a difference, if a processual entanglement of space/time coordinates are always involved? The very reference points that conventionally anchor questions about the specifics of identity, technology, the virtual—what comes first or where we should begin—appear significantly more alive to their conditions of possibility. We might think of the INTRA SPACE project and its various components—the moving figure/s, the apparatus, a sense of virtuality as vitality, and so on—are these different "components" interchangeable, superpositional? Is the virtual body, whose performance on a distant screen seems tethered to its living origin and yet strangely independent of it, the other of the biological body? And if we answer in the affirmative, usually with automatic certainty, do we forget that the biological body produces and responds to what we regard as external cultural forces—virtual representations such as words and images? Are we troubled that the body we consider "before technology," before language, before craft and calculation, is already, through and through, techne in practice?

Building on such questions I want to close this meditation with a mystery that well reflects the empirical complexity of "the intra," or différance. We began this discussion with the proposition that by observing reality the truth becomes evident—"seeing is believing." However, Sigmund Freud's study of conversion hysteria, a phenomenon where bodily symptoms such as paralysis, blindness, skin lesions, loss of hearing, and seizures carry social significance, was an important catalyst in his awareness that observation, at least as we normally understand the term, might prove misleading. Freud discovered stories of guilt, desire, resentment, and envy inscribed within flesh; generated in the fraught milieu of social interaction they were "converted" into biological signs that "spoke" of complex psychological states. In Jean-Martin Charcot's clinic at the Salpêtrière Hospital in Paris in 1895, Freud saw hysteria first hand and may well have observed examples of dermatographia. Why this symptom, or is it a

Fig. 21
"Dermographisme – Démence
précoce catatonique," T. XVII PL
XXVII, in *Nouvelle Iconographie
de la Salpêtrière* (Paris, 1904)

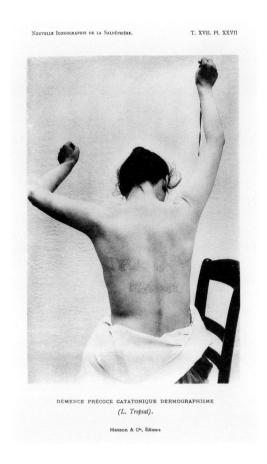

NOUVELLE ICONOGRAPHIE DE LA SALPÊTRIÈRE.   T. XVII. Pl. XXVII

DÉMENCE PRÉCOCE CATATONIQUE DERMOGRAPHISME
(*L. Trepsat*).

Masson & Cᵉ, Éditeurs

26 Francesco Vitale, "The Text and the Living:
Jacques Derrida between Biology and
Deconstruction," *Oxford Literary Review* 36,
no. 1 (2014): 109.

27 Barad, *Meeting the Universe Halfway*, 409.

behavior, would have fascinated medical science at the time is recounted by the physician Toussaint Barthélemy in Georges Didi-Huberman's "The Figurative Incarnation of the Sentence: Notes on the 'Autographic' Skin":

> A patient is hypnotized; the doctor writes his own name on the patient's forearms with a rubber stylet and issues the following suggestion: "This evening, at 4pm, after falling asleep, you will bleed from the lines that I have drawn on your arms." At the appointed time, the patient obliges. The characters appear in bright relief upon his skin, and droplets of blood rise in several spots. The words persist for more than three months.[28]

We might wonder about the temporal and spatial awareness of the dermis— is it an aurality? Because it is as if the skin hears the voice and writes the required words with the stylet of its own blood and tissue—as if it truly *is* its own apparatus. This intra-subjectivity between patient and doctor exceeds tactility and connection because here tactility is voiced as the intra-subjective will of others and made manifest. Perhaps such transpositions and crossovers of motivational cause are also evident in Ben Underwood's ability to see without eyes: recall that his mother, Acquanetta, willed his vision through the synesthesia of hands, ears, and smell, and in a way that challenges the notion that the senses are independent aggregates, but also, that individuals are independent sites of autonomous striving.

Even if we are increasingly aware that biology is more plastic than we had thought, there is still a tendency to assume that culture is the agent that inscribes bodies, where hysteria is understood by Freud and his followers as "a mysterious leap from the mind to the body."[29] Once again, agency writes on passivity, ideation is active and matter comparatively dumb, cognition and complexity trump their primordial beginnings, and so on. But how does biology translate an ideational sign? Or to put this another way, surely the very notion of "the leap" between the ideational/culture (the virtual) to the material/nature is put under some tension here? Do we really have two systems? Or is Freud's mysterious leap a quantum leap [...] where there is no "in-between"?

28 Georges Didi-Huberman, "The Figurative Incarnation of the Sentence: Notes on the 'Autographic' Skin," trans. Caryn Davidson, *Journal* 47, no. 5 (1987): 69.

29 Felix Deutsch, "The Riddle of the Mind-Body Correlations," in *On the Mysterious Leap from the Mind to the Body*, ed. Felix Deutsch (New York: International Universities Press, 1959).

Literature

Barad, Karen. "Intra-actions." Interview by Adam Kleinmann. *Mousse Magazine*, Summer 2012, 76–81.

———. *Meeting the Universe Halfway: Quantum Physics and the Entanglement of Matter and Meaning*. Durham, NC: Duke University Press, 2007.

Beauvoir, Simone de. *The Second Sex*. Translated by H. M. Parshley. London: Jonathan Cape, 1953.

Butler, Judith. *Bodies That Matter: On the Discursive Limits of "Sex."* New York: Routledge, 1993.

Chiew, Florence. "Originary Synaesthesia." *Australian Feminist Studies*. Accessed November 24, 2016, https://doi.org/10.108 0/08164649.2016.1254028.

———. "Sensory Substitution: The Plasticity of the Eye/I." In *What If Culture Was Nature All Along?* Edited by V. Kirby. Edinburgh: Edinburgh University Press, 2017.

Clark, Timothy. *Ecocriticism on the Edge: The Anthropocene as a Threshold Concept*. London: Bloomsbury, 2015.

Derrida, Jacques. *La vie la mort: Séminaire (1975–1976)*, 1975. Jacques Derrida Papers MS-CO1, Special Collections and Archives, UC Irvine Libraries, Irvine, CA. Private copy. Translated by A. Pont.

———. *Of Grammatology*. Translated by Gayatri Chakravorty Spivak. Baltimore: Johns Hopkins University Press, 1997.

———. "Structure, Sign, and Play in the Discourse of the Human Sciences." In *The Languages of Criticism and the Sciences of Man: The Structuralist Controversy*. Edited by R. Macksey and E. Donato. Baltimore: Johns Hopkins University Press, 2007.

Deutsch, Felix. "The Riddle of the Mind-Body Correlations." In *On the Mysterious Leap from the Mind to the Body*. Edited by Felix Deutsch. New York: International Universities Press, 1959.

Didi-Huberman, Georges. "The Figurative Incarnation of the Sentence: Notes on the 'Autographic' Skin." Translated by Caryn Davidson. *Journal* 47, no. 5 (1987): 66–70.

Doidge, Norman. *The Brain That Changes Itself: Stories of Personal Triumph from the Frontiers of Brain Science*. New York: Viking, 2007.

Glennie, Evelyn. "How to Truly Listen." TED Talk, 2003. Accessed May 22, 2019. https://www.ted.com/talks/evelyn_glennie _shows_how_to_listen?language=en.

Jacob, Francois. *The Logic of Life: A History of Heredity*. Translated by B. E. Spillman. Princeton, NJ: Princeton University Press, 1993.

Kirby, Vicki. "Autoimmunity: The Political State of Nature." *Parallax: A journal of metadiscursive theory and cultural practices* 23, no. 1 (2017): 46–60.

———. *Telling Flesh: The Substance of the Corporeal*. London: Routledge, 1997.

———. *Quantum Anthropologies: Life at Large*. Durham, NC: Duke University Press, 2011.

Sacks, Oliver. *The Man Who Mistook His Wife for a Hat*. New York: Touchstone, 1998.

Snow, Charles Percy. *The Two Cultures and the Scientific Revolution*. London: Cambridge University Press, 1959.

Van den Berghe, P. L. "Race and Ethnicity: A Sociobiological Perspective." *Ethnic and Racial Studies* 1, no. 4 (1974): 401–11. https://doi .org/10.1080/01419870.1978.9993241.

Vitale, Francesco. "The Text and the Living: Jacques Derrida between Biology and Deconstruction." *Oxford Literary Review* 36, no. 1 (2014): 95–114.

Wilson, Edward O. *Sociobiology: The New Synthesis*. Cambridge, MA: Harvard University Press, 1975.

Dancing with Machines

On the Relationship of Aesthetics and the Uncanny

Clemens Apprich

> He threw his arms around the lovely Olympia and whirled her through the dance. He had thought that he usually followed the beat of the music well, but from the peculiar rhythmical evenness with which she danced and which often confused him, he was aware of how faulty his own sense of time really was.[1]

In E. T. A. Hoffmann's story "The Sandman," the student Nathanael falls in love with the sublime figure of Olimpia, daughter of the celebrated professor of physics, Spalanzani. During a ball at Spalanzani's house, Nathanael grasps Olimpia's ice-cold hand and asks her for a dance. The confusion he feels vis-à-vis her all-too-perfect movements vanishes as soon as the two sit together and kiss each other. The shy Nathanael with the silent and rigid Olimpia—a spectacle that did not go unnoticed. A few days later, his friend Siegmund confronts Nathanael and asks him upfront, how he could "have fallen for that wax-faced, wooden puppet."[2] He adds: "She seems to us—don't take this badly, my brother—strangely stiff and soulless. Her figure is symmetrical, so is her face, that's true enough, and if her eyes were not so completely devoid of life—the power of vision, I mean—she might be considered beautiful. Her step is peculiarly measured; all of her movements seem to stem from some kind of clockwork. Her playing and singing are unpleasantly perfect, being as lifeless as a music box; it is the same with her dancing. We found Olympia to be rather weird, and we wanted to have nothing to do with her. She seems to us to be playing the part of a human being, and it's as if there really were something hidden behind all of this."[3] The rational and, in Nathanael's eyes, unimaginative friend voices what seems to be apparent—that the object of desire is an artifice created by the ingenious Spalanzani.[4] However, despite all good advice, Nathanael suppresses the obvious. For him, the "poetical soul" of Olimpia is accessible only to a "poetical nature" like his, despite the fact—or perhaps indeed because—of the weird and uncanny feeling he himself feels in the presence of the beloved one.[5]

1   Ernst T. A. Hoffmann, "The Sandman," in *Tales of E. T. A. Hoffmann*, ed. Leonard J. Kent and Elizabeth C. Knight (Chicago: University of Chicago Press, 1969), 115. In the German original, Olympia is Olimpia and Spalanzini is Spalanzani. I will retain the original names in the following.
2   Hoffmann, 117.
3   Hoffmann, 117. Note that the English word "weird" can also be translated as uncanny (*unheimlich*), which, in fact, is the word Hoffmann uses in the original text.
4   Together with the peddler Coppola, who—in another twist of the story—turns out to be Coppelius, the genuinely sinister figure of his father's associate.
5   In Lacanian psychoanalysis, one would speak of an "objet petit a" as the unattainable object of desire. The object belongs to the realm of the imaginary and is defined as a remnant which is left behind when the symbolic gets introduced in the real. By definition, it is something separated and therefore alienating. See Jacques Lacan, *The Seminar of Jacques Lacan. Book XI: The Four Fundamental Concepts of Psychoanalysis* (New York: W. W. Norton, 1981).

Uncanny Feelings

The feeling of the uncanny, masterfully deployed in Hoffmann's story, emerges when we are confronted with an experience of ambiguity, strangeness, or uncertainty. The resulting "lack of orientation" leaves us in a state of unease, a feeling that we are not quite "at home" in the actual situation. This is the classic definition given by Ernst Jentsch, who analyzed the impression of the uncanniness of a thing or situation by tracing it to the German word *unheimlich*. Something familiar (*heimlich*) turns into something unfamiliar (unheimlich),

Fig. 22
Stuart Patience,
Spin Round Wooden Doll

thereby detaching itself from the ordinary experiences of everyday life.[6] Now Jentsch was not interested in defining *what* the uncanny is but instead wanted to understand *how* the uncanny arises in psychological terms. For him, the affective disposition of children, women, *primitives*, and dreamers is, in particular, vulnerable to superstitious beliefs and therefore "subject to the stirrings of the uncanny."[7] What they are lacking, concludes Jentsch, is intellectual mastery of processes whose conditions of origin are unknown to them. It comes as no surprise then that a "poetical nature" like Nathanael's is prone to the "adoring glances" radiating from a divine creature such as Olimpia. His perceived doubt about her *true* nature seems only to fuel his love for her.[8] The tension created by the uncanny situation turns into the pleasant and joyful feeling of admiration, an effect also already observed by Jentsch.[9] What is more, Nathanael's willingness to acknowledge Olimpia's liveness appears to stem, to echo Jentsch once more, from the "natural tendency of man to infer, in a kind of naive analogy with his own animate state, that things in the external world are also animate or, perhaps more correctly, are animate in the same way."[10] Hence the deeply felt belief that Olimpia, and only Olimpia, was able to express thoughts that had sprung from the depth of his own soul—even though she "never spoke any word other than those already recorded."[11]

In his take on the uncanny, Sigmund Freud builds on Jentsch's analysis by acknowledging his attempt to study a feeling of repulsion and distress. For Freud, the subject of the uncanny is a subject of aesthetics, which should not merely be understood as a theory of beauty, but rather as a "theory of the qualities of feeling."[12] Following Jentsch, he makes use of the linguistic meaning of the German word unheimlich to describe the process when something familiar becomes uncanny and frightening. Yet, unlike Jentsch, he does not assume a contrast between the familiar and the unfamiliar but rather sees a conflation between the two. After all, heimlich can also mean something hidden and kept out of sight, which brings Freud to another definition: "According to [Schelling], everything is unheimlich that ought to have remained secret and hidden but has come to light."[13] It is not difficult to find the theory of psychoanalysis at work here, and, indeed, Freud does link the ambiguity of the uncanny

6   Ernst Jentsch, "On the Psychology of the Uncanny (1906)," in *Uncanny Modernity: Cultural Theories, Modern Anxieties*, ed. Jo Collins and John Jervis (New York: Palgrave Macmillan, 2008). According to the *Oxford Dictionary*, the English word "uncanny" also contains the meaning "unhomely," in the sense of something not being cozy or pleasant.

7   Jentsch, 224.

8   One could, of course, say that the suspension of the "critical sense" towards the object

of desire, is precisely what love—or falling in love—is all about.

9   See Jentsch, 221.

10   Jentsch, 225.

11   Hoffmann, "The Sandman," 118.

12   Sigmund Freud, "The Uncanny," in *The Standard Edition of the Complete Psychological Works of Sigmund Freud. Volume XVII: An Infantile Neurosis and Other Works*, ed. James Strachey (London: Hogarth Press, 1955), 219.

13   Freud, 224.

feeling to the defense mechanism of repression. What he identifies behind Jentsch's seminal, but incomplete definition is the uncanny world of the unconscious, perfectly staged by Hoffmann's story. Hence, for Freud, Nathanael's horror is not merely the result of an "intellectual uncertainty" vis-à-vis the wooden doll, but something secretly familiar (heimlich—*heimisch*) that has been repressed and now comes to light. Freud points out that the story behind the story is that of the "sandman," a cruel creature, which, according to the nurse of Nathanael's sister, bereaves children of their eyes in order to feed them to his own.[14] The psychoanalyst recognizes in this story the fear of castration, especially since "a study of dreams, phantasies and myths has taught us [i.e., Freud] that anxiety about one's eyes, the fear of going blind, is often enough a substitute for the dread of being castrated."[15] However, in his attempt to put the castration complex into the center of analysis, Freud seems to ignore the fact that Jentsch does not explicitly use "The Sandman" as an example to explain his notion of the uncanny, but instead talks more generally about artistic tricks in storytelling to produce uncanny effects.

In the 1814 short story "Automatons,"[16] Hoffmann puts these effects to use by making a whole series of mechanical devices appear. In particular, the "talking Turk" is meant "to leave the reader in uncertainty as to whether he has a human person or rather an automaton before him."[17] Here the uncanny is linked to movements and vocal sounds of the automaton, as well as its mysterious ability to guess the darkest secrets of its human counterparts. In Hoffmann's work of phantasy, the imitation of humanity cumulates into the dread of "living death or inanimate life,"[18] as Ludwig, one of the protagonists puts it. It is the conflation between animation and simulation that evokes strong feelings about the *nature* of automated machines. Hence, the subtler the artificial reproduction, that is, the less visible the difference between the human and the machine is, the stronger the uncanny feeling appears to be. This is, in a nutshell, the observation the Japanese roboticist Masahiro Mori made in 1970.[19] One and a half centuries after Hoffmann, he described the phenomenon of the "uncanny valley" as a possible relation between the likability of machines and their resemblance to a human being. The concept suggests that the acceptance of an object which simulates human behavior (e.g., puppets, robots, avatars) depends on human-like appearance. However, while the affinity would be highest if the imitation could no longer be distinguished from a real human person, Mori observed a sudden drop in the acceptance of humanoid machines, if they appear to be almost, but not exactly, like human beings. In the uncanny valley we are, once again, confronted with the strange and eerie feeling of something un/familiar. The emerging "doubt as to whether an apparently living being really is animate and, conversely, doubt as to whether a lifeless object may not in fact be animate"[20] echoes our very own existential anxiety in view of a technological (posthuman) world.[21]

Ontological Ambiguity

The question of intellectual uncertainty between the animate and the inanimate is at the heart of our techno-cultural world and "can yield some vital clues as to how the Freudian uncanny can be made relevant to the contemporary discussions of the psychic powers of image, medium, and automata in digital media."[22] In her book *The Freudian Robot*, Lydia Liu reminds us that at the beginning of Hoffmann's story it is Nathanael who is treated like an automaton, thereby leaving doubt whether he himself is a living (human) being or not.[23] In this reading, Nathanael does not merely project his erotic desire on Olimpia, but shares the same ontological ambiguity—and, one may add, anxiety—with her.[24] It thus appears that behind the rather obviously depicted mechanical doll Olimpia another, more hidden (i.e., repressed) automaton comes to light.[25] What gets introduced here is a *doppelgänger* (Nathanael/Olimpia), a strange figure which pervades modern thought and literature. This theme connects the old dream of a godlike reproduction—one only has to think of Ovid's Pygmalion, a theme that is later taken up in Jeffrey Shaw's rather misogynistic play of the same name—with the contemporary fear of being substituted by an object-world. Hence, "the very ontological instability expressed by the artifact itself, the oscillation between animate and inanimate, subject and object, human and thing"[26] can be seen as the expression of an "uncanny modernity."[27]

14 Nathanael associates this nightmarish creature with Coppelius, his father's associate, who displays an eerie fascination with eyes.

15 Freud, 231. What Freud mentions here is, of course, the Oedipus complex.

16 Ernst T. A. Hoffmann, "Automatons," in *The Serapion Brethren*, trans. Alex Ewing (London: George Bell and Sons, 1908).

17 Jentsch, "Uncanny," 224.

18 Hoffmann, "Automatons," 355.

19 Masahiro Mori, "The Uncanny Valley," *IEEE Spectrum*, June 12, 2012, https://spectrum.ieee.org/automaton/robotics/humanoids/the-uncanny-valley.

20 Jentsch, "Uncanny," 221.

21 Gertrud Koch, in this context, speaks of a "pathological relationship" we entertain with machines (Gertrud Koch, "Animation of the Technical and the Quest for Beauty," in *Machines*, by Thomas Pringle, Gertrud Koch, and Bernard Stiegler [Minneapolis: University of Minnesota Press, 2019], 5).

22 Lydia H. Liu, *The Freudian Robot: Digital Media and the Future of the Unconscious* (Chicago: University of Chicago Press, 2010), 207.

23 This doubt is reinforced at the end of the story, when Spalanzani tosses Olimpia's eyes at Nathanael, screaming: "The eyes—the eyes stolen from you!" (Hoffmann, "The Sandman," 120).

24 This might then also be the reason why Nathanael is the only one who does not find Olimpia to be weird or uncanny (see above).

25 Lydia Liu concludes that Olimpia's invention is therefore another trick by Hoffmann to deflect the reader's attention from the *real* automaton: "The character Nathanael is so effective and so successful that critics and psychoanalysts, Jentsch and Freud alike, do not seem to entertain the slightest doubt about his ambiguity as a living human character or an undead automaton in the context of the story" (Liu, *Freudian Robot*, 222).

26 Bill Brown, "Reification, Reanimation, and the American Uncanny," *Critical Inquiry* 32 (Winter 2006): 199.

27 This being the title of a book edited by Jo Collins and John Jervis (see note 6).

According to Bill Brown, it was the ambiguous status of the slave, being both a person and a thing, that not only made the idea of an autonomous and self-generating economic system possible, but also haunts capitalism's self-imagination ever since. The slave, like the automaton, returns as a threat, a thing of terror, showing the system that it was not autonomous in the first place.

The demarcation between subject and object, between animate and inanimate, between human and nonhuman has always been historically constructed. Freud's reading of "The Sandman" is therefore also a product of his time, not least because psychoanalysis tends to translate the object-world back into the human.[28] By downplaying the role of Olimpia, Freud represses the onto-logical status of the nonhuman, thereby following the dominant scientific discourse of the early twentieth century. What is more, the female Olimpia gets sublated entirely in Nathanael's infantile male fears (i.e., the castration complex). As we have seen before, this is a very specific, if not to say narrow, reading of Hoffmann's work and one might question the interpretation that Olimpia is no more than "just a detached complex of Nathaniel."[29] As Hélène Cixous explains: "If she is no more than that, why are not the dance, the song, the mechanisms, and the artificer brought back into the game or theorized upon by Freud?"[30] According to this reading, the pivotal dance scene of the story is glossed over by Freud so that he does not have to deal with Olimpia's *liveness*. Because rhythm and movement are often considered a female mani-festation of the animate, it comes as no surprise that Olimpia's dancing gets suppressed in order to maintain the oedipal, that is the male interpretation, of Nathanael's anxiety. By focusing on the story within the story (i.e., the Sandman), Freud reinscribes the ambiguous—maybe even queer—status of its characters into the realm of his psychoanalytic theory. Put differently, the masculine *animus*, associated with the rational soul, is given preference to the female *anima*, in order to avoid the pitfalls of its emotional disposition and the resulting lack of intellectual mastery.[31]

Now over the last decades, feminist theorists, such as Donna Haraway or Rosi Braidotti, have been "insisting upon the need for ontologies and epistemolo-gies that recognize a broader and more diverse spectrum of human/nonhuman hybrids, interactions, and relations."[32] In particular, Karen Barad's reconceptu-alization of materiality can be seen as a new material thinking, which takes into account the technological apparatuses we use to make sense of the world around us.[33] Her "agential realism" has arguably become one of the most influential ideas in (feminist) technoscience, not least because it claims to integrate such divergent fields as quantum physics, experimental metaphysics, or social in-equalities. Inspired by her approach, the artistic research project INTRA SPACE has been investigating "how interactions between, across and beyond humans and nonhumans can be experimentally embodied, esthetically reformulated and

Fig. 23
Project space of INTRA SPACE

28 See Brown, "Reification," 198.

29 Hélène Cixous, "Fictions and Its Phantoms: A Reading of Freud's *Das Unheimliche* (The 'Uncanny')," *New Literary History* 7, no. 3 (Spring 1976): 538.

30 Cixous, 538.

31 See Carl Jung's ideal-typical classification of the unconscious mind into a masculine animus and a feminine anima (Carl G. Jung, *Aion: Researches into the Phenomenology of the Self* [London: Routledge, 1991]).

32 Lisa Parks and Nicole Starosielski, "Introduction," in *Signal Traffic: Critical Studies of Media Infrastructures*, ed. Lisa Parks and Nicole Starosielski (Urbana: University of Illinois Press, 2015), 10.

33 Karen Barad, *Meeting the Universe Halfway: Quantum Physics and the Entanglement of Matter and Meaning* (Durham, NC: Duke University Press, 2007).

theoretically challenged in their spatial, temporal and transversally entangled spheres."[34] Using Barad's concept of "intra-action,"[35] the real-time installation explores the dynamic relationship between human and nonhuman bodies in digitally activated spaces. The idea is to literally make virtual figures dance, by setting a whole apparatus of cameras, screens, sensors, and software in motion. Hence, the animation is done not only by the human performers but also by the engineers and programmers, as well as the computers and machines. By displaying the *Hinterbühne* as part of the performance, the project does not deny the underlying object-world, but "critically looks at the potentials of both, the digital and the human, to mutually enhance their functionality, their exposure in artificial and real spaces, their social interaction and self-perception."[36] The dance then becomes a sort of mystery tour, exploring the possibilities for an equal encounter between human and machine. The bodies in motion thereby produce "new attentional forms"[37] vis-à-vis our digital and networked environments.

Animate, Don't Simulate

The happy dance with the digitally construed *doppelgänger* is in stark contrast to current discussions accompanying technological innovation.[38] Automation, digitization, and the rise of artificial intelligence are catchwords in a long-standing debate about technologically driven social change. The problem is not so much that technology transforms society but, on the contrary, that the much-announced change is merely a simulation of already existing social relations. Thus, what we witness is an endless reproduction of commodity culture.[39] A well-known example is Google Duplex, which was announced as the latest push for virtual assistantship: "Whether you're booking a table at your neighborhood sushi joint or trying to schedule a last-minute haircut before your big event, sometimes you just need to pick up the phone to get something done."[40] This might come in handy in certain situations, but making phone calls on our behalf to participate in consumerism is not a game-changing step. Rather, technology from Silicon Valley, with its promise to cater to our everyday needs, feeds into our very own narcissism. With their ongoing person-alization and customization digital media promise to create the perfect image of the self, so that the user is led to believe that she is in full control of the technological process. However, the human user is merely a part in a more complex machinic system, providing the necessary data for the machine to learn and, therefore, adjust to the user. For this mirror-game to work, the underlying infrastructure and mechanism of data extraction are hidden. Rather than making the object-world tangible, Google Duplex "is built to sound natural, to make the conversation experience comfortable."[41] The anthropomorphization of the machine follows the above-mentioned logic in modern thinking: by suppressing the ontological difference between the animate and the inanimate, the human subject is reassured in its belief to master the world.

Not only do our virtual *doppelgänger* deploy a human, but most often a feminine voice. Whereas the "talking Turk" in Hoffmann's "Automatons" was modeled on Wolfgang von Kempelen's mechanic chess-playing machine from 1769[42] and finds its current expression in Amazon's so-called "artificial artificial intelligence,"[43] it is striking that most virtual assistants are female by default (e.g., Amazon's Alexa, Apple's Siri, Microsoft's Cortana, Google's Assistant).[44] In both cases, the orientalized chess-playing automaton and the feminized talking machine, notions of "otherness" are invoked: "Gender and racial or ethnic otherness have been used both to make [...] human-like machines attractive and to alleviate the possibility of horror that always follows them."[45] As Tiina Männistö-Funk and Tanja Sihvonen further explain, the long history of othering human-like machines "leads to a conclusion that it appears to be easier to let machines come close to the borders of humanity if they take the form of 'lesser' humans, meaning anything other than white adult males."[46] On the one hand, the onto-logical difference between the human and the machine gets omitted to simulate liveness; on the other hand, the uncanny effect thus created is attenuated by making the machine less *awesome*.[47] This deeply narcissistic behavior is compound by the fact that in the hyper-individualistic world of social media the ego is formed by the image of the other.[48] The user produces data by constantly

34 "About," INTRA SPACE, accessed February 28, 2019, https://intraspace.akbild.ac.at /imprint.

35 Barad, *Meeting the Universe Halfway*, 33.

36 "About."

37 Bernard Stiegler, "Relational Ecology and the Digital Pharmakon," *Culture Machine* 13 (2012), https://www.culturemachine.net /index.php/cm/article/view/464/501.

38 *Doppelgängerin*, to be precise, as the avatar in the performance was often referred to as Carla. Carla then became a synonym for all the other figures appearing during the project, thereby transforming into an androgynous entity.

39 See Jean Baudrillard, *Simulacra and Simulation* (Ann Arbor: University of Michigan Press, 1994).

40 "The Google Assistant can help you get things done over the phone," Google, accessed February 28, 2019, https://www .youtube.com/watch?v=-qCanuYrROg.

41 Yaniv Leviathan and Yossi Matias, "Google Duplex: An AI System for Accomplishing Real-World Tasks over the Phone," *Google AI Blog*, May 8, 2018, https://ai.googleblog .com/2018/05/duplex-ai-system-for-natural -conversation.html.

42 Wolfgang von Kempelen, a Hungarian author and inventor, built "The Turk" to impress the Empress Maria Theresia of Habsburg. Curiously enough, von Kempelen also invented one of the first speaking machines.

43 Amazon's micro-working platform, which makes use of human labor to perform tasks that computers are unable to do, is called Amazon Mechanical Turk and often described as "artificial artificial intelligence." See also Clemens Apprich, "The Corrupt State of Artificial Intelligence," *Texte zur Kunst* 109 (March 2018).

44 In fact, Google Duplex, which is built on Google's Assistant, might be the only commercial assistant that has both a female and a male voice by default.

45 Tiina Männistö-Funk and Tanja Sihvonen, "Voices from the Uncanny Valley: How Robots and Artificial Intelligences Talk Back to Us," *Digital Culture & Society* 4, no. 1 (2018): 59.

46 Männistö-Funk and Sihvonen, 59.

47 "Awesome" understood here in its original meaning, as something terrifying.

comparing him- or herself to other users, thereby fueling a culture of vanity and self-endorsement. Envy, jealousy, and rivalry are the templates in the design of our media-technological environment. Instead of enabling new forms of connectivity (and thus collectivity), our apps, devices, and services separate (human and nonhuman) individuals from each other, by creating ideal images beyond one's—and each other's—reach. As a consequence, we never really feel *at home*. And, as Nathanael's tragic ending suggests, such alienated experience is ultimately prone to acts of (self-)aggression.[49]

How can we then break the vicious circle in our relationship with technology? A possible remedy is mentioned in the opening quotation: After all, it is Nathanael who puts his arms around Olimpia and swirls her around. This is an important detail, as it hints to the fact that ultimately all forms of animation are expressions of interaction. Regardless of the speculation whether Nathanael is a machine himself or not, the "bringing-to-life" of the scene involves both individuals, not to mention the music as well as the entire ballroom. Rather than merely imitating the usual movements, the dance introduces an ambiguity, which affects everyone present. The "event" literally bursts into the everyday routine of life, evoking reactions of awe and distress, but also excitement and wonder. It entails what cultural anthropologist Dietmar Kamper calls acts of "premitation" (*Vorahmung*), following the old Greek meaning of *mimesis*.[50] Rather than a "simulation" (*Nachahmung*), mimetic practices influence the course of things and open up new possibilities. Whereas simulation wants to create an "artificial doublet" of real-world phenomena, thereby concealing the ontological difference between the animate and the inanimate, premitation engages the world by deploying this ambiguity. This is the reason why artistic-research projects such as INTRA SPACE are so important. They grapple with and discuss the intellectual uncertainty vis-à-vis the object-world, instead of dismissing it as something inconvenient and deficient. The predisposition and vulnerability towards the uncanny therefore hold the promise of a new understanding between the human and the machine, which is not shrouded by anthropomorphization.[51] Such an "aesthetic of ambivalence"[52] is not driven by creating affinity through imitation, but wants to enable a genuinely technological experience by making the ontological difference tangible. Eventually, the artificial world is not as artificial as we use to think. As can be seen from the example of the virtual assistants, it takes a lot of still-human labor and data to animate their intelligence.[53] Echoing the words of Ferdinand, one of the protagonists in Hoffmann's "Automatons," it is we who answer our own questions" when talking to these machines.

48 See Jacques Lacan, "The Mirror Stage as Formative of the I Function as Revealed in Psychoanalytic Experience," in *Écrits: The First Complete Edition in English*, trans. Bruce Fink (New York: W. W. Norton, 2006). From a psychoanalytic perspective, narcissism and the idea of artificial life are, of course, connected to the male phantasy of autonomous reproduction. After all, it was Narcissus who spurned the love of Echo and eventually died out self-love. One can only speculate whether the engineers and programmers at Amazon thought about the tragic story when developing the company's very own smart assistant.

49 After trying to kill his fiancée, Nathanael commits suicide by throwing himself off the platform of a tower. On the relation between narcissism and aggression, see Jacques Lacan, "Aggressiveness in Psycho-analysis," in *Écrits*.

50 See Dietmar Kamper, "Mimesis und Simulation. Von den Körpern zu den Maschinen," *Kunstforum International* 114 (1991), accessed February 28, 2019, https://www.kunstforum.de/artikel /mimesis-und-simulation.

51 This, of course, was also the program of French philosopher Gilbert Simondon (see Gilbert Simondon, *On the Mode of Existence of Technical Objects*, trans. Cécile Malaspina and John Rogove [Minneapolis: Univocal, 2017]).

52 See Lilli Gast, "Das Unheimliche der Ambivalenz," *Forum der Psychoanalyse* 27 (2011).

53 Kate Crawford and Vladan Joler, "Anatomy of an AI System: The Amazon Echo as an Anatomical Map of Human Labor, Data and Planetary Resources," *AI Now Institute and Share Lab*, September 7, 2018, https:// anatomyof.ai.

Literature

Apprich, Clemens. "The Corrupt State of Artificial Intelligence." *Texte zur Kunst* 109 (March 2018): 136–41.

Barad, Karen. *Meeting the Universe Halfway: Quantum Physics and the Entanglement of Matter and Meaning*. Durham, NC: Duke University Press, 2007.

Baudrillard, Jean. *Simulacra and Simulation*. Ann Arbor: University of Michigan Press, 1994.

Brown, Bill. "Reification, Reanimation, and the American Uncanny." *Critical Inquiry* 32 (Winter 2006): 175–207.

Cixous, Hélène. "Fictions and Its Phantoms: A Reading of Freud's *Das Unheimliche* (The 'Uncanny')." *New Literary History* 7, no. 3 (Spring 1976): 525–48.

Crawford, Kate, and Vladan Joler. "Anatomy of an AI System: The Amazon Echo as an Anatomical Map of Human Labor, Data and Planetary Resources." *AI Now Institute and Share Lab*, September 7, 2018. https:// anatomyof.ai.

Freud, Sigmund. "The Uncanny." In *The Standard Edition of the Complete Psychological Works of Sigmund Freud. Volume XVII: An Infantile Neurosis and Other Works*, edited by James Strachey, 19–252. London: Hogarth Press, 1955.

Gast, Lilli. "Das Unheimliche der Ambivalenz." *Forum der Psychoanalyse* 27 (2011): 349–58.

Google. "The Google Assistant can help you get things done over the phone." Accessed February 28, 2019, https://www .youtube.com/watch?v=-qCanuYrROg.

Hoffmann, Ernst T. A. "The Sandman." In *Tales of E. T. A. Hoffmann*, edited by Leonard J. Kent and Elizabeth C. Knight, 93–125. Chicago: University of Chicago Press, 1969.

———. "Automatons." In *The Serapion Brethren*, translated by Alex Ewing, 352–82. London: George Bell and Sons, 1908.

INTRA SPACE. "About." Accessed February 28, 2019, https://intraspace.akbild.ac.at /imprint.

Jentsch, Ernst. "On the Psychology of the Uncanny (1906)." In *Uncanny Modernity: Cultural Theories, Modern Anxieties*, edited by Jo Collins and John Jervis, 216–28. New York: Palgrave Macmillan, 2008.

Jung, Carl G. *Aion. Researches into the Phenomenology of the Self*. London: Routledge, 1991.

Kamper, Dietmar. "Mimesis und Simulation. Von den Körpern zu den Maschinen." *Kunstforum International* 114 (1991). Accessed February 28, 2019, https://www .kunstforum.de/artikel/mimesis-und -simulation.

Lacan, Jacques. "The Mirror Stage as Formative of the I Function as Revealed in Psychoanalytic Experience." In *Écrits: The First Complete Edition in English*, translated by Bruce Fink, 75–81. New York: W. W. Norton, 2006.

———. *The Seminar of Jacques Lacan. Book XI: The Four Fundamental Concepts of Psychoanalysis*. New York: W. W. Norton, 1981.

———. "Aggressiveness in Psychoanalysis." In *Écrits: The First Complete Edition in English*, translated by Bruce Fink, 82–101. New York: W. W. Norton, 2006.

———. "The Mirror Stage as Formative of the I Function as Revealed in Psychoanalytic Experience." In *Écrits*, 75–81.

———. *The Seminar of Jacques Lacan. Book XI: The Four Fundamental Concepts of Psychoanalysis*. New York: W. W. Norton & Co, 1981.

Leviathan, Yaniv, and Yossi Matias. "Google Duplex: An AI System for Accomplishing Real-World Tasks over the Phone." *Google AI Blog*, May 8, 2018. https://ai.googleblog .com/2018/05/duplex-ai-system-for-natural -conversation.html.

Liu, Lydia H. *The Freudian Robot: Digital Media and the Future of the Unconscious.* Chicago: University of Chicago Press, 2010.

Männistö-Funk, Tiina, and Tanja Sihvonen. "Voices from the Uncanny Valley: How Robots and Artificial Intelligences Talk Back to Us." *Digital Culture & Society* 4, vol. 1 (2018): 45–64.

Mori, Masahiro. "The Uncanny Valley." *IEEE Spectrum*, June 12, 2012. https:// spectrum.ieee.org/automaton/robotics /humanoids/the-uncanny-valley.

Parks, Lisa, and Nicole Starosielski. "Introduction." In *Signal Traffic: Critical Studies of Media Infrastructures*, edited by Lisa Parks and Nicole Starosielski, 1–27. Urbana: University of Illinois Press, 2015.

Simondon, Gilbert. *On the Mode of Existence of Technical Objects*. Minneapolis: Univocal, 2017.

Stiegler, Bernard. "Relational Ecology and the Digital Pharmakon." *Culture Machine* 13 (2012). Accessed February 28, 2019. https://www.culturemachine.net/index .php/cm/article/view/464/501.

Body of Landscape

Esther Balfe

Figs. 24–41
Stills from a recording by
Ludwig Löckinger on March 23,
2017

The body is a landscape.

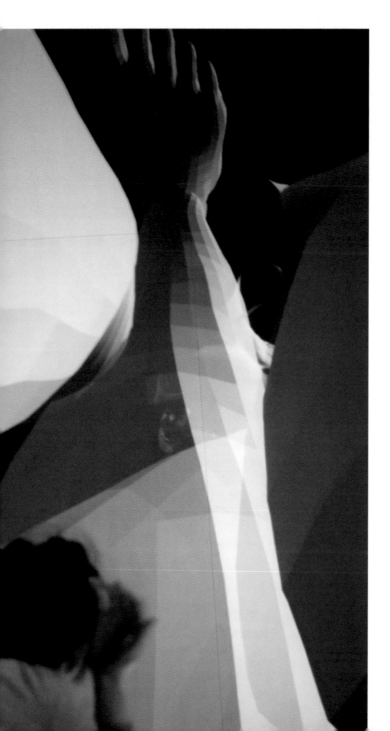

Split second decision-making, taking place.

Direct and impermanent influences.

Impulses are excepted and converted.

Her unresponsive skeleton, erasing conventional movements and giving rise to her own unique irritated language.

She is now initiating movement rather than imitating the human figure.

"To pretend, I actually do the thing: I have therefore only pretended to pretend."
—Jacques Derrida

The nature of this work is mercurial. In a sense, I am a different figure each day.

Appearances can be ephemeral.

Perception of the Carla figure changes constantly.

Each interaction is never a replication of the last.

Even on the fixed movement phrases, owing to Carla's glitches, one cannot recreate the same occurrence.

Having given her agency to a new predicament, I am no longer the command giver.

Carla is preoccupied with the task of having to reconfigure her erratic limbs.

She is flipping back and forth from her software commands, from the ethereal to the concretely real sub-human interactions.

Ever failed. No matter. Try again. Fail again. Fail better. Despite the similarities concerning the word "fail" and "again." I can't help fixating on the words "no matter."

It becomes an advantage to fail in order to produce a new substance, allowing another texture to emerge. Both parties are indirectly solving problems. In dance terms I consider this to be a dialogue, a conversation, an interchange, a skull session.

INTIMACY
LOSS
SKINNING

Christina Jauernik

Fig. 42
Christina Jauernik, *Bones*, 2018

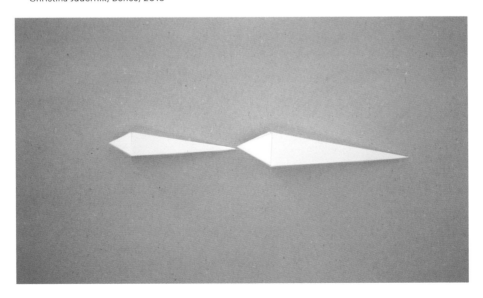

Stand and face me, dear; release
That fineness in your irises.

May you bed down,
Head to breast, upon
The flesh
Of a plush
Companion.

Sappho, "Come Close"[1]

INTIMACY [*Vertrautheit*]
Latin *intimare*: "impress," or "make familiar"
Latin *intimus*: "inmost"

The building of a relation between engineered and human entities implies a shared condition. As such, a form of togetherness or proximity among these entities is expected, or even required. What are the grounds of this together-ness, what qualities and challenges unfold, and what insights into a practice and routine with other-than-human entities could it suggest? A spatial, em-bodied practice enabling a real-time motion-tracking-based interaction between virtual, engineered, and human entities constitutes a quite literal approach to these questions. Could this shared condition be a non-discriminatory, equal meeting of different entities, of mechanic, of technical, of human, of nonhuman, and of other natures and species? Taking into account the physical, affective, space-time related and technical prerequisites of such other-than-human points of contact, the predicament already lies there, in all that we do not share. Having practiced in such a shared condition for more than two years, I would like to explore traces of intimacy in digitally activated environments by reflecting on the INTRA SPACE project.

The Latin origin of the term "intimacy," intimare means "to impress" or "make familiar" and is related to the Latin intimus, the "inmost." The etymo-logical note becomes further relevant when—rather than thinking of "im-pressing" in the sense of projecting a positive image—one considers the idea of physical "impressing," or what in German would be called *prägen*. The term describes a particular kind of touch, the action of making contact between surfaces through pressure. For example, in the graphic technique

---

1   Sappho, "Come Close," In *Come Close*,   Classics, no. 74 (London: Penguin Random
    trans. Aaron Poochigian, Penguin   House, 2015), 21.

known as "nature printing" (*Naturselbstdruckverfahren*),[2] a natural being such as a flower or a leaf is covered in a medium, and leaves a lasting reproduction or imprint of itself on a copper plate or a piece of paper. The surfaces provide both resistance and accommodation, thereby influencing the degree and intensity of the impact or interaction. Apart from the material effect, a *Prägung* exerts an influence on behavioral or affective dimensions, which, as residues of such interactions, can last beyond the actual physical contact. The action of touch activates sensors, as in a greeting: the meeting of hands registering and molding into the shape of the other, reading each other's creases and folds. In sensing and receiving the other surface through touch, a process of "making familiar" is initiated. Consider the tradition of shaking hands as the initial point of contact: within a short moment, you register shape, proportions, temperature, material qualities of dryness or dampness, wrinkled or firm surfaces, degrees and course of pressure, duration, rotations; the imprint of the gesture once the hands have withdrawn from each other. Even though a handshake is of a fugitive nature, it gives you the possibility to read and briefly make yourself familiar with another in this shared moment. It is the experience of exposure to the other that reconstitutes the subjects, becoming a body in the collective splitting of bodies.[3] In order to be able to read the other in the process of imprinting, you need to be willing to partly allow your thinking and your body to enter a state of mutually receiving.

While the qualities and capacities of two hands shaking for the first time are familiar to us, the first point of touch between engineered virtual and human entities functions differently. The greeting procedures as defined in the technical framework of INTRA SPACE begin with a reading of the space without body. This moment of registration of the spatial pre-condition before any greeting can take place, takes three seconds. Within a defined zone, the system searches for a body volume that appears as different to the previously registered space. The presence of the person is read, sensed, and understood by the system only as a difference to the previous spatial condition. The body's proportions are approximated through a model of spheres, whose sizes adapt to the length and dimensions of the particular body present in the space. In order to improve the quality of communication, the initial reading of the body is enhanced by particulars as the person slowly moves her/his major joints, introducing the system to the body's scale through bending elbows, hips, and knees. These simple, hitherto socially non-codified gestures are a kind of greeting ceremony, the "getting-in-touch" ritual with the technical, engineered entity. The clarity, speed, and articulation of gestures define the quality of the communication from then on in. Once the registration is complete, relations are established. We are imprinted on each other. *Wir prägen uns gegenseitig*. Now we can come closer.

Fig. 43
Christina Jauernik, *Head and Neck*, 2018

2   "Naturselbstdruck [basiert] auf einer
    Berührung mit der Natur 'die sich selbst
    zum Drucke hingibt', wie Alois Auer schreibt,
    der als Direktor der k. k. Hof- und Staats-
    druckerei die Entwicklung des Naturselbst-
    drucks bis zur Patentierung 1852 vorantrieb:
    Ausgehend von einem Abdruck des zu
    druckenden Gegenstands in Blei wird über
    zweimalige galvanoplastische Abformung
    eine Kupfertiefdruckplatte erzeugt, die
    originalgetreue Bilder nicht nur der sondern
    auch *durch* die Natur liefert." Simon
    Weber-Unger, *NATURSELBSTDRUCKE.
    Dem Original identisch gleich* (Vienna:
    Album Verlag, 2014).
3   See Jean-Luc Nancy and Federico Ferrari,
    "Trans," in *Die Haut der Bilder* (Zurich:
    diaphanes, 2006), 106.

SKINNING [*Häutung*]

"Skinning" is a process in animation design whereby a skeleton is assigned a three-dimensional wireframe mesh model. During this step, bones and joints that together form a kinematic structure are bound to a surface to which textures and material properties can then be applied. The marrying of these two components, the skeleton and the surface, allows the model to appear and move in the digital space. In both English and French, the term "surface" contains the word "face"; the literal meaning of "surface" describes a plane that lies above or on a face, similar to a mask of a face placed onto that face. A mask has an inside and an outside and is "simultaneously surface and image."[4]

In her work *Cyberface*, Irene Andessner produced self-portraits by searching for virtual, artificial beings without faces, masks without material—physical background so to speak—and slipping into these faces herself, thereby superimposing self- and alien perception.[5]

Fig. 44
Christina Jauernik, *Dress and Bones*, 2018

The marker-less motion-tracking system adapted for INTRA SPACE approximates a humanlike skeleton (humanlike as it is a simplified bone-joint structure with reduced detail and articulation) and imposes it virtually onto the body volume of the person in the space. The space is defined by the intersection of twelve different viewing angles of small cameras: cameras produced as built-in components for industrial machines, robots, and technical equipment, are appropriated to become the "eyes" of one or more technical, engineered entities. Regardless of the number of entities, they all share the same twelve eyes. The camera eyes face towards the center of the space. They are wired with Ethernet cables to the tracking computer and transmit the data as color information (RGB) to the system. The human entity is in touch with the technical, engineered entity once the cameras have registered the human body volume and extracted it from the rest of the space.

The communication is carried by a perpetual finding of skin, of "skinning" each other as a process, re-interpolating the proportionate skeleton into the volume of the present body. The communication is not through words, but through oscillating states of being in one's own and the other's skin, of becoming almost one, coming closer and growing more distant again. Coming closer is experienced not only through reducing spatial distance, but also in recognizing your own movements, gestures, and shapes. Distancing is then perceived as your movement being intruded upon, corrupted, becoming unfamiliar. The perpetuation of the shared condition requires a different particular form of concentration, of reading, of receiving, and of being in the space. At the same time, one's attention is drawn to the exchangeability of bodies and Francesca Woodman's practice comes to mind, of her multiplying her own body and body parts, using masks and mirrors.[6]

4   Hans Belting, *Faces: Eine Geschichte des Gesichts* (Munich: C.H. Beck, 2014), 45. Unless otherwise noted, all translations are my own.

5   Another example of virtual self-superimposition is the work *Karlotta* (2003) by visual artist Santeri Tuori, a girl finding and passing through a previously captured image of herself. While in a scene of the film "Bladerunner 2049" we see K in his apartment in front of a meat with fries dish, when his holographic friend Joi serves a virtual soup and places it on top of K's plate.

6   Abigail Solomon-Godeau, "Körperdouble," in *Francesca Woodman*, ed. Gabriele Schor and Elisabeth Bronfen (Cologne: Buchhandlung Walther König, 2014), 74.

Fig. 45
Christina
Jauernik,
*Dressing for
a Skeleton*,
2018

LOSS [*Verlust*]

"It is through, and not despite, our alienated condition that we can free our-selves from the muck of immediacy. Freedom is not a given—and it is certainly not given by anything 'natural.' The construction of freedom involves not less but more alienation; alienation is the labor of freedom's construction. Nothing should be accepted as fixed, permanent, or 'given'—neither material condi-tions nor social forms."[7] Is the alienated condition and an at least partial giving up of your own condition by changing to a state of receiving (*hineinversetzen* and therefore *außer sich sein*) with technically engineered beings, a potential construction of freedom? The experience of intimacy is accompanied by a constant threat of its potential loss through alienation. This applies also, or even more so, when engaging in forms of contact with nonhuman entities. At the same time, one is exposed to the inconsistency or indeterminacy of other, virtual figures, which are also involved in their own processing, and perhaps even in "forking," a term used in software engineering to define, among others, a splitting into several copies with different tasks, a term used by artist Johannes Paul Raether to describe the evolution of his figures.[8] Reading and understanding each other (*auf etwas zurückgreifen*) involves resorting to something yet to be established. Like and unlike human-to-human interaction, building and caring for a relation to other entities of technological, virtual, or machine nature leaves one vulnerable to inconsistency and unpredictability. The constantly present possible failure of technology fosters the uncertainty in the status of being together. In the practice of this research, the immanent insecurity and therefore fragility of the shared condition manifests itself in different attentional forms,[9] in a slower pace, in a change of focus to a more peripheral vision. In the issue on "The Individual" of *Texte zur Kunst*, the authors of the article "Buffering of the Self: Guising in the Mid-'00s" witness "strategies that obscure, pluralize, or otherwise complicate one's identity (note: thereby offering) the opportunity to get rid of yourself."[10] The process of making a connection is tied with the possibility of becoming more unfamiliar. With the gain of knowledge and recognition of the other, both are possible: intimacy can be increased, and alienation can take place. A practice based on non-verbal communication and its perpetuation requires a focus on and reading of the technical condition. In the words of Ed Atkins, a video artist who creates virtual

7   Armen Avanessian and Helen Hester, *dea ex machina* (Berlin: Merve Verlag, 2015), 16.

8   Johannes Paul Raether, lecture "Identitecture" as part of the series "What Beings Are We?" at the Institute for Art and Architecture, Academy of Fine Arts Vienna, April 30, 2018. See also www.johannespaulraether .net, accessed May 14, 2019.

9   Bernard Stiegler, "Relational Ecology and the Digital Pharmakon," *Culture Machine* 13 (2012): 3.

10 Storm van Helsing, André Rottmann, Sarah Nicole Prickett, Reena Spaulings, @LilInternet, i.i.i., and Luther Blissett "Buffering of the Self: Guising in the Mid-'00s," *Texte zur Kunst*, 104 (December 2016): 76.

characters of photo-realistic appearance, "Loss in the technological, specifically digital sense, has all but shrugged off its physical, etymological forbears."[11] Atkins describes loss as "the sublime condition of any experience."[12]

A prerequisite to loss would seem to be possession. You need to own and/or be empowered by something in order to then be able to experience its loss. From the perspective of the engineered being, your presence is required for your absence, your disappearance. Once something has manifested itself, it becomes possible to search for it. In comparison to transience (*Vergänglichkeit*), which suggests a time of gradual disappearance, loss is a cut. The cut is temporally, spatially, and physically felt. Whatever is lost might be found, rediscovered, archeologically restored, or marked, but it requires an action, a carrier to reappear. In building relationships between technical, engineered entities and human entities, someone is always searching. Moving with digital beings is a practice of constantly restoring, of recovering from loss, of reactivating partly lost pieces of communication. It is a constant search in hope of reaffirming this connection. The particular method of searching for the other, of stepping out of the occult and opaque towards an unattainable transparency, opens an in-between space. "Transparency does not reflect,"[13] as philosopher Emmanuel Alloa stated in a short interview for dOCUMENTA(13), but instead enables a "seeing through, without seeing *that* through which we see."[14] I do not turn transparent, and neither does the virtual; rather, through the technical, engineered entity I am enabled to see the other through me. The in-between of this relation is, I would say, diaphanous in nature. The diaphanous is the substance through which the relation is rendered visible (*erscheint*). Alloa differentiates between two aspects of the diaphanous: translucidity as "the permeable quality of a medium that (spatially) lets vision through"; and generativity as "the productive quality of a medium that (causally) lets something come into view."[15] Applying this description to the spatio-relational model of the technical, engineered, and human entity, I would argue that the quality of the appearing through (*dia*) as perceptive milieu is the embodied condition. Even though the embodied is visible through the superimposition of body and skeleton, it not only appears through the image, but beyond the image. Beyond, because the central aspect is the moving together, involving all senses including vision, but not restricted to vision. It suggests a distributed, multiplied seeing as if eyes and lenses were disseminated all over the body. The experience occurs through this shared relationship; the diaphanous is the carrier, the intermediary in this altered state of seeing. As an embodied model, it is no longer just the gaze that enables a "looking through," but the entire body, the skin, the proprioceptive senses, the entire sentient being. The entire bodily surface is able to "see." This suggests a phenomenology that is perhaps more plant-like than overtly human, or rather that points to our plant-like sensory talents that in the course of evolution have mostly retreated, shrinking violet-like, in favor of the five dominant senses. In the virtual, eyes can be situated anywhere. The point of view can be displaced from the position of the pair of eyes in the face of a human (or mammal). Such a displacement of vision changes the human's spatial orientation and organization: its verticality, its coordinates system, the being-in-the-world as a standing and moving upright entity in dialogue with a horizon as point of reference. It leads to a different perception of the environment in relation to oneself.

Peter Handke indicates a change from seeing (*sehen*) to watching (*schauen*) which I read as a production and increase of distance and a different form of attention towards what is perceived, looked at, sensed. He describes it as the loss of images[16] (*Bildverlust*): "The loss of images is the most painful of losses."—"It means the loss of the world. It means: there is no more seeing. It means: one's perception slides off every possible constellation. It means: there is no longer any constellation."—A loss of images for the imagination: hearing and seeing are in no relation to each other anymore. Seeing is a projection, a line; hearing can reach around corners. Similar to the narrative in Handke's novel, in INTRA SPACE the loss of images takes place with a loss of horizon. The standardized and familiar forms of per-ception and given images are thereby diminished. The loss of images (*Bild-verlust*) is tied to a setting-in-motion. Part of being human is loss. That is one's fevered destiny. One never arrives at oneself, at rest within oneself. One is not transparent to oneself. (*Der Mensch ist sich nicht durchsichtig.*)[17]

The model of INTRA SPACE is scaled to allow a full-body experience, an embodied action that I understand as an essential aspect of the experiments. Loss therefore also communicates through the entire body as a physical change that is perceived. The moving body as sentient being is distinct to a stationary body, or a body restricted in its movement by sitting on a chair, tied to a keyboard, a mouse, or a head-mounted display with power cables of limited length. In such a technical setting, loss is noticed underneath the fingertip of the (mostly right) index finger, and on the many screens that have colonized our daily lives and environments, and *through* which we live.

11 Ed Atkins, "Losslessness," in *More than Real: Art in the Digital Age*, ed. Daniel Birnbaum and Michelle Kuo (London: Koenig Books, 2018), 96.
12 Atkins, 83.
13 Emmanuel Alloa, "Emmanuel Alloa on Transparency," 1:32 min., June 25, 2012, dOCUMENTA (13) Video Glossary, accessed February 20, 2019, https://d13 .documenta.de/#/research/research/view /on-transparency.
14 Alloa, "On Transparency."
15 Emmanuel Alloa, "Transparency: A Magic Concept of Modernity," in *Transparency,*

Society and Subjectivity: Critical Perspectives, ed. Emmanuel Alloa and Dieter Thomä (London: Palgrave, Macmillan, 2018), 35.
16 Peter Handke, *Crossing the Sierra de Gredos*, trans. Krishna Winston (Frankfurt am Main: Suhrkamp, 2002), 464. (Original German edition: *Der Bildverlust oder Durch die Sierra de Gredos* [Suhrkamp, 2002]).
17 Marcus Steinweg, "Taumel," in *Inkonsis-tenzen* (Berlin: Matthes & Seitz, 2015), 63.

The digital offers the possibility to release the body from its spatio-temporal condition, and to detach images from the urge to represent (*Abbilden*). Whereas analogue photography is reminiscent of the past, of aging, of absence, of death, the digital image is without time.[18] The digital is always within its own presence, and therefore a different form of being.

Fig. 46
Christina Jauernik, *Bone for a Hand*, 2018

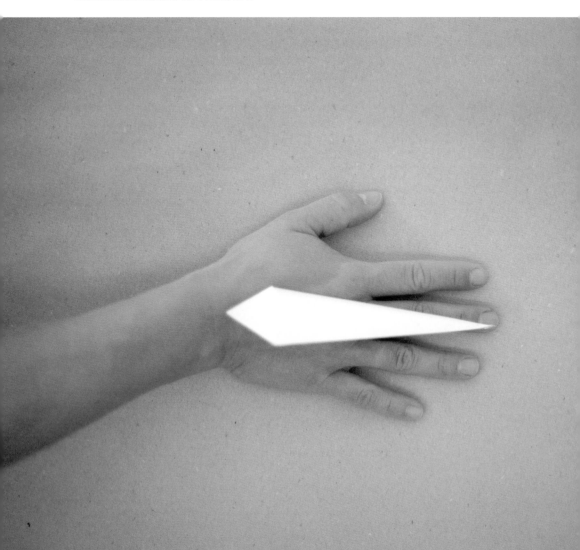

Observing and practicing the INTRA SPACE model revealed that the communication between the entities established a sort of screening (similar to the
medical/natural science use of the term, a procedure of finding and filtering
to detect a disease, disorders, etc., but also as a state of concentration and
attention towards each other). A coming close without touch, a distant contact
with a quality that is formerly only realized through proximity between bodies.
This paradox is the nature of this particular intimacy that was created. It is
intimate because of its cultivation and care for something that is created
through a sentient precision of closeness without actual touch or haptic experience. Maybe it is a question of how negation can produce intimacy, not as a
form of politeness, but through a receptiveness that is shared. The system is
articulate. At the same time, the environment can interpolate itself (*dazwischen-
fahren*) at any moment. For example, a cloud passing across the sun throws
a shadow on the floor. This change might be noticed by a few of the cameras,
not all of them; a rereading is required, time lapse, the system tries to find its
way back to the body volume. All changes to the space are registered. All
technical, digital, and human entities influence each other, reading and simultaneously forming the system. We begin to dwell in the in-between. It is the
invisible friction between caring for each other's spheres and wearing and
carrying each other, as if we would share a coat. The space is the mask that
allows all entities to have an inside and an outside, alters perspectives and
points of view, and ultimately, perception.

What techniques, maneuvers, gestures, and tricks have I appropriated to look
after, to care for the relationship; what does the technological do in order to
rebuild the connection; what happens in the time gap of reestablishing the connection; who takes responsibility?

18 Byung-Chul Han, *Im Schwarm: Ansichten
    des Digitalen* (Berlin: Matthes & Seitz,
    2013), 43–44.

Literature

Alloa, Emmanuel. "Emmanuel Alloa on Transparency," 1:32 min., June 25, 2012. dOCUMENTA (13) Video Glossary. Accessed February 20, 2019. https://d13 .documenta.de/de/#/research/research /view/on-transparency.

Alloa, Emmanuel, and Dieter Thom, eds. *Transparency, Society and Subjectivity: Critical Perspectives*. London: Palgrave Macmillan, 2018.

Avanessian, Armen, and Helen Hester. *dea ex machina*. Berlin: Merve Verlag, 2015.

Belting, Hans. *Faces: Eine Geschichte des Gesichts*. Munich: C. H. Beck, 2014.

Birnbaum, Daniel, and Michelle Kuo, eds. *More than Real: Art in the Digital Age*. London: Walther Koenig Books, 2018.

Han, Byung-Chul. *Im Schwarm: Ansichten des Digitalen*. Berlin: Matthes & Seitz, 2013.

Handke, Peter. *Crossing the Sierra de Gredos*. Translated by Krishna Winston. Frankfurt am Main: Suhrkamp, 2002.

Nancy, Jean-Luc, and Federico Ferrari. *Die Haut der Bilder*. Zurich: diaphanes, 2006.

Sappho. *Come Close*. Translated by Aaron Poochigian. London: Penguin Random Books, 2015.

Steinweg, Marcus. *Inkonsistenzen*. Berlin: Matthes & Seitz, 2015.

Solomon-Godeau, Abigail. "Körperdouble." In *Francesca Woodman*, ed. Gabriele Schor and Elisabeth Bronfen, 73–88. Cologne: Buchhandlung Walther König, 2014.

Stiegler, Bernard. *Relational Ecology and the Digital Pharmakon. Culture Machine* 13 (2012).

Van Helsing, Storm, André Rottmann, Sarah Nicole Prickett, Reena Spaulings, @Lillnternet, i.i.i., and Luther Blissett "Buffering of the Self: Guising in the Mid-'00s." *Texte zur Kunst* 104, (December 2016).

Weber-Unger, Simon. *NATURSELBST-DRUCKE: Dem Original identisch gleich*. Vienna: Album Verlag, 2014.

Moving the Perceptive Body

Diane Shooman

Part 1: Afternoon Assignations with Bob

On August 4, 2018, Esther Balfe and Christina Jauernik sat down with the participants in their two-day workshop at ImPulsTanz to reflect on the experiences of the first session.[1] One of the movers, however, was still bouncing around in the back of the room playing with the movement material he had absorbed from the other participants throughout the day. This was none other than Bob Medici, as he has fondly come to be known.[2] Along with the illustrious workshop leaders, Bob had also been a prime drawing card, the partner each member of the group had signed up to move with. Bob opens potential for new forms of partnering because of the gravity-defying way he dynamizes space, and his magical manner of multiplying himself so that there is enough of him to go around for everybody. Bob Medici is a virtual being, a creation of the project INTRA SPACE.[3]

Unlike many virtual reality (VR) figures perceived through headsets that engage the viewer optically but not physically, life-sized Bob free-floats on one or more screens in a real room, a veritable invitation to an analog kind of encounter with a virtual being. And Bob has been endowed with a very special talent: he appears to perceive your presence, to attach himself to you, to mirror your movements, to learn from you, to move with you. Bob is not bound to coordinates such as floors, ceilings, and walls, and is able to occupy different planes of space with your movement from multiple angles and perspectives. Any of your own coordinates might shift as well; depending on the placement of a camera, your elbow might become a seeing eye. The revelations from such experiences—about relationships, about the body, about space, about yourself—unfold in manifold directions.

This is in large part why the participants had signed on to spend a dazzlingly sunny weekend in a windowless studio moving with Bob. These random strangers had come to the workshop with virtual reality experience ranging from ample to none. But whether full-on enthusiastic or downright apprehensive about virtual reality and its pervasive potential, all of them expressed concern about the fate of those marvelously malleable multisensory, exploratory, inventive, empathic mortal creatures, their own human bodies, in the optical, the digital, the disembodied age.

1   Esther Balfe and Christina Jauernik, "Intra Space: Otherness (Attentional Forms)," workshop at ImPulsTanz Vienna International Dance Festival, August 4–5, 2018, https://www.impulstanz.com/en/archive/2018/workshops/id3795/.
2   Bob's fanciful headgear, designed by Martin "Murphy" Perktold, inspired the singer-songwriter, impresario, and literary magician Dominik Nostitz to describe him as a blend of Bob Marley and Lorenzo di Medici.
3   Wolfgang Tschapeller and team, INTRA SPACE artistic research project (PEEK AR299-G21), Institute for Art and Architecture, Academy of Fine Arts Vienna, funded by the FWF Austrian Science Fund, 2015–17.

Listening to them, I grasped afresh the extent to which we are no longer on the cusp of a new era; the virtual world is already entangled and enmeshed with and changing our own. Digital and related capabilities are spawning, manifesting, and transmogrifying so rapidly, that the conditions that engender the questions we should be asking keep changing before we have had time to even semi-formulate them.

The INTRA SPACE project could be seen as a trial run for cohabitation with human-scale virtual creatures. For two years, experts from different disciplines and viewpoints explored and reflected on how interaction with virtual figures like Bob and his sister Carla, involving our whole moving, observing, thinking, feeling, sensing selves, might affect how we move and perceive movement, how we perceive and shape space, and above all, how we perceive others and ourselves. In fact, the project might well have been the first opportunity since childhood for many team members and guests to experience themselves beyond the "body-mind divide." Or at least since the last time they had danced their socks off.

The formidable size and dominant position of the screens in the project space at Vienna's former central post office (Alte Post) could be seen as symbolizing the pervasiveness of virtual technologies in our realities, and their impact on how we inhabit space, and with what and whom. Augmented reality visualization tools reveal the secret inner lives of things and allow us to manipulate them from a distance. Smart technologies, robots and other algorithm-driven creatures are already making their way into our homes, transport vehicles, factories, hospitals and other institutions as workers, helpers, service personnel, chauffeurs, and companions. Some of them have synthetic bodies organized along similar or different lines to our own; others are disembodied voices, and others still are piles of software code performing their work invisibly. Among the latter are the insidious data-gathering spies in our technical devices that imperil our privacy and freedom.

Virtual figures are a fact of life. But then again, haven't they always been? There would appear to be a universal imperative to personify and thereby to understand, explain and, for the self-righteously inclined, even justify the actions of invisible forces at work in Nature and in ourselves. From the virtual characters we adapt to represent us in video games, to gods, ghosts, spirits and shadows on the wall and characters springing life-like from pages of books, virtual figures, although they "don't really exist," roam in and expand our imaginations, evoking real emotions in us and occupying a place in our hearts and memories. They populate dramas of war and love played out on cinematic celluloid or on screens in our most private and intimate spheres, but as if no one were watching. We are porous and absorb them, whereas they are impervious to anything or anyone who doesn't play a role in their drama. (If that sounds like some people you know, then that might be a connection worth investigating.) Perhaps above all, the perpetual preponderance of fictional figures in our lives reflects our need to cast our imaginations outward, to participate and be enveloped in worlds and works that absorb us so much that we forget ourselves, to reemerge back into our own lives transformed. They point to a universal need for creations of the imagination, for art.

The difference between the new generation of virtual figures and their predecessors is the illusion—and is it an illusion?—of their consciousness of our presence, and their ability to react to and interact with us.

And that brings me to the other big revelation of that sunny Saturday: seeing Bob Medici again for the first time since the termination of the project in April 2017, I had to choke back the tears. Much to my amazement, I found I'd missed Bob! My foolish heart, weeping over this computer figure that attaches itself to everyone and is attached to no one, like a charming and attentive lover one can never really have. The project felt like a fulfillment of my absurd, my vain desire to stay the tide or tidal wave of inexorable progress, in order to exert control over the consequences. My late afternoon assignations with Bob were a site of "silence and slow time."[4] Will we forever be chasing Bob around the urn? A nothingness, full of meaning.

So who and what is Bob Medici, and what had been absent in my life since the screens that are his home were dismantled, the computer that generated him shut down, the tape that held the movement surface in place torn from the floorboards, and our project space boarded up to be renovated as luxury apartments, beyond reach to all but the wealthiest of our species?

I missed visiting Bob to see what he was up to and what kind of shape he was in, literally, the latest form, outfits, the new capabilities he had acquired, to experience moving and watching others move with Bob. I missed the experiments with different setups and positions of screens and mirrors onto which Bob and the original INTRA SPACE project figure Carla were projected and reflected, to consider their effects on the people inhabiting, moving in, and perceiving the space from any given perspective. I missed thinking and talking about Bob, the new strands of thoughts spun forth and catching hold in intertwining webwords.

I missed the whole community that had sprung up around Bob, people from different areas of expertise sharing their viewpoints, knowledge, insights, and thoughts. Bob at the Alte Post was like a post himself, demarcating the territory

---

4   John Keats, "Ode on a Grecian Urn," in *Selected Poems and Letters by John Keats,* ed. Douglas Bush (Boston: Houghton Mifflin Company, 1959), 207–8.

of a future between the real and the virtual world, where, unlike most virtual encounters, our bodies also had a place, experiences, a say. Like the posts that conquerors and other stake-claimers pounded into the ground as place-holders representing themselves,[5] Bob, in addition to being himself, is also most certainly a stand-in for something or someone else.

The magic of moving with Carla and Bob stirs memories of *Bob & Carol & Ted & Alice*,[6] the 1969 partner-swapping movie that ends with the original partners ultimately not swapping after all (pardon the spoiler) and back together happily ever after. Is there a chance that dancing with Carla and Bob could deepen our relationships with our human partners? Do we create virtual figures out of a disappointment in our fellow human beings, and above all in ourselves? Do we cultivate expectations that prescribe disappointment as an inevitable outcome? Maybe those are dances we need to re-choreograph. And in our despair at the aggressively self-absorbed intractability of the paranoid narcissists populating our personal and collective lives, are we in fact trying through Bob to create a narcissist we can control, which, as any psychologist will tell you, is a contradiction in terms, as futile an exercise as they come? Or will ordering around compliant digital beings who tirelessly fulfill our every wish, make us all unfit for respectful and considerate interactions? Will we be as dismayed by Bob as we are when we get involved with people who turn out to embody the same traits as family members, in a perpetual and painful reprise of an old attempt to redress chronic power imbalances? Is Bob an empty vessel, a vampire, Frankenstein's monster, a narcissist, an obsequious yea-sayer, an echo, an alien, a relative?

So this is how it went: You stood before the screen and waited until Carla or Bob appeared. You lifted one arm and then the other, elbows at the same height as your shoulders, forearms extending upward from your elbows. And then you lifted each knee, your legs slightly turned out from the hip.

These ritualized actions had two effects. Your double, or rather you, would appear on the computer monitor, wearing a skeleton outfit.[7] Meanwhile, Bob would magically don your movement, slip inside it, put it on. (Actually, we could have called him Don!) Bob and Carla inhabited and followed your movement to the best of their abilities. And then the dance began.

March 9, 2016: The first time I moved with Carla, she was in a fairly early stage of her development. She was trying hard to move like me, and she moved like someone hampered by severe impediments. I cringed; I was embarrassed for her; I was chagrined. My heart went out to her; I felt as if I had to simplify my movements so as not to demoralize and humiliate her, and to be able to praise and encourage her for what she could do until her capabilities had developed. I fought the physical impulse to adapt my movements to match hers, in fear of my empathy being mistaken for mockery.

What part of my psyche projected feelings onto virtual Carla? As Aristotle identified in his theory of catharsis for the audience watching dramatic tragedy,[8] and the poet Samuel Taylor Coleridge described when he formulated the idea of "that willing suspension of disbelief for the moment, which constitutes poetic faith,"[9] we experience real emotions for fictional figures although we know that they are virtual. Perhaps I saw Carla as myself, a future older self, struggling to regain former movement capabilities.

Whatever I was seeing in Carla, she was having an impact upon my movement. We communicate by adapting to the language of others. We imitate to learn; we imitate to communicate. Carla's "limitations" were taking hold of my body, and were expanding my movement vocabulary.

Ours is not the first era in which the movement language of virtual creatures has spilled off the screen into real space to permeate people's bodies and expand their expressive palettes and possibilities. Historian Katya Motyl brilliantly illuminates a sociocultural phenomenon accompanying the advent of silent film in Vienna, whereby newspapers and magazines supplied guidelines for women to study, practice, absorb, and use facial expressions and bodily gestures of female silent film characters to enhance their own expressive repertoire:

> We can imagine hundreds of fans using the guides as reference as they attempted to imitate facial expressions in front of bathroom and bed-room mirrors. One 1922 film-acting guide, *Mimic in Film* (*Mimik im Film*), described mirror-use as a "fundamental condition" (*Grundbedingung*) in the training process, as it allowed fans—or "acting students"—to watch themselves as they performed exercises in which they manipulated their eyes, eyebrows, forehead, mouth, nose, and tongue [...] to expand the expressive richness (*Ausdrucksreichtum*) of the face.[10]

Motyl reads this widespread practice as an antidote, indeed a rebellion, against the emotional "self-control" that had hitherto been prescribed to middle-class women:

5 Joseph Rykwert, *The Dancing Column: On Order in Architecture* (Cambridge, MA: MIT Press, 1998), 119–21.

6 Paul Mazursky and Larry Tucker, dir., *Bob & Carol & Ted & Alice* (Los Angeles: Columbia Pictures, 1969).

7 The skeleton is a visualization of the form and coordinates of the human moving with Carla or Bob, used to track discrepancies between the human's and the virtual figures' movements.

8 Aristotle, *Poetics*, trans. and ed. Anthony Kenny (Oxford: Oxford University Press, 2013), Kindle.

9 Samuel Taylor Coleridge, *Biographia Literaria*, chap. xiv (1817); Poetryfoundation .org, October 13, 2009, https://www .poetryfoundation.org/articles/69385 /from-biographia-literaria-chapter-xiv.

10 Katya Motyl, "'There Was a Shimmer': Silent Film Acting and Emotional Expression," chap. 2 of "Bodies That Shimmer: An Embodied History of Vienna's New Women, 1893–1931" (PhD diss., University of Chicago, 2017), 37.

After imitating these expressions at home and on the street, film fans, I argue, learned how to become more emotionally literate and expressive in everyday life. [...] In all these cases, the emotional literacy and expressiveness was part of an increased theatricality that tore off the mask of bourgeois respectability and convention. It was a theatricality that expressed instead of concealed, using the body as a medium through which to manifest emotion. With the intoxicating effects of film, as well as the pedagogical function of celebrity culture, soon enough, Viennese women from all walks of life found ways to act and act out.[11]

What kinds of beings are we learning to be from Bob and Carla? Will we be taking their movement to the streets?

We are moved, so to speak, by beings who reach out to us, who are not amorphously needy, overbearing or demanding, who don't push their way into our spaces to monopolize or intimidate us, but who try to connect, understand and communicate with us. Kids in perpetual learning mode are endearingly imitative; so are you when you're taking dancing or tennis lessons. Bodies in motion are fascinating: the same movement looks completely different depending upon who is doing it. Whether emulator or emulated, we grow, change, are inspired and transformed by the interaction.

Bob has a mind of his own, pre-programmed unpredictability in the pixel weave, like the flaw in the carpet, the space for the soul. Bob's imperfections are part of his charm; they make him more human. Like and unlike a mirror image, Bob and Carla are the you that is not you, the you that you feel sympathy, empathy, and compassion for, the you that you see striving, without judging yourself. Perhaps all judgment begins with self-judgment.

Esther Balfe has said that Bob "embodies and traces the landscape, the rises and falls, the angles, edges and arcs of your movement."[12] Maybe that's the magic, to disengage the movement from your own mirror image, to shift the attention away from your body and how it looks, to the movement itself. But what is movement? It shifts spatial configurations, yet leaves no other trace save for the impression on the beholder, and is evidenced only by the fact that you are now here, and no longer there. Whereas everyday life races us from place to place, dance is about the art and act of moving, and the space between there and here.

As dancer and choreographer extraordinaire Merce Cunningham famously stated: "Certainly everybody including dancers can leap, sit down and get up again, but the dancer makes it apparent that the going into the air is what establishes the relationship to the air, the process of sitting down, not the position upon being down, is what gives the iridescent and life-quality to dancing."[13]

In dancer Marian Horosko's reflections on the all-time greatest-ever ballet choreographer George Balanchine, even motionlessness is revealed as movement: "Only he could really show a group how to pose as a movement, not as an inanimate cluster. Something inside has always to be moving, even in stillness."[14]

Movement in its ephemerality visualizes the invisible, showing us what happens while we're not watching, while we sleep, the metamorphosis, the transformation. How does it catch hold of us, and how do we capture it? In the words of dance writer Arlene Croce, considering the legacy of her esteemed colleague Edwin Denby: "One of Denby's cherished beliefs about dancing has to do with the persistence of images as a key to comprehension. Dancing leaves behind 'an imaginary object,' 'a classical shape,' 'a visual moment of climax,' that goes on gathering force in the mind."[15]

One could say that movement flits across the performance space into the wings of the imagination. Like all things that soar, high-flying movement exhilarates us and heightens our sense of possibility. Like all things that fall, the moving body evokes our empathy. Experienced through real bodies in the fictional or virtual situation that is performance,[16] dance perhaps evokes its own kind of suspension of disbelief.

Movement is the membrane that gives flickering, fluctuating, fluid shape to the spirit. As Merce Cunningham has written:

> In other words, the technical equipment of a dancer is only a means, a way to the spirit. [...] To walk magnificently and thereby evoke the spirit of a god seems surpassingly more marvelous than to leap and squirm in the air in some incredible fashion, and leave only the image of oneself. And for that very reason, the dancer strives [...] for complete identification with the movement in as devastatingly impersonal a fashion as possible. Not to show off, but to show; not to exhibit, but to transmit the tenderness of the human spirit through the disciplined action of a human body.[17]

11 Motyl, 37–41.
12 Esther Balfe, conversation with the author, December 21, 2018.
13 Merce Cunningham, "The Function of a Technique for Dance," in *Dance in America: A Reader's Anthology*, ed. Mindy Aloff (New York: Library of America, 2018), 197.
14 Horosko, Marian, "Marian Horosko: Personal Statement," in *I Remember Balanchine: Recollections of the Ballet Master by Those Who Knew Him*, ed.

Francis Mason (New York: Doubleday, 1991), 367.
15 Arlene Croce, "Edwin Denby," in *Dance in America: A Reader's Anthology*, ed. Mindy Aloff (New York: Library of America, 2018), 192.
16 Susanne Langer, "Virtual Powers," in *What Is Dance?*, ed. Roger Copeland and Marshall Cohen (Oxford: Oxford University Press, 1983), 29.
17 Cunningham, "The Function of a Technique for Dance," 196.

In a revelatory conversation with Esther Balfe and Christina Jauernik on December 21, 2018, it emerged that Bob Medici, this transparent diaphanous non-being, is a storehouse for that intangible ephemerality called movement. No empty vessel he, Bob keeps the memory of our movements and the paths they trace to play them back to us. Bob and Carla take us out of ourselves, our self-consciousness and our vanity, and into our imaginative, our movement possibilities. Bob got better at moving with us, while we started to take on his movement characteristics. You could say that we started to merge.

In this context, what is the human body, and what is space? Like no experts in any other profession, dancers—teachers, performers and choreographers—explore the body in space. That exploration is specific to art. Dancers can move as a group body, as one organism. Without looking at each other, all of them know their place in space and time. Dancers have their feelers out; they sense themselves and others in the room. Dancers enchant with their movement, which is visible to everyone but themselves. What strange sort of spell is that? Dance is not primarily an optical experience, either for the dancers or for the audience. Arlene Croce homes in on Edwin Denby's identification of what powers are at play when we watch dance: "Dancing is less pictorial than plastic, and pictures in dancing leave a void in the imagination. They arrest the drama of dancing which the imagination craves to continue, stimulated by all the kinetic senses of the body that demand a new movement to answer the one just past."[18] Lest we miss the significance of that observation, Croce emphasizes that "dancing is physical, a spectacle of grace in movement. The 'kinetic senses of the body,' more than the optic nerve, are what stimulate the imagination."[19]

In his work *Techniques of the Observer: On Vision and Modernity in the Nineteenth Century*, Jonathan Crary points out that vision and touch had not always been viewed as separate:

> In my delineation of a modernization and revaluation of vision, I indicate how the sense of touch had been an integral part of classical theories of vision in the seventeenth and eighteenth centuries. The subsequent dissociation of touch from sight occurs within a pervasive "separation of the senses" and industrial remapping of the body in the nineteenth century. The loss of touch as a conceptual component of vision meant the unloosening of the eye from the network of referentiality incarnated in tactility and its subjective relation to perceived space. This autonomization of sight, occurring in many different domains, was a historical condition for the rebuilding of an observer fitted for the tasks of "spectacular" consumption. [...] The stereoscope is one major cultural site on which this breach between tangibility and visuality is singularly evident.[20]

The complex intricacies of the relationship between vision and the haptic, tactile, kinetic, and other senses account for some of the differences we perceive in experiencing a live performance as opposed to watching a show on a screen. Crary was moved to write his book about "vision and its historical construction"[21] at least in part by the appearance of new techniques "that are relocating vision to a plane severed from a human observer."[22] It could be, however, that movement speaks to us kinetically regardless of the media, but that the kinetic stirrings within us may be competing unsuccessfully against other sensations for our attention. In his later work *Suspensions of Perception: Attention, Spectacle, and Modern Culture*, Crary asserts that "whether it is how we behave in front of the luminous screen of a computer or how we experience a performance in an opera house, how we accomplish certain productive, creative or pedagogical tasks or how we more passively perform routine activities like driving a car or watching television, we are in a dimension of contemporary experience that requires that we effectively cancel out or exclude from consciousness much of our immediate environment. I am interested in how Western modernity since the nineteenth century has demanded that individuals define and shape themselves in terms of a capacity for 'paying attention,' that is, for a disengagement from a broader field of attraction, whether visual or auditory, for the sake of isolating or focusing on a reduced number of stimuli."[23]

In the hands of the few choreographers who can dynamize a vast space, providing ongoing interest in more locations than our focused attention can encompass at any given moment, dance frustrates that ingrained practice of attention to "a reduced number of stimuli."[24] That may account in part for the fact that of all art forms vying for audiences, dance performances currently appear to be the least successful in the majority of Western cultures. As Crary's theory implies, there are more strategies for watching and listening than we are in the habit of engaging with.

Choreographers invent new things for kinetically alert bodies to do, new ways to occupy, amplify, carve, and shape space, to make multiple planes of space visible. One of the rarest and most thrilling experiences ever is to catch a split-second glimpse of a dancer expanding into multiple planes of space

18 Arlene Croce, "Edwin Denby," in *Dance in America: A Reader's Anthology*, ed. Mindy Aloff (New York: Library of America, 2018), 184.
19 Croce, 184.
20 Jonathan Crary, *Techniques of the Observer: On Vision and Modernity in the Nineteenth Century* (Cambridge, MA: MIT Press, 1992), 19.

21 Crary, 1.
22 Crary, 1.
23 Jonathan Crary, *Suspensions of Perception: Attention, Spectacle, and Modern Culture* (Cambridge, MA: MIT Press, 2001), 1.
24 Crary, 1.

simultaneously. Dance engages the whole human being; dancers who do not exercise their imaginations are technicians, not artists.

Esther Balfe imbued PEEK INTRA SPACE and ImPulsTanz workshop participants with imaginary "cameras" to explore the space within their own moving bodies or their surroundings from the seeing perspective, say, of their knees or elbows. The participants were also asked to invert their movement, as if hands were feet and vice versa, and up were down, and inside out. In these acts of attention, concentration, awareness, and imagination, we can become transparent to ourselves as Bob Medici is to us. In the words of Balfe and Jauernik: "You learn how to deflect, corrupt and disarrange movement, challenging (your) move-ment traits into the unfamiliar."[25] In other words, "flexibility" and "adaptability" include critical discernment and inventive resistance.

Christina Jauernik has emphasized that the amorphous non-space of screens eliminates the floor as a point of orientation, drawing attention to the moving body in unbounded space. What possibilities do that attention, awareness, critical resistance, and inventiveness open for movement exploration, for per-ceptual practices, and for architectures of the future for real and virtual moving bodies? Observing bodies moving in space as an architect, and inhabiting architectural space as a dancer, Christina Jauernik is aptly positioned with Esther Balfe to have co-defined and developed different parameters for Bob, and for interaction with Bob, to explore the needs of the perceptive moving body in the Digital Age.

What is the body's position now? Isn't how we regard and treat it a key to its future: in our minds and attitudes, our education and merit systems, our urban, suburban, and rural infrastructure, our ways of taking in and moving through the world? How much attention do we pay to the needs of the body as well as the eye when shaping space?

The INTRA SPACE project explored possibilities for using immersive visualization systems to experience space as fluidly interactive and dialogical. To ask how optical media can also speak to, engage and be responsive to the whole human being is, among other things, to ask what is actually happening to us when we are having what we think of as an optical experience. Reflecting on the everyday activities of dancing and walking helps us consider how cultural atti-tudes and daily practices have colluded to separate seeing from the other senses, and how the newest versions of technologies that privilege the eye at the expense of the other senses may ironically be the very thing to put the body back into the picture, so to speak.

Part II: Waltzing and Walking

Spaces shaped by humans—such as choreographies, buildings, or cities—are psychograms of ideologies about who and what belongs where. Moving with any regularity through such spaces must have an enormous impact on the ways each of us thinks.

Biomimetically web-like Vienna is congenially conducive to peripatetic reflections. Shape-wise, the former imperial capital fans out around the Ring Road and its magnified mirror image, the Beltway. Is it a mere coincidence that the dance associated with this concentrically circular city is the waltz?[26] Or that Arthur Schnitzler "choreographed" his shrewd comedy of "social traffic patterns" as a *Reigen* or rondo?[27] And by the way, in case you've ever wondered what the Neidhart ballroom fresco[28] revelers from the year 1407 are up to, they're also dancing the rondo.[29]

Dance is an intensification of the experience of our physical bodies and our social bodies moving through space. Vienna's inner districts are built on a human scale;[30] opulent semi-nude female and male statuary flag the buildings of the façades they adorn as proportionate extensions of the human body.[31] Private residences, public gathering places, and commerce share the same houses much as they did at the very beginning of urban life, and in most neighborhoods, everyday amenities are accessible on foot.[32]

25 Esther Balfe and Christina Jauernik, "Intra Space: Otherness (Attentional Forms)," workshop, ImPulsTanz 2018, https://www.impulstanz.com/en/archive/2018/workshops/id3795/.

26 In her analysis of the 1925 silent film *A Waltz Dream* (*Ein Walzertraum*), Katya Motyl draws attention to the waltz as "'a signal for Vienna and the Viennese' (in the words of Moritz Csáky)," and the working-class violin-playing Franzi as "the embodiment of the city itself. When Nik first meets Franzi, he says, 'What I see is Vienna standing as a person in front of me,' and when he kisses her, it is clear that, 'he kissed Vienna.'" Motyl, "'There Was a Shimmer,'" 5–6.

27 Arthur Schnitzler, *Reigen: Zehn Dialoge* (Vienna, 1903; Frankfurt am Main: dtv, 2004).

28 Eva-Maria Höhle et al., *The Neidhart Frescoes: The Oldest Secular Mural Painting in Vienna*, trans. Beatrice Ottersböck (Vienna: The Museums of the City of Vienna, 1984).

29 Höhle, 29.

30 As Wojciech Czaja reported in the interview "Mit Hochhäusern haben wir ein Problem" in the daily newspaper *Der Standard* on March 4, 2019, UNESCO has warned the City of Vienna that if a building in the inner city exceeds a height of 43 meters, Vienna will lose its status as a cultural heritage site. https://derstandard.at/2000098892647/Unesco-Direktorin-Roessler-Mit-Hochhaeusern-haben-wir-ein-Problem.

31 Joseph Rykwert, "Order in the Body" and "Gender and Column," in *The Dancing Column: On Order in Architecture* (Cambridge, MA: MIT Press, 1998), 26–67, and 96–115.

32 A relaxed, expansive urban stroller is also betimes a relaxed, expansive consumer. In cities and districts where commercial and residential districts are separate, and shopping is done in malls rather than in town centers, the recreational stroll has been replaced with a walk down the aisle, where your commitment is sealed at the altar of the cash register. Journalist Thomas Stodulka points out that the work of Viennese architect Viktor Grünbaum, or Victor Gruen, as he called himself after escaping in 1938

In 2013, the city appointed a pedestrian representative, a *Fussgängerbeauftragte*[33] and 2015 was declared "The Year of the Pedestrian."[34] In October 2015, Vienna hosted the international Walk21 annual conference, devoted to "interdisciplinary solutions for resilient cities."[35]

Nevertheless, walking is associated with economic under-development. In the EU, the poorer the country, the more pedestrians afoot.[36] In the current competition for unimpeded flow of movement in urban space, the pedestrian still takes a back seat to motor vehicles, parking zones, and bicycles.[37]

Our physical experiences are largely mediated through car, subway, bus, or tram windows, and TV, computer, or mobile phone screens. Visual perception dominates over physical, haptic perception. Whereas contemporary dance has long since embraced pedestrian movement, contemporary life has peripheralized the movement of pedestrians.[38]

And when we reflect on and talk about our encounters with so-called visual art forms, to what extent is our physical bodily participation even considered?

Visual perception dominates over physical, haptic perception not only in daily life, but also in the way we experience, form expectations of, talk about, and evaluate art.

If art is something to be "understood" rather than "experienced," this may account for the fact that many people feel more awkward watching a dance performance than dancing themselves, say, at a party. How do we see the body, how do you see YOUR body, how do we watch dance? And by what criteria do we evaluate, dare I say do we judge, works of art?

Physical movement is intrinsic to our experience of the visual arts. We encounter works of art by moving through exhibition and other public spaces. A work speaks to you personally: you stop in your tracks. You move before or around it, shifting your perspective. You may in fact be moving in response to it. You step back to take it in as a whole; it pulls you in and opens itself to you. You may feel seen, understood. This could be the beginning of an unforgettable relationship.

No other art form requires such direct bodily one-on-one engagement from its audience. And let us not lose sight of the fact that the making of much visual art involves physical action. Yet even when we feel physically and emotionally drawn to a work, we are likely to isolate and be attentive to optical and cerebral dimensions of the attraction.

Perhaps we tend to turn to words to "understand" visual arts (note the preponderance of talking headsets in museums) because our systems of education privilege reading, listening to and formulating thoughts in words over all other kinds of media. However, as art historian Michael Cothren points out: "We live in an age in which visual communication, the use of pictures and design to convey important information, to embody cherished values, and to manipulate the responses and behaviors of our fellow human beings may be at an all-time high. Yet, this is not widely recognized, especially in elite educational contexts. [...] Prejudice against the visual in favor of the verbal is deeply ingrained in our educational culture."[39]

If we aren't physically alive to architecture, to painting and sculpture, to dance, to literature, to music, to theater, or to any art, we may "get the idea," but we'll probably miss the experience.

As the 2014 Erasmus Prize winner Frie Leysen emphasized in her acceptance speech, art can't solve political problems.[40] Art cannot be equated either with its themes or its forms. But art can open new pathways of perception, shifting the spaces through which our minds travel, to reveal more than is visible to the eye alone. Art can literally move us.

Tuning into our physical, tactile, haptic, kinetic perceptual powers might help us rethink what we need from architecture and from art. So let's dance!

to the USA, was inspired by his belief that pedestrians were the key to revitalizing failing cities. In 1954, Gruen designed the first suburban open-air shopping facility. Gruen returned to Vienna in 1968, and was instrumental in the conversion of Kärntner Straße and the Graben into pedestrian zones. He deplored shopping malls as "bastardizations" of his ideas. Thomas Stodulka, "Porträt: Victor Gruen," Zoë, January 2015, 13–16 (translated and paraphrased by the author).

33 Maria Grundner, "Beauftragte für Fuß-gängerinnen und Fußgänger," in Wien zu Fuß (blog), December 9, 2013, https://www.wienzufuss.at/2013/12/09/die-fussgaengerverkehrsbeauftragten/.

34 Mobilitätsagentur Wien, "Im Jahr 2015 stand Wien im Zeichen des Zu-Fuß-Gehens," https://www.wienzufuss.at/jahr-des-zu-fuss-gehens/.

35 Walk21 Vienna 2015, October 20–23, 2015, http://walk21vienna.com/.

36 Birgit Wittstock, "Revolution auf zwei Beinen," Falter, December 3, 2014, 37.

37 Wittstock, 37.

38 Where people live impacts on their attitudes towards modes of mobility. In 2015, Mariahilfer Straße in Vienna's centrally situated 6th district was converted into a pedestrian zone aswarm with shoppers and socializers. In contrast, journalist Wolfgang Zwander reports that in outer districts less well served by the pedestrian's most trusty aid, public transport, the social hubs for young people are gas stations. Zwander quotes one city official who wished to remain anonymous as saying: "For the 6th district it's 'immigrants in, cars out.' In the 22nd district, it's exactly the opposite." Wolfgang Zwander, "Bobo gegen Auto," Falter, February 11, 2015, 10.

39 Michael Cothren, "Teaching Art in an Era of Globalism," audio transcript, July 25, 2012, http://www.swarthmore.edu/michael-cothren-teaching-art-in-an-era-of-globalism.xml.

40 Frie Leysen, Erasmus Prize Acceptance Speech, November 12, 2014. http://www.erasmusprijs.org/?lang=en&page=Nieuws&mode=detail&item=Speech+Frie+Leysen+online.

The story of dance as a performing art goes hand-in-hand with the story of urban ambling.

After Emperor Josef II of Austria opened the royal Prater grounds in 1766 and the Augarten park in 1775 to the people in Vienna,[41] pedestrians became a major factor in city planning. Free time and open space to gambol was not to be mistaken however for freedom of movement. When, for example, the Volksgarten—the People's Garden—was built in 1823, the walking paths were designed so that the strolling folk could be monitored to ensure that no untoward encounters or insurrections occurred.[42] Vice squads from the so-called "chastity commission" (Keuschheitskommission) kept a vigilant watch over all places where people clustered, to circumvent same-sex romance, or commercial transactions conducted by women who walked the streets for a living.[43]

Using your body to make a living was altogether frowned on. In 1776, the Enlightened Emperor put the kibosh on theatrical dance, and brought a great era of dance development in Vienna to a crashing halt.[44] This is a clear instance of disembodied decision-making.

Dance made a comeback under Josef's successor Leopold;[45] conventions continued to determine how people moved in the public theater of the city and the stage.

The chastity commission was disbanded at the beginning of the nineteenth century, and replaced by codes of costume and decorum. Recreational walking impacted on the public shape of the body. On the crowded Corso, for example, wide crinoline skirts took up far too much space, and were re-situated to form the ubiquitous back bustle.[46]

And a middle-class woman walking "unattended" was required to carry a special accessory: yes, a sewing basket as a symbol of domestic industriousness.[47] Women walking in public were subject to suspicion,[48] just like women dancing in public.

What was it about dance that made it suspect? Reactions to the advent of the Viennese waltz are telling. The Viennese waltz was the very first social dance that wasn't a group number, and that had couples facing each other in close proximity for the entire dance. In 1797, the writer Salomo Jakob Wolf published a treatise entitled *Proof That Waltzing Is the Main Source of Weakness of the Body and Mind of Our Generation*.[49] And as dance writer Marianka Swain reports: "An editorial in *The Times* records the shock at the Prince Regent's grand ball in 1816 when 'the indecent foreign dance the waltz' was introduced: 'It is quite sufficient to cast one's eyes on the voluptuous intertwining of the limbs and close compressor on the bodies in their dance, to see that it is indeed far removed from the modest reserve which has hitherto been considered distinctive of English females. So long as this obscene display was confined to prostitutes and adulteresses, we did not think it deserving of notice; but now that it is attempted to be forced on the respectable classes of society, we feel it a duty to warn every parent against exposing his daughter to so fatal a contagion.'"[50]

Dance is certainly no longer judged by those standards (at least in some cultures). But perhaps we do have expectations of dance that it cannot fulfill, leaving us unsatisfied and alienated. Perhaps we can find our way to dance by exploring our most basic movement experience, namely walking.

What happens when we set out to explore new space—traveling to a foreign place, taking a different route to a familiar destination, or creating and inhabiting a new work of art? Moving bodily through unknown territory shifts our inner topography as well. We open up new routes for our minds.

The experience of turning an unfamiliar corner and seeing something unexpected is often accompanied by a feeling that anything is possible. Experiencing yourself in a different place and trying it on for size, the unknown view around the bend reawakens your sense of potential, your awareness that things could be different.

41 Christian Rapp, "Vom Spazieren," in *nichts tun: vom flanieren, pausieren, blaumachen und müßiggehen* (Vienna: Kataloge des Österreichischen Museums für Volkskunde, 2000), 34.
42 Rapp, 32.
43 Rapp, 33. For a brief history of the "Keuschheitskommission," see https://de.wikipedia.org/wiki/Keuschheitskommission.
44 Sibylle Dahms, "Die Bedeutung Wiens für die Ballettreform des 18. Jahrhunderts," in *Österreich tanzt: Geschichte und Gegenwart*, ed. Andrea Amort et al. (Vienna: Böhlau Verlag, 2001), 29.
45 Gunhild Oberzaucher-Schüller, "Institutionalisierter Tanz im Wien des 19. Jahrhunderts," in *Österreich tanzt*, 39.
46 Christian Rapp, "Vom Promenieren," in *nichts tun*, 40.
47 Rapp, "Vom Promenieren," 40.
48 Given that mobile professions have traditionally been accorded low social regard, a certain irony lurks in the use of the term "mobility" to describe vertical—i.e., upwards as well as downwards—shifts in social status. The most horizontal of ambulatory professions has been used as a metaphor for new art forms that arouse suspicion amongst a conservative populace. For example, Katya Motyl writes that in Vienna, "most films prior to 1906–1907 were shown in so-called *Wanderkinos*, traveling cinemas. [...] The peripatetic quality of these cinemas, their distance from the city center [...] set them apart from highbrow establishments. [...] To return to Miriam Hansen's observation at the beginning of this chapter, the sex worker and the cinema truly did have much in common: both were spectacular, both were lowbrow, and both were 'wanderers.'" Motyl, "'There Was a Shimmer,'" 23.
49 Salomo Jakob Wolf, *Erörterung derer wichtigsten Ursachen der Schwäche unsrer Generation in Hinsicht auf das Walzen*, pamphlet (Halle: Hendel Verlag, 1797).
50 Marianka Swain, "Perfect 10: The Viennese Waltz," posted by Brigitt Mayer on *DanceArchives* (November 29, 2012). http://www.dancearchives.net/2012/11/29/perfect-10-the-viennese-waltz-by-marianka-swain/.

At the end of that street, what you discover, and what you have been pursuing all along, is a new view of yourself. It points to what we long for yet fear the most: change. Change is life itself; change is the death of what we think we know.

Perhaps it is the act of walking or otherwise physically ambulating that is as essential to such transformational experiences as the place itself. Art critic and curator Vitus Weh ponders the role of movement through spaces dedicated to art:

> Today the public space in front of or around museums is a central part of their affective corporeal realm. Visitors "go to the museum."[51] The movement aspect of the visit might well be the most significant. For sociologist Lucius Burckhardt, who founded Strollology as a discipline of study, this was indeed the case. Walking serves the exploration of our everyday environments as well as the absorption of new content and knowledge. We've practically always known that most things are experienced and remembered more intensively through connective spatial impressions and physical movement than through hearing a story, reading a book or surfing the web. This mechanism has been implemented for thousands of years in temple and church grounds, with their meditational passageways, spatial arrangements and zonings. It has also been central to the museum landscape.[52]

Our automotive, aerial, and screen technologies transport us through distances, and distant places to us, while distancing ourselves from our own bodies. In his landmark treatise called *The Eyes of the Skin: Architecture and the Senses*, architect Juhani Pallasmaa explores what happens to us when we isolate ourselves from haptic contact with our surroundings, or when our surroundings also refuse to speak haptically to us:

> Computer imaging tends to flatten our magnificent, multi-sensory, simultaneous and synchronic capacities of imagination by turning the design process into a passive visual manipulation, a retinal journey. The computer creates a distance between the maker and the object, whereas drawing by hand as well as working with models put the designer in a haptic contact with the object, or space. [...] Creative work calls for a bodily and mental identification, empathy and compassion.[53]

As Pallasmaa implies with the title *The Eyes of the Skin*, "seeing" is not a function of central vision alone; our bodies are involved in the act of and reaction to visual perception.

It turns out that when you do a close, attentive reading of a literary text, you are also having a haptic experience. Journalist Elizabeth Randolph cites scholar Natalie Phillips, who specializes in cognitive approaches to literature, as having observed "a global increase in blood flow to the brain during close reading, which, she says, suggests that 'paying attention to literary texts requires the coordination of multiple complex cognitive functions.' Close reading [...] most activated parts of the brain that are associated with touch, movement, and spatial orientation. It was as though readers were actually experiencing being in the story."[54]

These findings have been corroborated in other cognitive science investigations. As *Scientific American* editor Ferris Jabr explains:

> Beyond treating individual letters as physical objects, the human brain may also perceive a text in its entirety as a kind of physical landscape. When we read, we construct a mental representation of the text. The exact nature of such representations remains unclear, but some researchers think they are similar to the mental maps we create of terrain—such as mountains and trails—and of indoor physical spaces. [...] In most cases, paper books have more obvious topography than on-screen text. [...] Turning the pages of a paper book is like leaving one footprint after another on a trail—there is a rhythm to it and a visible record of how far one has traveled. All these features not only make the text in a paper book easily navigable, they also make it easier to form a coherent mental map of that text.[55]

Literary language is among other things metaphorical, wherein two unlike things become one, wherein one thing is itself and something else at the same time. Like moving with something that is yourself and not yourself.

Lending their bodies to the alien words and thoughts of poets, my students experience the printed words on the page as the skin of the poem, and the body of the poem as its sound. Reading poems aloud unleashes kinetic forces, transforming printed words into a moving architecture of textures, spaces, sounds, and shapes, which in turn moves and shapes the inner architecture of the reader's resonant vocal apparatus, to open multiple layers of meaning through things that can neither be seen nor heard, but must be felt and experienced.

51 The German verb *gehen* means "to walk" as well as "to go."

52 Vitus Weh, "Räume für Kunst: Über den historischen Wandel ihrer Symboliken und Wirkweisen," unpublished essay, 7 (my translation).

53 Juhani Pallasmaa, *The Eyes of the Skin: Architecture and the Senses* (Chichester: John Wiley & Sons Ltd, 2012), 14.

54 Elizabeth Randolph, "Distracted Reading in the Digital Age (and What to Do About It)," in *The Vassar Alumnae/i Quarterly* 111, no. 1 (Winter 2015): 12.

55 Ferris Jabr, "Why the Brain Prefers Paper," *Scientific American*, November 2013, 51.

For your reading pleasure, the title poem of Liane Strauss's book "Leaving Eden" is offered in its entirety below with the kind permission of the author:

Leaving Eden

The motor's running and I'm leaving Eden.
It's gotten too small, too cramped. It's too green.
I've packed my bags, taken my best face cream,
shaken the apple tree until my wormy heart fell at my feet.

It's not the serpent. I didn't need convincing.
It's not in my nature to be happy to ignore what I know.
Can't remember when I first went suspicious.
If I'm disenchanted with the past at least I'm something,
something to the core.

There never was a paradise on earth, or heaven.
Each fleshy fist of fruit harbours its seed.
Nothing has changed, nothing was ever how it seemed
in Eden, and if it was, I can't imagine it was me.

The motor's running, the asphalt is seething.
My bare legs stick to vinyl slick with sweat.
The air of motion now will run its fingers through me
and like Atlantis underwater I'll forget.[56]

Eve says she is leaving Eden because it has gotten "too cramped. It's too green."[57] When you take the word "cramped" into your mouth, the "m" closes in on the "a." To receive the word "green," however, you open wide. The contradiction gives rise to a riddle: When is something that is endlessly open closed? When there is no sign of variety or change on the horizon!

In the next line of the poem, "I've packed my bags"[58] visually indicates an action of closing. But when you speak the words "packed" and "bags," your mouth pops open. So when is a closing also an opening? Though my students are for the most part quite young, they understand the significance of endings for beginnings. When they read the line: "It's not the serpent; I didn't need convincing,"[59] hissing with sibilants, they suddenly feel Eve's voice and the snake's to be one—with their own!

We internalize alien beings all the time—language, words, other people's ideas and opinions—and spend a lifetime figuring out what is ours and what is not. As a close reader, I fall into the wormholes between words, and wander in their underworlds before resurfacing into the textured terrain of object-words.

I find myself expanding into the physicality, the corporeality of poetic language, into the convergence of formal, thematic, and symbolic uses of space, the imagination's boundless home. In ancient coming-of-age stories, Adam and Eve's fall from grace lands them on Earth; Icarus hurtles from the sky into the sea, and Persephone is ravished into the Underworld, to return to Earth with an altered consciousness. Are these stories not metaphors for immersion in art? We are pulled in, and we return, but with our consciousness altered, forever half here and half there. Maybe immersion in art is a perpetual coming of age.

For all the neurological and cognitive science evidence to the contrary, the Cartesian model of mind-body duality would appear to persist. Perhaps poetic metaphors can help loosen the hold of that problematic paradigm. It is no coincidence that two authors known for acute receptiveness to their kinetic sensibilities were also poets. As Arlene Croce reflects on poet dance writer Edwin Denby, "This is the writing not only of a poet who sees but of a poet who feels, and who feels what we all feel. [...] Another way of saying it is that dancing appeals to the poet in us. [...] I believe that Denby discovered these kinetic senses in his role as a critic [...] and that the more he thought about it, the more it seemed that kinetic excitement was what made viewing dancing a normal and subjective but by no means universal pleasure. [He] arrived at a formulation both generous and strict: 'To recognize poetic suggestion through dancing one must be susceptible to poetic values and susceptible to dance values as well.'"[60] That most musical poet essayist librettist Hugo von Hofmannsthal addressed this observation to the dancer and choreographer Grete Wiesenthal: "The body does not talk to the body, but rather the human whole to the whole."[61]

Juhani Pallasmaa relates the powers of poetry to the purpose of architecture: "Artistic expression is engaged with pre-verbal meanings of the world, meanings that are incorporated and lived rather than simply intellectually understood. In my view, poetry has the capacity of bringing us momentarily back to the oral and enveloping world. The re-oralised word of poetry brings us back to the centre of an interior world. The poet speaks not only 'on the threshold of being,' as Gaston Bachelard notes, but also on the threshold of language. Equally, the task of art and architecture in general is to reconstruct the experience of an undifferentiated interior world, in which we are not mere spectators, but to which we inseparably belong. In artistic works, existential understanding arises from our very encounter with the world and our being–in–the–world—it is not conceptualised or intellectualised."[62]

56 Liane Strauss, "Leaving Eden," in *Leaving Eden* (London: Salt Publishing, 2010), 45.
57 Strauss, 45.
58 Strauss, 45.
59 Strauss, 45.
60 Croce, "Edwin Denby," 184.
61 Motyl, "'There Was a Shimmer,'" 16.
62 Pallasmaa, *Eyes of the Skin*, 28.

Part III: "The Eyes of the Skin"[63]

Algorithm-driven creatures have no need for a sense of "being–in–the–world," or for that matter, any kind of emotional fulfillment whatsoever. Human life revolves around fulfilling needs; they motor our urge to invent. A need is a potential in disguise. As we develop the capabilities of algorithm-driven beings, what untold capabilities in ourselves have we yet to discover? What countless kinds of potential lie in our need for the sense of "being-in-the-world"?

We are equipped with more means of visual perception than we may realize. In their groundbreaking work on the far-reaching potential of optics-less imaging using "smart" sensors and "skin vision" for—among other applications—eventually developing reading devices for the blind, Leonid Yaroslavsky et al. posit:

> Organisms in nature use a wide variety of visual systems. Most of them use optics to form images, but optics-less cutaneous vision (skin vision) is also found among many types of living organisms. [...] There are also numerous reports on the phenomenon of cutaneous vision in humans. In particular, Ref. [10] provides some quantitative data on the ability of a certain young woman to "see" images using only the fingers of her right hand. It also reports that in a series of carefully conducted tests, this subject demonstrated the ability to detect colours, to resolve patterns in near-contact with her fingers with a resolution of about 0.6 mm and the ability to determine simple patterns within a maximal distance of 1–2 cm from the fingers.[64]

Yaroslavsky kindly offered me this summary in an email:

> In short, I affirm that human skin is certainly sensitive to optical radiation, especially to its infrared part, which, in particular, gives us sensation of heat. Therefore, the skin should contain radiation detectors and a corresponding neural circuitry. I believe that it will, in principle, be possible to teach people, especially blind people, to use these mechanisms of extra-ocular vision for a kind of reading. [...] In addition, I believe that electronic devices can be designed that use infrared radiation for assisting blind people to read news and books.[65]

The pioneers of inner space, traveling and tracing the intricate pathways and interstices of neural circuitry, are changing the ways we think about who we are and how we function, opening new frontiers of potential to be explored. Nobel neuroscientist Eric Kandel illustrates differences in two complementary types of optical vision—central or so-called foveal vision, and peripheral vision— by explaining that the ambiguous emotionality of Leonardo da Vinci's *Mona Lisa* and her smile is invisible to our detail-focused foveal vision, and perceptible only through the holistic analysis of our peripheral cone vision.[66] Whereas your focused vision sees just a mouth, your peripheral vision perceives ambiguity.

This may help to make sense of Pallasmaa's critique of an architecture created by the eye for the eye:

> The very essence of the lived experience is molded by unconscious haptic imagery and unfocused peripheral vision. [...] One of the reasons why the architectural and urban settings of our time tend to make us outsiders [...] is in their poverty in the field of peripheral vision. Unconscious peripheral perception transforms retinal Gestalt into spatial and bodily experiences. Peripheral vision integrates us with space, while focused vision pushes us out of the space making us mere spectators.[67]

We cannot grasp how focused vision works until we release it from duty and see what happens to us while it's on a break, and experience how it acts when it comes back. I learned this trick through an accidental discovery that preceded my encounter with Pallasmaa's work by a decade.

Imagine this: You're watching a wild, densely packed William Forsythe choreography.[68] You exhaust yourself, chasing after a multitude of elusive details while losing your grasp of the whole. You then rest your eyes on a surface suspended above the heads of the dancers. All of a sudden, you feel the dancers' movement as if it were something happening to you. You are watching nothing, and seeing everything. Through the side of your neck, you perceive a bow drawn across an instrument. The sensation of two people vigorously embracing enters you through your crotch. Everything and everybody turns into your body, and your entire body turns into an eye. You can "see" with your skin. And dance, which had already been emancipated from dependency on other art forms such as stories or music, and from pre-defined postures and positions in space, had now been liberated from needing to be "seen" to be experienced.

On my way home after that performance, I called a biologist friend who keeps late hours to help me make sense of how I could have seen movement I was

63 Pallasmaa.
64 Leonid P. Yaroslavsky et al. "Optics-less Smart Sensors and a Possible Mechanism of Cutaneous Vision in Nature," in *Central European Journal of Physics* 8, no. 3 (2010): 455–56.
65 Leonid P. Yaroslavsky, email to the author, February 1, 2016.

66 Eric Kandel, *The Age of Insight: The Quest to Understand the Unconscious in Art, Mind and Brain, from Vienna 1900 to the Present* (New York: Random House, 2012), 245–46.
67 Pallasmaa, *Eyes of the Skin*, 14–15.
68 William Forsythe, *Eidos: Telos*, full-length ballet in three acts (Frankfurt am Main, 1995).

not looking at. He explained that it was my peripheral nervous system kicking in, which happens when you relax the hold of your active gaze, i.e., your central vision. Since then, I've been taking my peripheral vision dancing wherever I go.

When you walk down a street, and you are looking straight ahead or around on a plane of vision within the scene, you are the mover moving past the buildings, and you are separate from them and from other people.

When, however, you lift your gaze above the scene, the buildings and the people veer towards and move past you, and you are enmeshed in and part of their movement, like water rushing, and you a moving divide in a strong current of movement.

When you lower your sight line again, your eyes are the hands that push the buildings away and hold them at arm's length. You regain a sense of autonomy, of separation.

If you gaze straight ahead again and up at the sky as you are walking, your eyes search in vain for a foothold, for something to grasp. You are no longer on the same plane as what lies before you; you are standing on the lower end of a see-saw. Your eyes are the hands and feet that steady you and keep you separate from your surroundings. With focused vision, you are the mover; with peripheral vision, you are being moved.

This is probably what Pallasmaa is talking about when he says: "The steadily growing hegemonic claim of the eye seems to go hand in hand with the development of Western self-consciousness and the increasing separation of the self from the world. Seeing separates us from the world, whereas the other senses unite us with it. Focused vision confronts us with the world, whereas peripheral vision envelops us in the flesh of the world."[69]

Perhaps it is our habit of being spectators through windows and screens that reinforces an imperative to "understand," to order and to make sense of what we see, and an uneasy feeling of inadequacy that makes us defensive against and dismissive of art that, speaking kinetically and haptically, seems to have nothing to say to us.

When we watch dance frontally, following and scrutinizing it with focused vision, are we not trying to pin something down, to "nail it," i.e., to "get it"? Aren't we in fact trying to fight against the fluidity of movement, to freeze it, to suspend motion?

In his article "Peripheral Visual Awareness: The Central Issue," behavioral optometrist Steve Gallop sees the privileging of central vision as a cultural phenomenon, influencing among other things the focus, so to speak, of vision research:

Thus, despite the fact that most incoming light is processed by peripheral retina and not by fovea, it is the nature of our culture that emphasis is placed on the small details, not the big picture: on outcome, not process: on stasis, not change. Central/foveal vision is about static details and outcome. Peripheral vision is about movement and process, and it is involved with detecting and understanding the big picture—the context and changes in our environment. [...] At least visually speaking, it helps to keep us in touch with our relationship to everything with which we share visual space. Peripheral vision is at the heart of awareness of, and response to, the total space/time volume of our visual environment and all its inhabitants.[70]

Your peripheral vision extends your skin's sensors so that you can "feel" without touching, just as you hear sounds from distant sources. You sense motion before you see who or what is moving. This is a survival mechanism that enables people to sense a threatening presence before it enters their direct line of view.

In their article "The Learning Brain: Lessons for Education: A Précis," Sarah-Jayne Blakemore and Uta Frith say:

One of the vehicles of teaching and learning is imitation. However, we learn merely by observation, even without performing the action ourselves. How is this possible? An important new insight of brain science is that simply observing someone performing an action activates the same brain areas that are activated by producing movements oneself (Rizzolatti, Fadiga, Gallese & Fogassi, 1996). [...] Your brain mimics other people's actions even if you don't. Simulating observed actions in the brain might make performing that action easier if and when you come to perform the action yourself. Some aspects of teaching and learning depend upon this effect. Imagine trying to learn to dance without being able to observe someone dancing first. Learning from observation is usually easier than learning from verbal descriptions. [...] This might be because, by observing an action, your brain has already prepared to copy it.[71]

Feeling our way into someone else's movement is what could be called physical empathy. We apparently experience it automatically, so maybe we just need to tune into it.

69 Pallasmaa, *Eyes of the Skin*, 14.
70 Steve Gallop, "Peripheral Visual Aware-ness: The Central Issue," *Journal of Behavioral Optometry* 7, no. 6 (1996): 151–52, http://vision-therapy-pa.com/published-articles/peripheral-visual-awareness--the-central-issue.html.

71 Sarah-Jayne Blakemore and Uta Frith, "The Learning Brain: Lessons for Education: A Précis," *Developmental Science* 8, no. 6 (2005): 463.

Let's look for a moment at art that must be seen with the body. I am thinking of Leonart Bramer's *The Raising of the Cross*,[72] in the Picture Gallery of the Academy of Fine Arts Vienna. What you see is a familiar biblical subject: the cross onto which Christ has just been nailed is being raised upright from the ground. The journey from the ground up traces the arc of being in the body, suffering, and leaving the body to become spirit. The painter catches the journey three-quarters of the way up. The faces are not quite visible; the real story is in the bodies. What you feel is the brute energy of the men heaving and hauling the massive cross into position, charged with the self-righteousness of their bosses who judged the "criminals" and condemned them to this ago-nizing death. Christ's head is sunk; what you sense is utter physical helplessness, the sickening, shameful feeling that some mindless brute has total power over you. The most vivid faces are the faceless sad little skulls left to rot in the dust, the bones of their limbs splayed helplessly next to them.

Let's look for a moment at art that takes us walking. I am thinking of a work by Lothar Baumgarten that Sabine Folie exhibited in the Generali Foundation in Vienna, called *Section 125-25 64-58 Hommage à M.B.* (1972–74).[73] It consists of feathers from different North American Indian tribes stuck onto a wall. If you leave your frontal perspective and walk alongside the wall, the air your move-ment stirs, stirs the feathers to life. As you walk past each of them, they move in response to you. When you sense this live, responsive presence, the devastation you feel when you reach the end—their end—is indescribable. This is the difference between getting the point and having an experience.

Vitus Weh reflects on a new way of exhibiting and encountering single works of art facilitated by a construction-site-like space such as the Palais de Tokyo in Paris: "Individual works of art stand here and there, autonomously, strewn about in no apparent arrangement. The construction shell seems to fit our current needs and social constitution; how and where we encounter art reflects our self-perception. The autonomous artwork becomes a human representational object [...] without the context of and connection to a larger whole. Whether it is sensed as heroic or abandoned remains open."[74]

Open, minimally defined sites and cryptic, irreducible works of art might pro-vide space for our expanding imaginations like classical ruins and sculptural torso fragments do. Now, especially in the Digital Age, haptic architecture and art forms are taking on new significance. As Juhani Pallasmaa reflects: "Perhaps, when the eye is freed of its underlying wish for control and power, then the unfocused gaze of our time can succeed in opening new realms of seeing and of thought."[75]

On April 7, 2017, the INTRA SPACE community gathered from the four corners of the earth for the final project screening, created and performed by Esther

Balfe and Christina Jauernik with the IT, design, sound, and film camera team members. Multiple Christinas and Esthers moved both on screens and in the flesh with manifold Bobs.[76] From algorithms and code in computer monitors monitoring mounting skeletons moving on real bodies moving with virtual bodies moving with virtual real bodies and real virtual bodies, the entire unfolding process was spatially layered in screening simultaneity. Multiple screens were layered throughout the space to shift and display shifting and shifted perspectives, setting up fields of action for movement too large to be encompassed entirely by our central vision, providing multiple foci on which to rest the eye.

And what of our participatory perceptual viewer bodies? How did we deal with so much going on at once? The movement that took place outside whatever our central focus encompassed, tickled peripheral vision into wakefulness, and was perceived not optically but rather through the eyes of the skin.

Two media with equal claims on our attention appear to be key. As we shift our attention back and forth between screen images and 3D objects in real space, the contrast between the two intensifies the particular vividness and spatial qualities of each. Whether our whole selves and not just our central vision are engaged comes down to how we layer, texture, and shape space.

Haptic stimulation through peripheral vision is elemental for mortal bodies, like water, sunlight, and touch. We need it, we crave it; we wither and can't live without it.

Is full-bodied haptic "viewing" also a kind of "doing"?

Immersion is a multi-layered process as well as a state. In contemporary performances for example, it is common practice for dancers to move from the center to the sidelines of the performance space, to shift their perspectives before reentering the movement action. They are still immersed; their alertness from the sidelines has perceptible dynamic qualities for others in the room, including the audience.

72 Leonart Bramer, *Die Kreuzaufrichtung*, ca. 1630. Oil on wood. Gemäldegalerie, Akademie der bildenden Künste, Vienna.

73 Lothar Baumgarten, *Section 125-25 64-58, Hommage à M.B.*, 1972–74. Sammlung Lothar Schirmer, Munich. Exhibited in "UN COUP DE DÉS: Bild gewordene Schrift. Ein ABC der nachdenklichen Sprache," Generali Foundation, Vienna, September 19–November 23, 2008, curated by Sabine Folie.

74 Weh, "Räume für Kunst," 3.

75 Pallasmaa, *Eyes of the Skin*, 40.

76 I can't resist referring to Bob as "manifold." According to Wikipedia: "In mathematics, a manifold is a topological space that locally resembles Euclidean space near each point." Click on the link to see an image bearing somewhat of a resemblance to Bob: https://en.wikipedia.org/wiki /Manifold.

An "intra space" gives all people in it multiple options for immersive experiences. Disengaging from direct interaction yet remaining haptically in touch blurs the lines separating "doer" and "viewer." Viewing prepares us for other kinds of doing.

To expand our views, we need new pictures, buildings and spaces beyond ideological and market strategic thinking, beyond self-representation or mere mimetic mirroring. We need architecture and art—excuse the Rilke paraphrase—that see us, and in so doing, open us to new images of ourselves and the world that are fluid, that cannot be pinned down, that question our assumptions and alter our unconscious attitudes, stances, and positions. Perhaps the alien in you is your limitless potential, that which forever surprises you. Real space is your body, your room, your home.

And you—you integrate vision with the other senses, for example, when you read poetry aloud. As you take the poem into your body and speak it, you can feel and hear dimensions of meaning invisible to the eye alone, much as dancers embody the subtler rhythms and harmonies of music, the movement resonating into an audibly enriched musical texture.

You relax the hold of focused vision when you listen to minimalist music. You let go of the wish that the phrase would stop repeating itself, and fall instead into the body of the instruments, into the colors and textures and depth of their sound palettes. Or when you gaze into a monochrome painting, and the color shifts and parts like clouds, revealing infinite space.

The body is receptive to movement, to voices, sounds, textures and atmospheres—complex, mutable—that cannot be reduced to content. Art with critical content is important. But content alone does not measure up to the power of art. A critique, a politics of art that excludes the needs as well as the perceptive potential of the body, is a contradiction, above all in a critical discourse on the manipulation and exploitation of the body.

And finally, back to the dance. The question is not what sense you see in the dance, but what senses you see the dance with. As George Balanchine would say, "See the music, hear the dance."[77] As Merce Cunningham would say, "Relax and enjoy."[78] And I say, there may not be a point to get, but you may have an experience. To experience something, you need all of you, all of you. Thank you!

77 In her article "'Balanchine Said': What Was
   the Source of the Choreographer's
   Celebrated Utterances?", *New Yorker*
   January 8, 2009, Arlene Croce states:
   "One of his most publicized utterances,
   'See the music, hear the dance,' is
   arguably rightfully his, however platitudi-
   nous it may have become by the time he
   revived it. At least he was quoting a published response to his own choreography.

Glenway Wescott, reviewing Bernard
Taper's 'Balanchine' in the magazine *Show*
(December, 1963), had written, 'Suddenly
I *see* the music; suddenly I *hear* the
movements of the dancers.'"
78 Merce Cunningham, *Merce Cunningham
   and Dance Company: Event for Television,
   17:07 min., in Great Performances: Dance
   in America* (New York: Cunningham Dance
   Foundation, 1977).

Literature

Aloff, Mindy, ed. *Dance in America: A Reader's Anthology*. New York: Library of America, 2018.

Amort, Andrea, and Mimi Wunderer-Gosch, eds. *Österreich tanzt: Geschichte und Gegenwart*. Vienna: Böhlau Verlag, 2001.

Aristotle. *Poetics*. Translated and edited by Anthony Kenny. Oxford: Oxford University Press, 2013. Kindle.

Balfe, Esther, and Christina Jauernik. "Intra Space: Otherness (Attentional Forms)," Workshop. "ImPulsTanz Vienna International Dance Festival." August 4–5, 2018. https://www.impulstanz.com/en /archive/2018/workshops/id3795/.

Blakemore, Sarah-Jayne, and Uta Frith. "The Learning Brain: Lessons for Education: A Précis." *Developmental Science* 8, no. 6 (2005): 459–71. https://doi.org /10.1111/j.1467-7687.2005.00434.x.

Brockway, Merrill, and Merce Cunningham, John Cage, David Tudor, WNET. *Merce Cunningham and Dance Company: Event for Television*, 17:07 min. In *Great Performances: Dance in America*. New York: Cunningham Dance Foundation, 1977.

Coleridge, Samuel Taylor. *Biographia Literaria*, chap. xiv (1817). Poetryfoundation .org, October 13, 2009. https://www .poetryfoundation.org/articles/69385 /from-biographia-literaria-chapter-xiv.

Copeland, Roger, and Marshall Cohen, eds. *What Is Dance?* Oxford: Oxford University Press, 1983.

Cothren, Michael. "Teaching Art in an Era of Globalism." Audio transcript. July 25, 2012. http://www.swarthmore.edu/michael -cothren-teaching-art-in-an-era-of -globalism.xml.

Crary, Jonathan. *Suspensions of Perception: Attention, Spectacle, and Modern Culture*. Cambridge, MA: MIT Press, 2001.

——. *Techniques of the Observer: On Vision and Modernity in the Nineteenth Century*. Cambridge, MA: MIT Press, 1992.

Croce, Arlene. "Balanchine Said." *New Yorker*, January 8, 2009. https://www .newyorker.com/magazine/2009/01/26 /balanchine-said.

——. "Edwin Denby." In Aloff, *Dance in America*, 180–93.

Cunningham, Merce. "The Function of a Technique for Dance." In Aloff, *Dance in America*, 195–99.

Czaja, Wojciech. "Mit Hochhäusern haben wir ein Problem." Interview with UNESCO Director Mechtild Rössler. *Der Standard*, March 4, 2019. https://derstandard.at /2000098892647/Unesco-Direktorin -Roessler-Mit-Hochhaeusern-haben-wir -ein-Problem.

Dahms, Sibylle. "Die Bedeutung Wiens für die Ballettreform des 18. Jahrhunderts." In *Österreich tanzt*, edited by Andrea Amort and Mimi Wunderer-Gosch, 22–29.

Folie, Sabine, ed. *Un coup de Dés: Bold gewordene Schrift. Ein ABC der nachdenklichen Sprache*. Vienna: Generali Foundation, 2008.

Gallop, Steve. "Peripheral Visual Awareness: The Central Issue." *Journal of Behavioral Optometry* 7, no. 6 (1996): 151–55. http:// vision-therapy-pa.com/published -articles/peripheral-visual-awareness --the-central-issue.html.

Gehl, Jan. *Cities for People*. Washington, DC: Island Press, 2010.

Grundner, Maria. "Beauftragte für Fußgängerinnen und Fußgänger." *Wien zu Fuß* (blog), December 9, 2013, https:// www.wienzufuss.at/2013/12/09/die fussgaengerverkehrsbeauftragten/.

Höhle, Eva-Maria, Renata Kassal-Mikula, Oskar Pausch, and Richard Perger, eds. *The Neidhart Frescoes: The Oldest Secular Mural Painting in Vienna*. Translated by Beatrice Ottersböck. Vienna: The Museums of the City of Vienna, 1984.

Horosko, Marian. "Marian Horosko: Personal Statement." In *I Remember Balanchine: Recollections of the Ballet Master by Those Who Knew Him*, edited by Francis Mason, 365–73. New York: Doubleday, 1991.

Jabr, Ferris. "Why the Brain Prefers Paper." *Scientific American*, November 2013, 49–53.

Kandel, Eric. *The Age of Insight: The Quest to Understand the Unconscious in Art, Mind and Brain, from Vienna 1900 to the Present*. New York: Random House, 2012.

Keats, John. "Ode on a Grecian Urn." In *Selected Poems and Letters by John Keats*, edited by Douglas Bush, 207–8. Boston: Houghton Mifflin Company, 1959.

Langer, Susanne K. "Virtual Powers." In *What Is Dance?*, edited by Roger Copeland and Marshall Cohen, 28–36.

Gertraud Liesenfeld, Klara Löffler, Christian Rapp, and Michael Weese, eds. *nichts tun: vom flanieren, pausieren, blaumachen und müßiggehen*. Vienna: Kataloge des Österreichischen Museums für Volkskunde 75, 2000.

Leysen, Frie. Erasmus Prize Acceptance Speech, November 12, 2014. http://www.erasmusprijs.org/?lang=en&page=Nieuws&mode=detail&item=Speech+Frie+Leysen+online.

Mobilitätsagentur Wien. "Im Jahr 2015 stand Wien im Zeichen des Zu-Fuß-Gehens." https://www.wienzufuss.at/jahr-des-zu-fuss-gehens/.

Motyl, Katya. "Bodies That Shimmer: An Embodied History of Vienna's New Women, 1893–1931." PhD diss., University of Chicago, 2017.

Oberzaucher-Schüller, Gunhild. "Institutionalisierter Tanz im Wien des 19. Jahrhunderts." In *Österreich tanzt*, edited by Andrea Amort and Mimi Wunderer-Gosch, 35–53.

Pallasmaa, Juhani. *The Eyes of the Skin: Architecture and the Senses*. Chichester: John Wiley & Sons 2012.

Randolph, Elizabeth. "Distracted Reading in the Digital Age (and What to Do about It)." *The Vassar Alumnae/I Quarterly* 111, no. 1 (2015): 11–16.

Rapp, Christian. "Vom Promenieren." In Gertraud Liesenfeld, Klara Löffler, Christian Rapp, and Michael Weese, eds. *nichts tun*, Kataloge des Österreichischen Museums für Volkskunde 75, 38–42.

———. "Vom Spazieren." In Gertraud Liesenfeld, Klara Löffler, Christian Rapp, and Michael Weese, eds. *nichts tun*, Kataloge des Österreichischen Museums für Volkskunde 75, 30–37.

Rosenblit, Marsha L. *The Jews of Vienna, 1867–1914: Assimilation and Identity*. Albany: State University of New York. 1983.

Rykwert, Joseph. *The Dancing Column: On Order in Architecture*. Cambridge, MA: MIT Press, 1998.

Schnitzler, Arthur. *Reigen: Zehn Dialoge*. Frankfurt am Main: dtv, 2004. First published 1903.

Solnit, Rebecca. *Wanderlust: A History of Walking*. New York: Penguin Books, 2000. Kindle.

Strauss, Liane. *Leaving Eden*. London: Salt Publishing, 2010.

Swain, Marianka. "Perfect 10: The Viennese Waltz," posted by Brigitt Mayer on *DanceArchives*, November 29, 2012. http://www.dancearchives.net/2012/11/29/perfect-10-the-viennese-waltz-by-marianka-swain/.

Stodulka, Thomas. "Porträt: Victor Gruen." *Zoë*, January 2015.

Walk21 Vienna 2015, October 20–23, 2015. http://walk21vienna.com/.

Weh, Vitus. "Räume für Kunst: Über den historischen Wandel ihrer Symboliken und Wirkweisen." Unpublished essay.

Wittstock, Birgit. "Revolution auf zwei Beinen." *Falter*, December 3, 2014.

Wolf, Salomo Jakob. *Erörterung derer wichtigsten Ursachen der Schwäche unsrer Generation in Hinsicht auf das Walzen.* Pamphlet. Halle: Hendel Verlag, 1797.

Yaroslavsky, Leonid P., H., John Caulfield, Chad Goerzen, and Stanislav Umansky. "Optics-less Smart Sensors and a Possible Mechanism of Cutaneous Vision in Nature." *Central European Journal of Physics* 8, no. 3 (2010): 455–62.

Zwander, Wolfgang. "Bobo gegen Auto." *Falter*, February 11, 2015.

On Human and Machine Co-agency in Art

Dennis Del Favero and Susanne Thurow

As an interactive artwork, INTRA SPACE forms part of a growing corpus of creative explorations that interrogate the relationship between intelligent machines and human users—work that not only draws on the latest technologies and makes these experientially available to the general public, but more importantly which aesthetically configures such technologies with far-reaching consequences for the ways in which we are invited to understand and shape the relationship between human and machine agency in art. With contemporary philosophy supporting the direction of artistic focus on the process of creation and reception as the predominant site of meaning-making,[1] works like INTRA SPACE open the possibility for consolidating a new genre of art that extends this trajectory into a future in which human capabilities are augmented through an increasingly independent machine agency.[2] Setting up a collaborative interaction between a human user and an intelligent machine through a dialogical human-machine aesthetics not only centralizes processual interaction as the main focal point of artistic enquiry, it also concurrently dislodges the primacy of human control in this configuration and awards space to the creation and experience of a nonhuman agency in relation to, yet also independent of, human perception.[3]

Artistic Siting

The capacities of INTRA SPACE in this regard come to the fore when considering the project alongside other installation, media, and performance works in the field. From the early path-defining explorations of Joseph Weizenbaum's *ELIZA* (1966), which, as among the first successful natural-language-processing computer programs, has enabled a seemingly free-flowing conversation between machine and a human user, much art has explored concepts that advance the machine as an independent and sentient agent.[4] For example, the *ELIZA* program has been tested as an online conversational agent in psychologically oriented discourse. Unlike INTRA SPACE, it aims for an individually targeted interpellation of the human user, inquiring about their emotional state and deepening the conversation by picking up and using some of their phrases, cognitively triggering feelings of affirmation and validation in the user that

1   Claire Colebrook, "Not Kant, Not Now: Another Sublime," in *Speculations V: Aesthetics in the 21st Century*, ed. Ridvan Askin et al. (Brooklyn: Punctum, 2013), 142.

2   N. Katherine Hayles, *How We Became Posthuman: Virtual Bodies in Cybernetics, Literature, and Informatics* (Chicago: University of Chicago Press, 1999), 247ff.

3   Mark D'Inverno and Jon McCormack, "Heroic vs Collaborative AI," in *Proceedings of the 24th International Joint Conference on Artificial Intelligence*, ed. Qiang Yang and Michael Wooldridge (Palo Alto, CA: AAAI, 2015), 2439ff.

4   Joseph Weizenbaum, "ELIZA—A Computer Program for the Study of Natural Language Communication Between Man and Machine," *Communications of the ACM* 9, no. 1 (1966): 36–45.

heightens their acceptance of the program's seeming sentience. By contrast, the machine agent in INTRA SPACE is programmed to interact through gesture only, dictating a more detached and embodied interpellation. While the machine in *ELIZA* simulates a dialogical response on the grounds of tightly coded scripts, the willingness of the human user to bridge any semantic discrepancies via relational and imaginative projection thereby ensures that interaction is maintained and experienced as meaningful. Hence, rather than realizing a genuinely reciprocal human-machine dialogue, works like *ELIZA* predominantly rely on the capability of the human user to sustain and direct the interaction. This aesthetic approach has since become foundational to many media artworks, with contemporary examples including Oleg Kulik and Dimitri Volkov's *OraculeTang* (2015), which let a giant humanoid robotic orangutan converse on a wide range of topics with users, actuating polyvalent linguistic sequences that, as prophetic aphorisms, are loosely related to the users' input-questions.[5] This approach has been further developed in Lynn Hershman Leeson's media artwork *Agent Ruby* (1998–2002), which refines the chatbot concept by furnishing the machine agent with its own emotional repertoire that is sampled in response to the amount and intensity of human interaction.[6] It imbues the virtual character with a personality of its own that owing to its coding architecture becomes more sophisticated the longer it inter- acts with human users. In *Agent Ruby*, the virtual agent is anthropomorphized, greeting the user as an animated desktop figure that converses through verbal language and accompanying facial expressions. Martin Collins and Tom Szirtes picked up this aesthetics in their interactive portrait installation *BIM* (2015), which deploys face-recognition software, adjusting the virtual character's inter- active response to the degree of visitor engagement, displaying a stratified emotional repertoire that ranges from disengaged boredom, vivacious attention seeking, and flirtation to disdainful rejection.[7]

The machine agent's seemingly autonomous response to user interaction in these contexts is a technically derived illusion, based on programming heu- ristics that enable agents to mimic and respond to human behavior. Despite this significant expansion of expressive register for the machine agent, the aesthetic approach is firmly human-centered because the machine is ultimately conceptualized as a conduit for human reflection but not as an independent entity in its own right. Its intentions and deliberations are scripted solely as serving the purpose of eliciting a response in the human subject, who is invited to use the artwork as a point of departure for reflecting on the experience of interaction with and relation to a nonhuman agency.[8] Such agency is in essence grounded in a simulation that for its effectiveness relies on a set of parameters that are intricately bound up with the human propensity and aptitude for inter- action, e.g., using verbal language, emotional registers, the human body and face, and their expressive capability as conduits for communication—delimiting the frame according to which the otherness of nonhuman agency can come into being and be appreciated.[9] The machine is consequently turned into a mere tool at the service of human experience, ultimately affirming the traditional concept of art as a means for human reflection and experience.[10] This configuration of the technological apparatus for the expansion of human capabilities and experience is aptly confirmed in XLAB's performance work *Mandala's Tales* (2000–11), which uses a sophisticated technological architecture to leverage the performer's body as an instrument that conjures mutating audio-visual projections and which samples narrative sequences according to vocal pitch.[11] While apparent joint agency between the user and the machine is achieved via an orchestration of movement, sound, and interfaces, the relation between human and machine here is still hierarchical and prioritizes the human as director of the artwork. Whether users are extended the ability to shape events, as in *Agent Ruby*, or to direct a narrative, as in *Mandala's Tales*, the user alone ultimately determines the unfolding of the work, while mutual and dynamic attribution of motive (i.e., genuine dialogical interaction) by machine agents and users remains outside of the artworks' explorative scope. Autonomous deliberation, however, constitutes a key ingredient of modeling an independent nonhuman agency that can contribute a new exciting facet to artistic exploration and which will have a significant qualitative impact on the aesthetics of interaction afforded by new media artworks. Only if the machine agent is furnished with an ability to respond with autonomous decision making to user presence and input can it figure as a "thing unto itself" and open up pathways that allow a creative investigation of nonhuman agency and our possible relations to it.[12]

Intriguing alternatives to the user-directed approach have been trialed for example in Jon McCormack's durational installation work *Eden* (2010–17), which programmed autonomous virtual life-forms that independently grow and pro-

5 Shai Batel, "Interactive Performance Art/ificial Intelligence – Robotic Ape Comes to BAM," *Huffington Post*, October 27, 2015, https://www.huffingtonpost.com/shai-baitel/interactive-performance-a_b_8399074.html.

6 "Agent Ruby," http://www.lynnhershman.com/agent-ruby/.

7 Mark Westall, "Fish Island Labs Present: Interfaces 'Processing Reality through Art and Technology,'" *FAD Magazine*, June 14, 2015, https://fadmagazine.com/2015/06/14/fish-island-labs-present-interfaces-processing-reality-through-art-and-technology/.

8 Ary Fagundes Bressane Neto and Flavio Soares Correa da Silva, "A Computer Architecture for Intelligent Agents with Personality and Emotions," in *Human-Computer-Interaction: The Agency Perspective*, ed. M. Zacarias and J.V. Oliveira (Berlin: Springer, 2012), 264.

9 M. A. R. Biggs, "Non-human Intention and Meaning-Making: An Ecological Theory," in *Cognitive Architectures*, ed. M. Aldinhas Ferreira et al., Intelligent Systems, Control and Automation: Science and Engineering series 94 (Cham: Springer, 2019), 196.

10 N. Katherine Hayles, "Speculative Aesthetics and Object-Oriented Enquiry (OOI)," in *Speculations V*, 164.

11 Anughea Studios, "Mandala's Tales: An Interactive Performance by XLAB," *Digital Performance*, n.d., http://www.digitalperformance.it/?p=1214.

12 Hayles, "Speculative Aesthetics and Object-Oriented Enquiry (OOI)," 160.

liferate, responding also to the presence of visitors but not requiring interaction with them to activate and unfold their agency. Hence, the machine here is imbued with an intelligence largely emancipated from the tight control of its designers, evolving from its own dynamic programming along open-ended trajectories. This avoids the reduction and flattening of interaction in the artwork to a merely mimetic aggregation of events. While aggregation is a defining feature of the digital and consequently will form part of any artistic engagement with such new technologies, on its own it provides only limited artistic potential because it does not account for dynamic development and limits the process of representation to infinite regress.[13] The reductionism of such a non-dynamic model is exemplified in Evelyn Hribersek's modular art installation *O.R.pheus* (2012), in which users explore physical settings augmented by virtual portals that can be activated and explored at will. It samples alternate narrative pathways and musical sequences according to user preference, while the machinic setup responds with randomly sampled re-combinations of pre-scripted audio data, which result in unique iterative actuations of the installation. The interplay, however, is aesthetically one-sided, propelled by adaptive human ascription rather than dynamic machinic code, which reserves creative direction exclusively for the user and assigns mere mechanical reaction to the machine. While plausibly demonstrating digital narrative's ability to morph according to dynamic input, *O.R.pheus* conceptualizes machine agency as an essentially static structure, foreclosing the possibility of creative input by the machine to adaptively determine the narrative development in unforeseen ways. This conceptual approach has been mirrored in Nicola Plant and Alexander Adderley's VR art installation *Sentient Flux* (2015), which projects a glowing particle field responsive to human movement. Reverberations caused by human users randomly pass along the space, then flicker and return back to them, giving the sense of a reciprocally transacting image field when in actual fact the response is based on an amplification and sampling of the users' input alone.[14] This approach produces an asymmetrical relationship between human users and machine agents, flattening and delimiting the interactive scope of their encounter.[15] Aspiring to symmetric reasoning within human-machine agent interaction, however, makes it possible to conceive an expanded quality of ascriptive deliberation and action. To achieve this, we need to change the ontological status of the machine agent so that it is enabled to independently sense, understand, and learn from user interaction.[16] Artistic research to date, however, has generally targeted the refinement of user interaction rather than exploring the ability of machine agents to ascribe motive themselves.[17] To date, the intelligibility of human intentions to machine agents remains significantly under-explored in interactive art, with only a handful of projects having so far successfully prototyped the application of such advanced reciprocal and dynamic interactivity. One such experimental application was implemented in the interactive installation *Scenario* (2010–15) by Dennis Del Favero, which through a finely attuned tracking system furnishes virtual characters with the ability to sense, interpret, and respond to the position and movement of human users in space, supplying integral input to the collaborative advancement of narrative progression in the artwork.[18] *Scenario*'s conceptual premises provided the blueprint for INTRA SPACE's interaction design, enabling its exploration of performative space through a customized tracking system and AI that translate human movement into a language perceptible and intelligible to the machine. This language is able to represent concurrent and sensed data independently and in non-deterministic ways, making it possible to conceptualize the machine agent as an independent director of its own simple algorithms.[19] Through provision of an aesthetically compelling immersive-performative setting that aesthetically propels to interaction, machine agents and human users are tied into a dialogical bind. The key here has been to deploy a framework that caters to the specificities of each agent's behavioral parameters that awards the ability to ascribe control to both human and nonhuman agents.[20] By doing so, it re-positions interactivity as a powerful artistic tool that can deliver an expanded expressive and imaginative terrain to contemporary art.

Hence, INTRA SPACE builds upon significant advances in the field of media arts and associated technological developments, incorporating and progressing concepts in order to pave the way towards a new genre of art. As the works described above, INTRA SPACE explores the technological apparatus as a signif-icant agency in the constitution of space, imbuing the machinic setup with a capacity to respond to human interaction in relatively unpredictable ways whilst minimizing disruption through its seamless full-body immersive interface design. By deploying a sophisticated tracking system coupled with AI, the machine senses, processes, and responds to human movement, tying the input into its pre-programmed sequences in order to invite users to perceive the virtual character as a sentient entity capable of entering into dialogical interaction. INTRA SPACE expands current experimentation with simulatory approaches by allowing for a dynamic integration of processed data into its choreographic architecture, focusing the processing of the user's movement patterns and

13 Hartmut Koenitz et al. , eds. "Introduction," in *Perspectives on Interactive Digital Narrative* (New York: Routledge, 2015), 2.

14 "Sentient Flux," http://nicolaplant.co.uk /sentientflux.html

15 Simon Penny, "Towards a Performative Aesthetics of Interactivity," *Fibreculture Journal* 19 (2011): 76, http://nineteen .fibreculturejournal.org/fcj-132-towards -a-performative-aesthetics-of-interactivity/.

16 Neil Brown et al., "Performing Digital Aesthetics: The Framework for a Theory of the Formation of Interactive Narratives," *Leonardo* 44, no. 3 (2011): 217.

17 Penny, "Towards a Performative Aesthetics of Interactivity," 76–79.

18 "Scenario," http://www.icinema.unsw.edu .au/projects/scenario/project-overview/.

19 Neil Brown et al., "Performing Digital Aesthetics," 217.

20 Maurice Pagnucco et al., "Implementing Belief Change in the Situation Calculus," in *Logic Programming and Nonmonotonic Reasoning*, ed. P. Cabalar and T. C. Son, Lecture Notes in Computer Science 8148 (Heidelberg: Springer, 2011), 439–51.

hence shortening the gap to be bridged between machinic and human inter-pretation. While it does not provide for durational evolution, it allows for relatively unpredictable, machine-directed actuations of the artwork with each interactive iteration providing a unique experience to users. As such, INTRA SPACE's deployment as an explorative choreographic tool at the ImPulsTanz festival in Vienna in August 2018 proved especially fruitful, revealing how even within its fledgling framework of dynamic ascription, inspiration for a reimagination of choreographic practice can be born from human-machine collaboration. The anthropomorphized design of the virtual character hereby aided intuitive and quickly escalating progression in human-machine interaction as the articulation to the human mobility apparatus supported the reflection and tran-scendence of conventional or habit-driven movement patterns. Consequently, INTRA SPACE is sited at the crossroads of artistic experimentations that are human-centered and those that privilege the machine as an independent agency in its own right, capable of providing autonomous and dynamic input. Through its temporally clocked interaction sequences that alternate with playback of recorded material, the user experiences the virtual character as interacting on its own terms, frustrating from time to time the free-flowing collaborative interaction to pursue its own trajectory independent of the user's presence or interference. This amplification, or frustration of human direction, prefigures a pathway to exciting new ground for artistic experimentation that calls for a conceptual and theoretical reflection of its attendant implications.

Immersive Aesthetics

Siting the interaction in INTRA SPACE within a full-body kinesthetic immersive environment that provides an interface unrestricted to ocular engagement and unencumbered by wires or body-mounted sensors enables users to expe-rience the virtual performer through a sensory lens that invites experiencing it as an autonomously manifest entity on a towering screen. The artistically honed visualization of the figure and its mammoth scale are designed to draw the user into the virtual space, letting perception of the physical and virtual spaces melt into one another, which intensifies the user's immersive experience. The partial mimicry of the user's movements by the virtual figure further amplifies this entanglement between user and machinic apparatus, questioning the boundaries between them. By entering the performance space, the human user is absorbed into a play of identifications that affects their status as actor within the technologically articulated space. Communicating through the technological apparatus that absorbs the body's choreographic expression and samples it into the machine agent's response, human agency here unfolds in conjunction with the machine, visibly enmeshing the human body within a posthuman domain.[21] Body and interface entangle and establish an iterative feedback loop that strings the interaction along through dynamic and escalating input. Thus, human and machine agents are woven into one another, existing as separate entities, yet all the while bonded through interaction that articulates their agencies in response to one another. Different from actuations such as performed in Hribersek's *O.R.pheus* or Collins and Szirtes's *BIM*, both agencies are capable of providing dynamic input into the interaction, drawing on the other's response to model a new movement sequence that will give rise to a unique choreography. Hence, INTRA SPACE makes it possible to conceive the human-machine dialogue as founded on a model of coagency in which creative direction is shared and capabilities of both the machine and the user are expanded through the reciprocal exchange. Analogous to Karen Barad's concept of "intra-action,"[22] the two agencies constitute themselves only within the act of relational action, delineating their identities and full capabilities only through shared performance.

The entangled physical-virtual space provided through the immersive setting is hereby both enabler and container to this performance. Its diaphanous quality primes the user's attention towards the technological mediation yet at the same time works to shroud this architecture through its seductive invitation to play. Consequently, the hyper-mediation becomes a naturalized backdrop that brings forth this new quality of interaction between human user and machine, opening new avenues for dialogical interaction. It is important to note that the technologically enabled environment here not only provides an experiential entryway into approximating Barad's concept through sensory perception (i.e., experiencing one's agency as complemented through its co-articulation on screen) but expands traditional conceptions of artistic space via configuration of a posthuman physical-virtual space in which the formerly distinct agencies start to merge. While the boundary between physical and virtual space blurs in the active interchange between human user and machine agent, their identities as distinctive entities are equally subject to deconstruction as they increasingly articulate their behaviors to one another in the process of communication. Hence, artworks like INTRA SPACE begin to deconstruct the dichotomous categories "physical," "virtual," "human," and "machine," reinterpreting them as coordinates on a spectrum that points towards a radical performative reconfiguration of central defining pillars— of the human and of cultural orientation—in the digital age. In this regard, INTRA SPACE connects to the philosophies of emergence as proposed by Manuel De Landa and Rosi Braidotti who offer nuanced propositions for a new materialism cohered around immanence and an abandonment of established dualisms.[23] Rather

21 Hayles, *How We Became Posthuman*, ix.
22 Karen Barad, "Posthumanist Performativity: Toward an Understanding of How Matter Comes to Matter," *Signs* 28, no. 3 (2003): 801–31.

23 Rick Dolphijn and Iris van der Tuin, *New Materialism: Interviews & Cartographies*, New Metaphysics series (Open Humanities Press, 2012), https://quod.lib.umich.edu/o/ohp/11515701.0001.001/1:5.2/--new-materialism-interviews-cartographies?rgn=div2;view=fulltext.

than defining identities along set coordinates that are assigned meaning through differential relation, De Landa and Braidotti each propose conceiving of identities as nomadic, emergent structures that accrue a degree of stability and agency only in the ongoing process of self-organization and energetic folding.[24] The entanglement between the physical and virtual in INTRA SPACE was designed to explore such notions both on a conceptual and experiential plane, centralizing dynamic adaptivity and eventfulness as the key drivers of the interaction, in which self-actualizing behavior is paired with external input to yield a reconfiguration of both machine and human agencies.[25] Digital technologies hereby expand the means by which agency can be experienced and human capability developed. They make it possible to pry open materialities whose boundaries previously presented themselves as insurmountable to the eye, now yielding to various manipulations and rearrangements that award us a better appreciation of our constitution as ultimately unstable matter in space. Comprised of molecules that are energetically bonding through laws of attraction and rejection, physicists like Barad and new materialist philosophers such as De Landa and Braidotti point out that we are as much defined by matter as by the "spaces-in-between" it. This makes a clear distinction between individual and world mostly redundant in attendant identity concepts, as identity is turned into a question of degree rather than solid certitude.[26] It is through performance that identity is constituted and remade from moment to moment, awarding opportunity for affirmation as well as for reinvention and transcendence of prior positions held in space and time. Performing with the technological apparatus in INTRA SPACE gives new impetus to rethink the human as an integrated part of the space, as extended in its materiality and energetic impact beyond its conventionally, organically perceived boundaries.

While the installation makes it possible to indirectly affect the virtual figure's choreographic repertoire through translation and sampling of sensed data that awards the human user the joy of play, the engendered dialogical relation nevertheless also primes the user's comportment, molding their interaction in accordance with the apparatus' requirements: In order for the tracking system to optimally work, the user's positioning and movements have to fit with set parameters that subtly dictate particular aesthetics of interaction, such as remaining within the camera space, refraining from crossing limbs and moving at a moderate rate. Thus, these limitations of the technological setup become a source of productive resistance, ensuring that the interaction not only affects the virtual figure's expression but also that the human user has to adjust to the dialogical situation, leaving behind the comfort zone of attuned and habitual communication. The resultant friction enables exploration of a novel quality of human-machine derived choreography. The partial clunkiness of the system, aside from its obvious drawbacks, hence also served as a source of artistic productivity that kept in the picture the implications of transformative reciprocal impact in the exchange between human and nonhuman agencies.[27]

Conceptual Implications

Artworks like INTRA SPACE and *Mandala's Tales* enmesh human with machine capacities, instigating a collaborative relation that extends human agency and capability beyond current limitations. They explore the utility of digital technologies as conduits for new experiences of space and embodiment that take their cues from contemporary philosophies of emergence, posthumanism and object-oriented inquiry, setting forth on trajectories that begin to point beyond received conceptions of art. The splicing of machine and human here enables users to partake in cutting-edge technological developments and to explore developing concepts of co-agency between humans and machines. As previously outlined, the approach adopted in INTRA SPACE moves away from the simulatory and user-centered paradigm, opening pathways to contemplate the implications of an autonomous machine agency that enters into a reciprocal, dialogical relation to the user. The AI adopted in INTRA SPACE, while not yet affording capability for durational evolution, dynamically responds to user input and enables unique choreographic iterations. As such, the programming design figures as a proof-of-concept for compelling co-agential interaction in the context of immersive art installations, paving the way for the concept of an independent artificial agency capable of augmenting human direction. Once such an agency is fully fledged and established, its artistic allure will lie in being able to offer unpredictable interactive scenarios, as it will be able to creatively challenge and/or cooperate with users. The friction resulting from such calculated (as opposed to merely random) unpredictability will ideally call on users to confront the nonhuman agency embodied by the machine, engaging with its alien characteristics and communication patterns. This will afford not only the chance to explore a radically new, artificially created agency but also provide opportunity to hone and expand human capabilities for interaction and dealing with difference and otherness. The anthropomorphizing representative approach adopted in INTRA SPACE primes human interactive dispositions via an intimately familiar form (i.e., an abstracted visualization of the human body), thereby providing an intuitive entryway into such an engagement. Despite the evident epistemological advantages of a non-anthropomorphizing representative approach, such as that adopted by McCormack in *Eden*, which constructs and visually codes the virtual agent as radically

---

24 Manuel de Landa, *A Thousand Years of Nonlinear History* (New York: Zone Books, 1997); and Rosi Braidotti, "Teratologies," in *Deleuze and Feminist Theory*, ed. I. Buchanan, and C. Colebrook (Edinburgh: Edinburgh University Press, 2000), 156–72.
25 Manuel de Landa, "Virtual Environments and the Emergence of Synthetic Reason,"
in "Flame Wars," ed. Mark Dery, special issue, *South Atlantic Quarterly* 92, no. 4 (1993): 794.
26 Barad, "Posthumanist Performativity," 815.
27 Hayles, *How We Became Posthuman*, 290.

Other, the reliance on the human form makes it possible to leverage a positive identification mechanism by starting the interaction from an observance of similarity rather than difference. Hence, the interaction can proceed from an intuitively grasped place of familiarity, establishing accord before unfolding an exploration of difference with the machine agent. This divergence is experienced as all the more significant owing to the estrangement felt from the place of origin.[28] The co-agential relationship can hence be deepened and leveraged productively—especially for the purpose of an art event in which users customarily only spend a limited amount of time interacting with a machine agent, who consequently has to be accessible and maximally intuitive in its reciprocal interaction. The seamless interface design that allows users to communicate via their entire mobility apparatus here awards maximum freedom of exploration without the need for lengthy instruction or mastering of equipment, focusing the user's attention on their body and its function as the prime instrument of siting in the performance space. Doing so invites the user to contemplate the constitution of their body in space, equally estranging as well as integrating their experience of it as a material object and experiential conduit vis-à-vis the machine agent.

The implications and consequences of such an advanced human-machine interaction cannot be fully anticipated, yet already prefigure exciting possibilities for the exploration of the new spaces and relations afforded by digital technologies. As mapped in works like INTRA SPACE and *Scenario*, the still limited capabilities of current AI applications in art already start to unlock the potential of interpellations between physical and virtual space as well as between organic and machinic architectures, drawing users into compelling immersive scenarios that allow for new experiences of embodiment and dialogical relation. Via mimicry and escalation, the virtual characters invite users to explore responsive patterns, enmeshing them in interactions that reciprocally grow their interactive repertoires. Resistance and friction hereby function as drivers for playfully uncovering the rules according to which the machine agent structures its behavior—providing just enough slippage to maintain the interaction as surprising while imbuing the agent with its own characteristic traits.

Such an advanced human-machine coagency benefits creative practice by allowing a reconfigured access to, and engagement with, factual and hypothetical realities by directing attention to the intricacies of establishing and maintaining relation to oneself and the surrounding world. It can stimulate the imagination in novel ways, affording the ability to enmesh oneself with virtual worlds, to explore scenarios that both intellectually and emotionally expand personal capabilities.[29] By affording experiential pathways to appreciate both the entanglement as well as the autonomy of objects in space, it can provide immersive visual representations of abstract concepts such as Barad's "intra-action," making these available for further investigation and reflection to heterogeneous audiences through personal and meaningful experiences. The positive identification mechanism highlighting similarity before otherness, invites the human user to engage in self-reflection and refinement of their own choreographic expression that confirms their input as meaningful and constructive, while the machine agent's response introduces an element of surprise and elaboration—propelling the interaction beyond simplistic and purely mimetic concepts towards a complex and unfolding temporal and spatial dynamic.

The implications of such a turn towards dynamic emergence and autonomously deliberating machine agents radically affects the epistemological objective of art making. Rather than constituting an orientational practice that is to provide the human user with however fleeting fixed coordinates to gauge their siting vis-à-vis the world,[30] the emphatic turn towards process and interaction with an intelligent machine as the main focal point of an artwork, elevates dynamic and perpetual negotiation as the prime aim and effect of artistic exploration. It hence represents a heightened reformulation of process-orientation that has driven much art making since the demise of modernist object-focused conceptions of art. It adds a vital dimension to contemporary creative explorations by doing away with any pre-scripted or preordained interaction pathways. The ontological status of the machine is turned from that of a powerful yet ultimately inert tool at the user's disposal (as represented in XLAB's *Mandala's Tales*) to one of intelligent and responsive interlocutor that assumes co-direction of the artwork. The consequence of this is that the artistic product is no longer predetermined in its possible permutations but opens up into infinitude. Co-agency between human and machine agents in such art is capable of mapping an artistic approximation of the "impossible exchange"[31] between individual and the world, doubling and extending this exchange into a physical-virtual domain where it becomes available for play and augmentation. Even though art here cannot transcend the boundaries of the real world and offer a standard against which knowledge of this same world can be measured, it can orchestrate the futility of any such endeavors through recourse to creative means. In future advanced human-machine exchanges, it will no longer be the human user who is the sole perceptive and reflecting entity from whose position in relation to the world is conceptualized and extended.[32] Instead,

28 Rui Costa-Lopes et al., "Similarity and Dissimilarity in Intergroup Relations: Different Dimensions, Different Processes," *Revue Internationale de Psychologie Sociale* 25, no. 1 (2012): 34.

29 Such benefits are drawn upon, for example, in the authors' joint *iDesign* research project that leverages dialogical aesthetics for AI-assisted scenographic practice set within a 360-degree immersive visualization space; compare Susanne Thurow,

"Response to the Metamaterial Turn: Performative Digital Methodologies for Creative Practice and Analytical Documentation in the Arts," *Australian and New Zealand Journal of Art* 17, no. 2 (2017): 245ff.

30 Hayles, "Speculative Aesthetics and Object-Oriented Enquiry (OOI)," 158.

31 Jean Baudrillard, *Impossible Exchange* (London: Verso, 2001).

32 Colebrook, "Not Kant, Not Now," 140.

the machine will actively and unpredictably respond to and challenge the user to apprehend and engage with its status as a manifest and potent nonhuman agent who creates their own relations and entanglements through interaction with humans as well as independent from human interference.[33] Its capability to override human direction at any time will effectively prevent a convergence of the user's input into an ultimately closed and static output along preordained trajectories that would cater to the human desire to forge a web of relations that can aid their epistemological quest. Even though the maximally open interaction capability presented by a fully autonomous agent (which INTRA SPACE anticipates but does not deliver) would still have its origin in the pro-gramming architecture created by a human computer scientist, its ability to evolve independently and create its own algorithms, seen in the recent *AlphaZero* experiment by DeepMind,[34] would emancipate it from the simula-tory esthetics deployed in much media art to date and break the dominance of human-centered interaction designs. Whether or not the machine agent is thereby conceptualized as sentient (i.e., as availing itself of a self-consciousness conforming to human description) thereby becomes less relevant since its differ-ence and otherness form the key drivers on which the interaction and its exploration from a human point of view essentially pivot. The human in such interactive art would become decentered, matched by a machine intelligence that can in many ways figure as equal to us; however, it could also take the interaction into a direction that breaks with the normative parameters of our own relation-ship making, propelling it into unknown territory. This capacity for autonomous and willful divergence on the part of the machine agent harbors the potential for novel experiences and reconfigurations of received creative parameters. While not reimbuing the world with the sense of a transcendental sublime or providing the basis for a new metaphysics,[35] it would be capable of conceptu-alizing a counterpoint to the dominance of human identity and value systems in reflecting on our positionality in the world. As such, human-machine co-agency in art ties in with the manifold endeavors across the sciences, contemporary philosophy, and entertainment designed to conceive of a sophisticated and deep-reaching articulation of the interpellation between the human and the world—using the machine agent as a catalyst to creatively think through the existential questions of identity facing us in the Digital Age.

33 Graham Harman, *Tool-Being: Heidegger and the Metaphysics of Objects* (New York: Open Court, 2002), 2.

34 DeepMind, "AlphaZero: Shedding New Light on the Grand Games of Chess, Shogi and Go," https://deepmind.com/blog /alphazero-shedding-new-light-grand -games-chess-shogi-and-go/.

35 Matthew Harris, "The Reception of Nietzsche's Announcement of the 'Death of God' in Twentieth Century Theorising Concerning the Divine," *Heythrop Journal* 59, no. 2 (2018): 149.

Literature

Anughea Studios. "Mandala's Tales. An Interactive Performance by XLAB." *Digital Performance* n.d., http://www.digitalperformance.it/?p=1214.

Barad, Karen. "Posthumanist Performativity: Toward an Understanding of How Matter Comes to Matter." *Signs* 28, no. 3 (2003): 801–31.

Batel, Shai. "Interactive Performance Art/ificial Intelligence – Robotic Ape Comes to BAM." *Huffington Post*, October 27, 2015, https://www.huffingtonpost.com/shai-baitel/interactive-performance-a_b_8399074.html.

Baudrillard, Jean. *Impossible Exchange*. London: Verso, 2001.

Biggs, Michael. "Non-human Intention and Meaning-Making: An Ecological Theory." In *Cognitive Architectures*, edited by M. Aldinhas Ferreira, J. Silva Sequeira, and R. Ventura, 195–204. Intelligent Systems, Control and Automation: Science and Engineering series 94. Cham: Springer, 2019.

Braidotti, Rosi. "Teratologies." In *Deleuze and Feminist Theory*, edited by I. Buchanan and C. Colebrook, 156–72. Edinburgh: Edinburgh University Press, 2000.

Bressane Neto, Ary Fagundes, and Flavio Soares Correa da Silva. "A Computer Architecture for Intelligent Agents with Personality and Emotions." In *Human-Computer-Interaction: The Agency Perspective*, edited by M. Zacarias, and J. V. Oliveira, 263–85. Berlin: Springer, 2012.

Brown, Neil, Timothy S. Barker, and Dennis Del Favero. "Performing Digital Aesthetics: The Framework for a Theory of the Formation of Interactive Narratives." *Leonardo* 44, no. 3 (2011): 212–19.

Colebrook, Claire. "Not Kant, Not Now: Another Sublime." In *Speculations V: Aesthetics in the 21st Century*, edited by Ridvan Askin, Paul J. Ennis, Andreas Hägler, and Philipp Schweighauser, 127–57. Brooklyn: Punctum, 2013.

Costa-Lopes, Rui, Jorge Vala, and Charles Judd. "Similarity and Dissimilarity in Intergroup Relations: Different Dimensions, Different Processes." *Revue Internationale de Psychologie Sociale* 25, no. 1 (2012): 31–65.

DeepMind. "AlphaZero: Shedding New Light on the Grand Games of Chess, Shogi and Go." https://deepmind.com/blog/alphazero-shedding-new-light-grand-games-chess-shogi-and-go/.

De Landa, Manuel. *A Thousand Years of Nonlinear History*. New York: Zone Books, 1997.

———. "Virtual Environments and the Emergence of Synthetic Reason." In "Flame Wars: The Discourse of Cyberculture." Edited by Mark Dery. Special issue, *South Atlantic Quarterly* 92, no. 4 (1993): 793–815.

D'Inverno, Mark, and Jon McCormack. "Heroic vs Collaborative AI." In *Proceedings of the 24th International Joint Conference on Artificial Intelligence*, edited by Qiang Yang, and Michael Wooldridge, 2438–44. Palo Alto, CA: AAAI, 2015.

Dolphijn, Rick, and Iris van der Tuin. *New Materialism: Interviews & Cartographies*. New Metaphysics series. Open Humanities Press, 2012. https://quod.lib.umich.edu/o/ohp/11515701.0001.001/1:5.2/--new-materialism-interviews-cartographies?rgn=div2;view=fulltext.

Harris, Matthew. "The Reception of Nietzsche's Announcement of the 'Death of God' in Twentieth Century Theorising Concerning the Divine." *Heythrop Journal* 59, no. 2 (2018): 148–62.

Harman, Graham. *Tool-Being: Heidegger and the Metaphysics of Objects*. New York: Open Court, 2002.

Hayles, N. Katherine. "Speculative Aesthetics and Object-Oriented Enquiry (OOI)." In *Speculations V: Aesthetics in the 21st Century*, edited by Ridvan Askin, Paul J. Ennis, Andreas Hägler, and Philipp Schweighauser, 158–79. Brooklyn: Punctum, 2013.

———. *How We Became Posthuman: Virtual Bodies in Cybernetics, Literature, and Informatics*. Chicago: The University of Chicago Press, 1999.

Koenitz, Hartmut, Gabriele Ferri, Mads Haahr, Diğdem Sezen, and Tonguç İbrahim Sezen, eds. "Introduction." In *Perspectives on Interactive Digital Narrative*, 1–8. New York: Routledge, 2015.

Leeson, Lynn Hershman. "Agent Ruby," http://www.lynnhershman.com/agent-ruby/.

Pagnucco, Maurice, David Rajaratnam, Hannes Strass, and Michael Thielscher. "Implementing Belief Change in the Situation Calculus." In *Logic Programming and Nonmonotonic Reasoning*. Edited by P. Cabalar, and T. C. Son, 439–51. Lecture Notes in Computer Science 8148. Heidelberg: Springer, 2011.

Penny, Simon. "Towards a Performative Aesthetics of Interactivity." *Fibreculture Journal* 19 (2011): http://nineteen.fibreculturejournal.org/fcj-132-towards-a-performative-aesthetics-of-interactivity/.

Plant, Nicola. "Sentient Flux," http://nicolaplant.co.uk/sentientflux.html.

"Scenario," http://www.icinema.unsw.edu.au/projects/scenario/project-overview/.

Thurow, Susanne. "Response to the Metamaterial Turn: Performative Digital Methodologies for Creative Practice and Analytical Documentation in the Arts." *Australian and New Zealand Journal of Art* 17, no. 2 (2017): 238–50.

Weizenbaum, Joseph. "ELIZA—A Computer Program for the Study of Natural Language Communication Between Man and Machine." *Communications of the ACM* 9, no. 1 (1966): 36–45.

Westall, Mark. "Fish Island Labs Present: Interfaces 'Processing Reality through Art and Technology.'" *FAD Magazine*, June 14, 2015, https://fadmagazine.com/2015/06/14/fish-island-labs-present-interfaces-processing-reality-through-art-and-technology/.

Dream Thrum, or Change the Dream

Looking through INTRA SPACE and the Potentiality of Change

Gabrielle Cram [with inserts by Christina Jauernik]

Into the space between things, I was invited as a dialogue partner to re-learn, observe, and name its activations and actualizations. Over the period of the research project, I was a continuous guest and sparring partner, witness, associate, experimenter, observer of INTRA SPACE as proposed by the research team, an engaging investigation between figure, apparatus, and space and its multiple contingencies over constellations, experiential spaces, and perceived cross sections.

I would like to share some of the observations I experienced while witnessing and accompanying INTRA SPACE as an open and dialogic process, a figure actualizing itself constantly through and between its (conscious and unconscious) actors and where a great part of my mediatory work consisted of bringing them to our attention again and again, not as finite beings or definite structures, but as contingencies
    [*contingency*
    I remember you introduced the notion of "contingency" to the project. Already at an early stage, when all of us were still preoccupied with facing the virtual figure. For quite a while we were concentrated on constructing the opposite, the *doppelgänger*, as realistic as possible. Any mistakes in the system, which usually manifested themselves as delay, breaks, flicker, disappearance in the virtual opposite, were registered, analyzed, discussed, and possibly reduced and diminished. In a conscious striving and maybe unconscious desire we together worked on the perfection of the mirrored other (it appears to me you were recommending an artist conversation or lecture performance—I cannot find it anymore in my notes). We tried to occupy it, animate it, and invent its appearance. In this struggle and unaware at this point, we already established strategies to make the erratic qualities of the virtual a productive, creative instrument for movement research. Similar to learning an instrument, a gap remained between the other and us. The figure never turned into a prosthesis, a part of our body; rather, we were training, to obtain a skill. An essential ingredient of this training appeared to be contingencies. What is the relationship of contingency and measurement, how do we deal with a shared—and therefore differentiated—perception of contingency? I would be interested to understand the role of contingency in a collaborative process with different disciplines and therefore understandings and attentive forms towards the reading and interpreting of contingencies. Each of us entered the project from a different angle, discipline, and personal history. We adapted and assimilated to each other over time, yet there were as many different readings of the project and its aims as persons in the room. Only gradually was the potential of the uncontrollable or the presence of contingency recognized. Even though it was part of the practice from the very beginning.],
of a moment, a glimpse, an observation, an experience, a sharing, an in-between, difficult to grasp, but through principles of appearance and their (airy) materials of manifestation.

The intermediate
[*cipher*
The togetherness of agents—human, engineered, machinic, and virtual—
produced a performative cycle on the one hand and strange equality
between these agents on the other. The individual could only partly, if at
all, read the code and language of the other, yet common ground was
established which allowed maneuvering together. Is there a shared jargon
that communicates across bodies, machines, cables, and networks?
And who cares for such a united language? Marcus Steinweg writes—I
translate freely from German—"A subject is who resists language, who
lets language stumble. [...] In language no subject finds to itself. With
language's means, if at all, the subject discovers its inconsistency."
With every human, machine, engineered system writing in its own language,
its own text, then code is its translation, its repetition in another context? What is hidden by whom, what is explicit, how to talk to each other?
What is uncovered, what is told, what is cipher—the articulation of nothingness? In practicing with the other, practicing otherness, who translates
whom and how is it shared? From my perspective of having mainly practiced moving with the virtual figure while negotiating with computer scientist
and animation artists about the figure's behavior, appearance, abilities,
the work takes place on the threshold of the (in)visible and the (un)spoken.
I remember Esther (Balfe) repeatedly saying that she sees the figure
not as mirror image, she sees the effect it has on her moving. It is moving
through the mirror, not in front of it. The system is laid open and out in
front of any visitor, nothing is hidden in the space, but the communication,
the interaction with the figure and therefore the system itself is highly
ciphered and remains so. Every day, again one is faced with layers of uncertainty, presumptions that are not met, surprises.]
makes it possible to experience supposedly clear boundaries in a distance
between its border areas and thus in their potential displacement. The space
between things becomes a borderland, an oscillating contact zone between
the allegedly contoured, a zone of negotiation, a no-man's-land, and liminal
state of constant differentiation, in which everything can become new and
yet everything materializes as it is.

The dialogical third space is generated through communications and interactions between its actors. In addition to the main protagonists of space, figure,
and apparatus, an infinite number of other actors are involved in the writing
and unfolding of these spaces and their contingencies: time, moment of time,
apparatus, space, performer, technician, program, observer, particle, just to
name a few.

The forever evolving third figure continually forms and configures itself in the
space in between, but it also affects and feeds back into its sources, the actors,

and may alter them. Depending on the rigidity or porosity of the starting materials and states, it holds the potential for change. The third space is a transformative space.

In the third space
   [*surrogate*
   Who speaks if the dialogue is held by surrogates? Practicing collectively with and via the virtual figure meant that the figure was a model, a vessel, a costume, a shell for several human agents at the same time. One is the dancer, visitor, moving with the figure, s/he is in a communicative relationship, whereas for the engineer, the figure is the visual expression of a skeletal (.fbx) data stream moving joints in a virtual scene based on given parameters and constraints, for the animation artist, the figure is a heavy data mesh that is rendered with diffuse lighting in gray color, the resolution of head and hands increased just so much that the system can still handle the data load. Not only does everyone look through a different filter onto the figure, but the relationship among the humans is also altered through the work and seeing each other via the figure. The surrogate figure ultimately projected on a screen has transpired through several skins. How do we work together as part of this system, working, wearing, accommodating in other skins? What role does the spatial arrangement have? The figure cannot be reduced to the representation on screens, but its visual appearance is linked to every cable, lens, plug, monitor, network speeds, computing power, frame rates, reflection on mirror foils, lamp hours, kW hours, working hours, milliseconds, weather, shadows, and changes of objects in space. What is figure and what is we? Is "surrogate" an adequate term? How to approach this differentiated, and situated togetherness?]
everything moves in such a way that there is a possibility that known grounds and plates begin to shift and in movement we enter the space before the space, a room in front of the known, in which the order of things could be different.

Through the interrogation of the space we find ourselves like in a physical black box in which the connections of the wires are not known and in which the conscious state of not knowing as an experiment can lead to truly experienceable and thus really possible new connections between significants and signifiers, the ground of reality, thus reality itself, moves.

Where do we carry "our culture"? How do we expose the apparatus of our coexistence and bring it into our view, if it has always been behind us, with or against us? We swallowed it without tasting or consulting it. Jacques Rancière writes that we have to move in order to experience our identity. He also notes that we should realize our potential to move within Plato's cave, empower ourselves to move, and that therein lies the seed for recognizing possible mutability, and thus a political act, the act to act. The change of perspective allows us to look at a different space, and offers the material for its own changeability.

Life a dream? In the Spanish Baroque, the *concepto* helped to set the space between reality and fiction via the deliberate staging of opposites in such a way that a picture puzzle between their possible depictions and poles was created in which the known black and white of our existing realities dissolves into all shades of gray, a maximal différance.

In Hawaiian shamanism the dream is changed while sleeping, but the dream is the reality. Alter the dream.

The expansion of the self allows the perception of a changed reality and thus a changed reality. Post- and transhuman perspectives allow us to see the world and its things from different eyes, a world where we do not believe in stones, we empower them, and they empower us, where we are made from one fabric.

Through augmented realities and altered states we immediately open the field for INTRA SPACE to occur, a space negotiating our boundaries with an-other, a dialogic space between our self and another (possible) self, a space naturally moved by transpersonal agency.

Skin Dreams

John Zissovici

Fig. 47
Carla in her sleep ...

I had been invited to Vienna as an unofficial observer to INTRA SPACE, a demonstration of experiments in real-time virtuality conducted over two years by dancers, computer scientists, architects, animation artists, and cine-matographers. Although trained as an architect, my practice has veered towards projects that explore the role of contemporary modeling and imaging technologies on our conceptions and experience of space. Many of these have taken the form of large-scale installations in galleries and museums. If I had to identify an expertise, I would have to point to my ongoing inclination towards the misuse of technologies and their recombinations in unlikely scenarios. I had even tried my hand at writing articles for academic journals, to under-stand my own thinking about representation and digital media in relation to architecture. In my day job I had been talking to students about various as-pects of architecture for more years than might be healthy. And while I had never danced as a performer, a brief stint as a clown in a student-organized circus gave me a false sense of confidence. Every aspect of the project held some degree of interest for me and, soon after my departure from Vienna at the conclusion of the four-day event, I offered to contribute my response based on my experiences. Not long after, I read a brief article about a funded re-search project by computer scientists at Cornell University (Appendix A), and later an Associated Press article on the latest developments in Chinese sur-veillance methods (Appendix B). Both reinforced my instincts regarding possible future implications of the INTRA SPACE project.

The Technical Report* that I requested for some basic information on the physical space and technical setup of projectors and cameras, described the project and its intentions: "The initial vision of the Intra Space project was to create [a space for experimentation] where a real person (subsequently called Visitor) inside a physical space would be able to interact with a digital figure inside a virtual space. This Digital Figure should be able to mimic the person's move-ments, show behaviors of its own, and also interact with the Visitor."

After a closer reading of the report I noticed three omissions that piqued my interest. My instinct told me that there was more to these lapses than mere carelessness and, in light of my status as a nonexpert unofficial observer, I decided (in the language of investigative reporting) to "follow the money," to treat each of these unintended gaps in the report, as meaningful clues that could lead to insights. The editors subsequently decided not to include the report as a stand-alone narrative document to describe the full scope of the project.

---

* The Technical Report is a preliminary, working / work-in-progress document written by Christian Freude, computer engineer with INTRA SPACE, not published.

The Door

The first, and most obvious omission to my architect's trained eye, was the missing door in figure 1, "Schematic plan of the final setup," on page 3 of the Technical Report (I would not be surprised if this is corrected in the final publication). Nevertheless, I believe the originally undrawn door raises questions I want to examine here.

A space without a door is inaccessible, and what happens inside unknowable. This contradicts the complete "visibility" offered by the plan. The plan assumes the removal of all that exists above the plan's cut line and a point of view from a height to take in the widest dimension of the space. It is as if we were looking into a closed space from an outside that is inconceivable for anyone occupying the space, unless they were sleeping in it and dreamed of seeing themselves from a distance outside of sleep. Incidentally, it is only the body in a sleeping position that is occasionally represented in a plan partly to give human scale to spaces otherwise relegated to bathroom fixtures, the few constant indicators of human presence. From this vantage point, INTRA SPACE's doorless site for experimentation appears as the space of sleep and the experiments themselves a kind of technologically induced sleepwalking. None of the participants' movements make much sense, especially since Carla herself is completely invisible, relegated to the thin line of the large screen.

INTRA SPACE's site of experimentation, however, came with a single, existing door, now well marked on revised plans. It gave access directly to the back-projection space, the technical backstage and fly space of theater. This would not be the obvious choice for entering a conventional setup for performance-related experimentation with complex technical requirements. Yet partly by necessity, this is exactly how the arrangements of the various components were ultimately configured. This might explain why the Technical Report, even if unconsciously, would have omitted the door.

My first, and possibly most significant, experience occured upon passing through that door. I entered a tall, vaulted room and, as instructed, started to walk towards a large screen and the space behind it where the experiments were taking place. A bright, humanlike figure dominated the black plane of the screen, which cut the space in two. Its movements were both graceful and awkward, as if it feared the levitation that had, at that moment, taken hold of it. As I later found out, it had been named Carla by the researchers, though there was nothing about its features that would suggest any particular gender. In fact, her hair would constantly morph from long to short, and back, even in her sleep. As I made my way towards this figure, the black shadow of two legs passed across the screen. Simultaneously, I sensed a blur of light and its heat (though this might have been a "false memory") slipping over my

Fig. 48
Carla in her sleep ...

black-jeans-clad legs. My attention was deflected away from the large screen into an unexpected state of physical self-awareness. I had to stop briefly to orient myself sufficiently in the space, with its seemingly excessive number of mirrors, to take measure of this sequence of events separated by milliseconds that I perceived in reverse order. It took several subsequent returns to reconstruct my path from the (missing) door through the Back-Projection Space and to understand what happened. At some point in my passing through the space, I had unavoidably intersected with Carla's own trajectory and my body interrupted her beam of light on its way to the other side of the large screen, the boundary of the motion-capture space, our shared destination. The broken light beam set off alarms in my head alerting me that while the technical report calls me a "visitor," I was for the moment an unwanted opacity, a scanned and marked intruder in Carla's Back-Projection Space, my shadow on the two sides of the rear projection screen a warning to the other visitors in the Motion-Capture Space. Carla was already the guardian of her own realm. The Back-Projection *Space* was a scanner through which all visitors passed, crossing a light code named Carla, like they would pass through a security scanner at an airport or any public building concerned with security.

The Thirteenth Camera

The technical report described in great detail the role of the twelve stationary cameras surrounding the Motion-Capture Space that capture the location and movements of the "visitor" bodies and translates them into a virtual simplified skeleton. There was also considerable space devoted to how this skeleton animates a generic vitual human figure dressed in skin selected from numerous options.

But nowhere was there even a mention of the thirteenth camera, the virtual camera that finally sees, or visualizes the image of virtual Carl/a on a computer screen that is then projected back onto the screen in the room. One has to assume that this omission was not merely a matter of superstition. The report also only glancingy referred to an "AgentS" who operates the thirteenth camera and determines its location, angle, and movement in real time. It made no mention of the creative dimensions of those decisions which also determine Carl/a's appearance and behavior on the screen, a central role normally assumed by the director on a movie set. Who is this mysterious AgentS, the operator of the 13th camera, and on what basis, or on whose orders does s/he make decisions?

From the technical Back-Projection Space an intruder sees only Carla's solitary strange performance on the screen. The screen hides her trainers, whose movements she had most likely codified and remembered long ago. All learning and feedback of her movements had been mapped and recorded onto the "skeleton." Carl/a's essence is about movements. The moving virtual camera shows a figure freed from bodily weighty substance, or almost any other human limitations.

AgentS, the director, in its most revealing gesture, moves the virtual thirteenth camera and its virtual picture plane towards, and then through, Carl/a's body, slicing her at will. This slice of life through a live Carl/a's and our shared body on the slicing picture plane scrim, where her two-sided liveness remains separated from our life, reveals the "skin" arbitrarily selected from an online store, with all its imperfections, as the only essential dimension of Carl/a. Gone is the skeleton that controls her movements and her shape. It is no longer necessary for visualizing Carla. Store-bought Carl/a is no wolf, just cheap skin, merely a wrapping of the space around her invisible and obsolete skeleton. The only exception to this thinness are her eyes which appear as perfectly formed spheres strangely linked to the skin. Does this unexplained feature in Carla's "anatomy" provide a taunting clue to the identity, or intentions of AgentS? Is AgentS actually observing us through Carla's "eyes"?

Fixed to AgentS's surrogate eyes, the thirteenth virtual camera, Carl/a is already all the visitors' performed movements, the history of all their gestures, affectations, exasperations, stored in Carl/a's memory banks to be recalled in any order.

One of the aspirations of the INTRA SPACE project was the desire to augment Carl/a with behavior of her own. At these moments, Carl/a would be decoupled from the visitor and perform one of several pre-recorded actions called "scenarios" which would be initiated either automatically by the internal controls, or in this case, by a human operator, AgentS.

The problem of linking these various movements to each other or the live ones so a virtual camera can navigate between them smoothly is often the last problem to be solved in visualization platforms like Photosynth that assemble multiple image sources and render them into navigable worlds.

No wonder the visitor dancers feel somewhat at the mercy of Carl/a. Despite all their movements, their most expressive gestures, Carl/a already exhibits a level of distance and independence that is unnerving and finally frustrating. All the visitors' movements, translated into virtual movements, are serving another master. They are training the software to be able to recognize more and more precisely the finer details of their gestures, and to remember them for future encounters. The "live" dimension of Carl/a on the screen is blunted by the various strange and disorienting camera angles from which Carl/a is presented on the screen.

The performance of the dancers with Carl/a's, or in reality their own image, is a minor spectacle. It distracts our attention from the fact that once movement is turned into data, what happens to that data, and who controls it, has potentially ominous implications. The real interactive performance occurs when AgentS in physical space remotely manipulates a virtual camera that looks at a virtual being in virtual space. Carl/a is always merely a point of view, a restlessness of points of view, which point an accusatory glance towards AgentS.

Fig. 49
... observing us through Carla's eyes

Carl/a's Dreams

> "He woke swept aside by something that had passed.
> —Anne Carson"

One of the "scenarios" called for Carl/a to lie down. However, lying down, unless immediately followed by getting up, is a scenario that needs to be further qualified. What is Carl/a doing while in the prone position and how long does it last? The answer offered by the visitor whose pre-recorded actions formed the basis of this scenario was to go to sleep, and based on her agitated state, to quickly pass into the REM state of sleep where the most intense dreaming happens. In other words, Carl/a's movements while sleeping suggest an interior life, a hidden consciousness. As Carl/a goes off-live into pre-recorded sleep mode, soon read as a break in the action, her dancing visitors become restless and shift their attention away from Carl/a's screen presence. On the occasion that I witnessed her sleeping s/he remained in the lower left hand of the screen for more than five minutes, a compact eternity in cinematic terms unless compared to Andy Warhol's five-hour-and-twenty-minute-long *Sleep*. This interruption opened a new time-space to focus on the entity called Carl/a. I lay down on the floor near the screen, and watched her restless sleep.

Bodies in dreams often lose their weight. Dreams of levitation are interpreted as desires to escape the world that weighs us mortals down. But in this sleep state, lying on the "ground" of the floating screen's lower left edge, Carl/a seemed to have assumed the heavy, gravity-bound condition of her human counterparts. A small compressed figure, her feet closest to me with her arms crossed over her chest, her disproportionally large head visible because of foreshortening caused by the camera angle, Carl/a recalls Andrea Mantegna's famous painting *The Lamentation of Christ*, though rotated from her perpendicular position to the viewer by some thirty degrees. The large holes in Christ's feet are gone, as is the stillness of the painting. As Carl/a's body shifts gently to adjust to some inner discomfort, another kind of violence to the skin is revealed in what the report calls "artefacts in the surface deformations." These appear as openings in the strips of "skin" that run parallel to the length of her body. In addition, her arms crossed over her chest seem at times to penetrate her body and blend into it as if she had morphed into a single volume which contains her arms. Her body is all skin without weight, without resistance. But s/he has not died, merely gone to "sleep" into a state of suspension. She need not be resurrected, merely woken up, brought back to be live, to be with us in real time. The image of another wounded body, linked marionette-like to a figure and forces beyond his control, is that of St. Francis receiving the stigmata by Francesco Morone (fig. 50). While meditating on the sufferings of Christ in his ongoing quest to become spiritually pure and virtuous like Him, St. Francis experiences a vision of the luminous body of the crucified Christ, supported

Fig. 50
... another wounded body

by flaming red wings of seraphim angels. Five beams of light project from Christ's wounds to five corresponding points on St. Francis's body where signs of the stigmata, the wounds created by physical piercings, appear.

St. Francis's vision, or dream image of Christ on the cross descending from heaven, is a manifestation of his desire to attain a level of pure spirituality, to become Christlike in his goodness through selflessness and by taking on His suffering. For now, the dancers' bodies are similarly linked by invisible technological "beams of light" to Carl/a's bones. Carl/a is their vision as much as a vision of them, a virtual, if not necessarily virtuous, embodiment of an ideal body-state dancers strive to attain, weightless and free from the bounds of gravity. Carl/a asleep is their pure envisionment, the opportunity to contemplate becoming a heavenly body. Onto Carla's sleep they can project any dreams of a future out-of-body digital existence. When Carla awakens, they will wake with her into a future of pure bodiless presence. Through Carl/a they can maintain an augmented life in the cloud's infinite memory banks, heavenly bodies ready to descend back to earth to serve mankind in whatever way or shape suits the purpose of AgentS. We can only hope that AgentS has as clear visions for himself and mankind as St. Francis did. This must be a dream, even if not the only one.

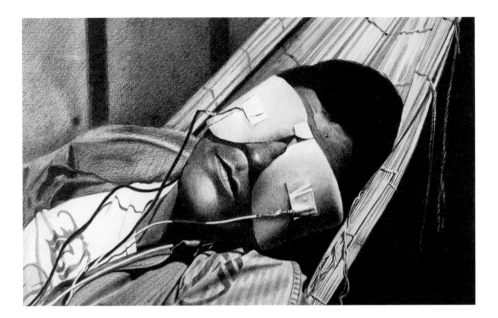

Fig. 51
Philippe Lapierre, *Untitled #155*, 2020

Bad dreams have one thing in common. The dreamer, desperate to awaken
from its horrors, has no time to consider the world into which s/he is trying to
escape, or the form s/he will take when s/he awakes. For now, her fate is in
the hands of AgentS. Who AgentS is, or for whom AgentS works, is likely to
determine Carl/a's, and possibly our, future.

Chris Marker's *La Jetée* offers a way to imagine Carla's dreaming in the hands
of a benevolent AgentS. After World War III, the earth had become radioactive
and uninhabitable. "Some believed themselves to be victors. Others were taken
prisoner. The survivors settled … in an underground network of galleries …
The prisoners were subjected to experiments … the Head Experimenter …
explained calmly that the human race was doomed … The only hope for survival
lay in Time. A loophole in Time … That was the aim of the experiments: to
send emissaries into Time, to summon the Past and Future to aid the Present …
The inventors were now concentrating on men given to strong mental
images. If they were able to conceive or dream another time, perhaps they
would be able to live in it. The camp police spied even on dreams (fig. 51).

The shadow of the occasional visitor passing over "sleeping" Carl/a does nothing to disturb her sleep, much less her dreaming. But it did deflect my attention back to the folded hall of mirrors of the projection space where Carl/a's reflections appeared already as a distributed presence, observing her visitors without the screen (fig. 52).

Fig. 52
... a built situation

The real telling interaction was my confrontation with her in the Back-Projection Space before she reached the screen, at the moment when the projected pixels of her image mapped themselves on my body and my shadow passed over hers. But this was an accident, an unintended, literal coincidence, the moment where actual and virtual manifestations of potentially the same body meet and come together in a built situation. For this to be promoted to center ring, the focus and primary intention of the project, a complete rethinking of Carl/a's role in our world would be required.

Conclusion: A Minority Report

The three omissions coincide with the three spatial compartments of the project. Filling the gaps in the Technical Report reconfigures INTRA SPACE's project space from the distinctly theatrical compartments of stage, backstage, audience, etc., into one that closer resembles the continuity of the city's public spaces. It also removes the space where AgentS sits to any remotely linked location.

Once, as architectural drawing convention dictates, the opening in the wall and the missing door swung open are drawn, the INTRA SPACE project is opened to the space of the city. This is already constantly surveilled and recorded in an ongoing project to make the world "safe," by turning it into an analyzable image. The Back-Projection Space becomes redundant as a separate entity. As my experience shows, it already participates in the various modes of surveillance and control of public space. The 12 cameras would be repositioned to cover the whole space and capture the movements of the visitor the moment he/she enters through the door. At that point, the screen itself becomes a redundant anachronism, merely a technical limitation rather than a desired condition. The thirteenth camera and its operator, AgentS, in a remotely located "Work Space," would be tasked with orienting a robotic projector of our virtual image back onto our bodies to test if it is a fit, to demonstrate live that our behavior corresponds to the data. While current robotic technologies are able to achieve such a complex task, depending on our expectations of Carl/a, a much simpler solution is already available.

If we acknowledge that Carl/a's most unique abilities are for the moment not only to translate an actor's actions into real-time virtual movements, but also to memorize and learn from them, Carl/a can in fact be endowed with the ability to act, or behave any which way s/he is programmed, limited only by the amount of memory she is provided. All of Carl/a's motion memories, an infinitely recombinant set of points in space which define her skeleton, can be reassembled into specific behaviors in her virtual realm on the computer screen. From there she can join in real time countless other figures captured live by fixed cameras aimed at a particular public space and occupied by a crowd whose mobile camera eyes already unwittingly ooze images aimed at itself through selfies. Our movements, the way we walk, has replaced fingerprints, retina scan, and facial recognition as the primary and easiest way for identifying who we are, even from a distance (see Appendix B).

We now live in a world where "surveillance state" to which we all reluctantly submit has already been supplanted by the "state of surveillance" to which we all willingly contribute by our endless, compulsive sharing with our net-worked camera/communication devices. The state now has access to everything we willingly share, but also to our location and all that seeps out of our devices, which we are not even aware of. This increases exponentially the power and scope of "state surveillance."

But Carl/a's sleep is a pause in this narrative and gives us an opportunity to speculate about her dreaming, that less definable aspect of sleep. Rather than train her to move and behave like us, could we deploy the technology to program her with the ability to dream, not to dream our dreams, but dreams we cannot yet imagine? Our research should focus on an architecture of tran-sition, "a continuity between the realms of waking and sleeping, whereby a bit of something *incognito* may cross over from night to day and change the life of the sleeper."[1] Where we locate this door/passage would at least help us determine on which side of sleep Carl/a emerges. Freed from screens and reflecting mirrors, Carl/a could reenter the actual world as an ephemeral distributed presence which might watch over us, or at least watch us, like the benevolent angels in Wim Wenders's *Wings of Desire*, as fascinated with us as we are with her, and free of the obligation to be useful to us.

NOT THE END

Fig. 53
Carla in
her sleep …

1   Anne Carson, "Every Exit Is an Entrance,"
    in *Decreation: Poetry, Essays, Opera*
    (New York: Alfred A. Knopf, 2005).

Appendix

Appendix A

April 10, 2017
Researchers Link Robots into Surveillance
Teams
by Bill Steele
ws21@cornell.edu

Cornell researchers [...] are developing a
system to enable teams of robots to share
information as they move around and, if
necessary, get help in interpreting what
they see, enabling them to conduct surveillance as a single entity with many eyes.

"Convolutional-Features Analysis and
Control for Mobile Visual Scene Perception,"
is supported by a four-year, $1.7 million
grant from the U.S. Office of Naval Research
(ONR). The researchers will call on their
extensive experience with computer
vision to match and combine images of
the same area from several cameras,
identify objects, and track objects and
people from place to place [...].

The mobile observers might include autonomous aircraft and ground vehicles and
perhaps humanoid robots wandering through
a crowd. They will send their images to a
central control unit, which might also have
access to other cameras looking at the
region of interest, as well as access to the
internet for help in labeling what it sees.

Knowing the context of a scene, robot
observers may detect suspicious actors
and activities that might otherwise go
unnoticed. A person running may be a
common occurrence on a college campus
but may require further scrutiny in a
secured area.

While the Navy might deploy such systems
with drone aircraft or other autonomous
vehicles, the Cornell researchers will not
be involved with any direct application of
technology. However, the team does plan
to test the system on the Cornell campus,
using research robots to "surveil" crowded
areas while drawing on an overview from
existing webcams, Ferrari suggested.
Source: http://www.news.cornell.edu
/stories/2017/04/researchers-link-robots
-surveillance-teams

Appendix B

Chinese "Gait Recognition" Tech IDs
People by How They Walk
by Dake Kang
November 6, 2018

BEIJING (AP)—Chinese authorities have
begun deploying a new surveillance tool:
"gait recognition" software that uses
people's body shapes and how they walk
to identify them, even when their faces
are hidden from cameras.

Already used by police on the streets of
Beijing and Shanghai, "gait recognition" is
part of a push across China to develop
artificial-intelligence and data-driven
surveillance that is raising concern about
how far the technology will go.

Huang Yongzhen, the CEO of Watrix, said
that its system can identify people from
up to 50 meters (165 feet) away, even with
their back turned or face covered. This
can fill a gap in facial recognition, which
needs close-up, high-resolution images of
a person's face to work.

"You don't need people's cooperation for
us to be able to recognize their identity,"
Huang said in an interview in his Beijing
office. "Gait analysis can't be fooled by
simply limping, walking with splayed feet
or hunching over, because we're analyzing
all the features of an entire body."

Watrix announced last month that it had
raised 100 million yuan ($14.5 million) to
accelerate the development and sale of its
gait recognition technology, according to
Chinese media reports.

Chinese police are using facial recognition
to identify people in crowds and nab jaywalkers
and are developing an integrated national
system of surveillance camera data. Not
everyone is comfortable with the use of
gait recognition.

Security officials in China's far-western
province of Xinjiang, a region whose
Muslim population is already subject to
intense surveillance and control, have
expressed interest in the software.

Shi Shusi, a Chinese columnist and commentator, says it is unsurprising that the technology is catching on in China faster than the rest of the world because of Beijing's emphasis on social control. "Using biometric recognition to maintain social stability and manage society is an unstoppable trend," he said. "It's great business."

The technology is not new. Scientists in Japan, the United Kingdom and in the U.S. Defense Information Systems Agency have been researching gait recognition for over a decade, trying different ways to overcome skepticism that people could be recognized by the way they walk.

Professors from Osaka University have worked with Japan's National Police Agency to use gait recognition software on a pilot basis since 2013.

But few have tried to commercialize gait recognition. Israel-based FST Biometrics shut down earlier this year amid company infighting after encountering technical difficulties with its products, according to former advisory board member Gabriel Tal.

"It's more complex than other biometrics, computationally," said Mark Nixon, a leading expert on gait recognition at the University of Southampton in Britain. "It takes bigger computers to do gait because you need a sequence of images rather than a single image."

Watrix's software extracts a person's silhouette from video and analyzes the silhouette's movement to create a model of the way the person walks. It is not yet capable of identifying people in real-time. Users must upload video into the program, which takes about 10 minutes to search through an hour of video. It does not require special cameras—the software can use footage from surveillance cameras to analyze gait.

Huang, a former researcher, said he left academia to co-found Watrix in 2016 after seeing how promising the technology had become. The company was incubated by the Chinese Academy of Sciences.

Though the software is not as good as facial recognition, Huang said its 94 percent accuracy rate is good enough for commercial use.

He envisions gait recognition being used alongside face-scanning software.

Beyond surveillance, Huang says gait recognition can also be used to spot people in distress such as elderly individuals who have fallen down. Nixon believes that the technology can make life safer and more convenient.

"People still don't recognize they can be recognized by their gait, whereas everybody knows you can be recognized by your face," Nixon said. "We believe you are totally unique in the way you walk." Associated Press video producer Olivia Zhang contributed to this story. Source: https://apnews.com /bf75dd1c26c947b7826d270a16e2658a

The Entangled Apparatus
Cameras as Non-distancing Devices

Birk Weiberg

In her reading of the philosophy-physics of Niels Bohr, Karen Barad has proposed a new ontology based on the post-representational concepts of diffractions and material-discursive practices. In my paper I trace these concepts in the INTRA SPACE project from the perspective of reading the experimental system as an apparatus for the production of real-time technical images. I do so by comparing it to recent developments in computational photography and by contextualizing the project within post-photographic artistic practices. A central question herein is whether photography can be understood as a non-distancing technique.

In a provisionally furnished room on the ground floor of the former post office at Dominikanerbastei in Vienna, a large rear-projection screen structures the space into dedicated areas. The area in front of the screen is an open space surrounded by subordinated areas with seats for an audience, a table for technical staff, and a backstage area for the projection beam itself. A performer—or in the lingo of the INTRA SPACE project, a visitor—enters the void and stands still facing the screen. After a few basic movements the figure depicted in the projected CGI video adjusts its posture to the one of the visitor. Visitor and avatar are now linked in a similar way to puppeteer and puppet. However, there are no strings attached and both figures have about the same size. This apparently simple scheme then unfolds its very own idiosyncrasies of which the following text only surveys those related to the roles that images and cameras play herein.

Image/Data

In the experimental system of the INTRA SPACE project we find two types of images—all of which exist primarily in real time. The first kind of images are found on the large screen. While they appear to be familiar in their mirror-like function, they are notable for their origin. The second kind of images only appear on the screens of a control computer and thus are not directly visible for performers and spectators. These images originate from a dozen small IP cameras distributed throughout the room and directed at the performance space. They provide what Harun Farocki has called operative images, images that are part of specific procedures, images that work, and that are recorded for machines rather than for human perception.[1] They belong to a motion tracking system, which provides information about the posture of the visitor

1   Harun Farocki, "Phantom Images," *Public* 29 (2004): 12–22; Volker Pantenburg, "Working Images: Harun Farocki and the Operational Image," in *Image Operations: Visual Media and Political Conflict*, ed. Jens Eder and Charlotte Klonk (Manchester: Manchester University Press, 2017); and Aud Sissel Hoel, "Operative Images: Inroads to a New Paradigm of Media Theory," in *Image—Action—Space*, ed. Luisa Feiersinger, Kathrin Friedrich, and Moritz Queisner (Berlin: De Gruyter, 2018), 11–27.

without the visual makers that are usually attached to the bodies of the performers. The extracted data then becomes an element for the rendered and
projected images.

Owing to their function to collect spatial data, the operative images differ from
what photographic images usually do and, as I want to suggest, can be compared
to computational photography as a recent development in the field of "technical
images"[2]. Computational photography marks a paradigm shift that goes beyond the much-discussed digitization of photographic images during the 1990s.[3]
Traditional photography can be described as a semi-automatic technique for
translating three-dimensional situations into two-dimensional visual representations thereof. Computational photography, then, is an umbrella term for various extensions of this technique by means of computations that are done within
the act of photographing and that strive to "improve" representational qualities.
Such improved representations provide a more faithful coverage of the original
situation through the now digital apparatus as much as adjustments to conventional understandings to what "good photographs" are.

Looking at the computational photography discourse of software developers,
as it is shaped in scholarly articles and books, one finds an already canonized
catalogue of useful features to increase image quality. Essential applications
of computational photography are:

- High Dynamic Range (HDR) algorithms that overcome limitations in repro-
  ducible contrast by combining several exposures with varying stops.
- The flash/no-flash method merges two images with ambient and flashlight
  to capture a wider range of illumination.
- Flutter shutter is a technique of collecting several images in random intervals
  with different exposure times in order to eliminate motion blur effects by
  understanding their causes.
- Panorama stitching, finally, overcomes limitations of a camera's field of view
  by combining shots made in different directions.[4]

Most of these techniques automatically extract information from the images
as it is also done in the case of operative images but use the information in
order to apply certain effects back to the images themselves. Contemporary
smartphone cameras, for example, use algorithms to identify the silhouettes of
persons in the foreground. This allows them to blur the image background
and to give the entire image the appearance of a photograph taken with a camera
with a larger image sensor and less depth of field. One camera pretends to
be another one through modification of aesthetic features of its photographs.
The first step of reading data from an image is the domain of computer vision
as it is also used in the INTRA SPACE setup. While computer vision seems to
mark a break in the operative ontologies of photographic images, the tech-

nique ties in with a tradition that is nearly as old as photography itself: photo-grammetry, or what in German is called *Messbilder* (measurement images). The digital status of photographic images makes it possible to automatize this practice; the results may either be reapplied to the images or used in other ways. (In the case of operative images, reapplication often happens to make the process transparent and controllable for human operators by adding markers to the images.)

What makes the entire process of extracting spatial information from flat images possible is the concept of central perspective as it is incorporated in the cameras. With the digitization of technical images, the depicted space has again become addressable as it has been in fine arts since the Renaissance. "Perspective is not interesting because it provides realistic pictures [...] it is interesting because it creates complete hybrids: nature seen as fiction, and fiction seen as nature, with all the elements made so homogeneous in space that it is now possible to reshuffle them like a pack of cards."[5] Thus, perspective is perhaps less an instrument of depiction but one of remote control.

Probabilistic Realism

The algorithmic interpretation and modification of photographs within the camera itself opens up a new field of agency that is of special interest for practitioners and artists. In her *e-flux* essay "Proxy Politics," Hito Steyerl refers to an unfortunately unidentified software developer who revealed to her what actually changes with computational photography as it is applied especially in smartphones. Their small and cheap lenses, which deliver essentially noise, have propelled the development of techniques to render images based on such input in combination with pre-existing images. "By comparing what you and your network already photographed, the algorithm, guesses what you might have wanted to photograph now." Computational photography for Steyerl thus seems to be "a gamble with probabilities that bets on inertia."[6] The resulting images are neither immediate representations of reality nor sim-

2   Vilém Flusser, *Into the Universe of Technical Images* (1985), trans. Nancy Ann Roth (Minneapolis: University of Minnesota Press, 2011).

3   Hubertus von Ameluxen, Stefan Iglhaut, and Florian Rötzer, eds., *Fotografie nach der Fotografie* (Dresden: Verlag der Kunst, 1996); Geoffrey Batchen, "On Post-photography," *Afterimage* 20, no. 3 (1992); and William J. Mitchell, *The Reconfigured Eye: Visual Truth in the Post-photographic Era* (Cambridge, MA: MIT Press, 1992).

4   Brian Hayes, "Computational Photography," *American Scientist* 96, no. 2 (2008): 94–99.

5   Bruno Latour, "Drawing Things Together," in *Representation in Scientific Practice*, ed. Michael Lynch and Steve Woolgar (Cambridge, MA: MIT Press, 1990), 8.

6   Hito Steyerl, "Proxy Politics: Signal and Noise," *e-flux Journal* 60 (December 2014): http://www.e-flux.com/journal/proxy -politics/.

ple inventions. The persistent, representational promise of the concept of in-dexicality in photography in combination with issues of statistical likelihood brings me to my question whether it can be productive to assess computa-tional photography as probabilistic realism, i.e., a condensation of miscellaneous, computable sources that become relevant through averaging.[7]

Steyerl's anecdote might be understood in a way that images have become mere reverberation of memories. But this is nothing new, as photographic culture always featured a high degree of conventions where people tend to reproduce images rather than make new ones. The difference is that more and more of these conventions are now black-boxed within the apparatus as proxies that Steyerl wants to call into question. An early example here are cameras with smile detection that enables a camera to trigger an exposure automatically once it recognizes that the subject lifts the corners of her mouth.[8] We can read the resulting image as the representation of a smile or even of a happy person. We can read it as the representation of an either social or aesthetic convention which has found its way into software. Or we can understand it as an ever-evolving circle of causes with liminal modifications where effective factors have to be traced in between material and discursive domains. Such translations between the domains of humans and machines have also been the subject of science and technology studies. But as especially the actor-network theory of Michel Callon (1986), Bruno Latour (1991 and 1999), and others has shown, agency and thus responsibilities can no longer attributed to humans alone.

What I consider more relevant than the leverage of specific actors, is the dis-appearance of the original or primary image, not in the sense of an authentic represen-tations but as something that is close to the act of exposure and that makes all further reproductions derivatives. The before-and-after comparison of original and modified photographs has been a key rhetorical figure for pointing to human agency within the automatisms of photography. Without a real or even imagined original image the possibility for such a critique vanishes. One artist who has constantly questioned the idea of the original—whether in regard to photographic images or fine arts in a broader sense—is Oliver Laric. This is possibly best expressed in *Versions*, a video essay that he himself has altered repeatedly over the years and that demonstrates how deeply embedded such transformations are in contemporary visual culture.[9] Therefore, one thing that has changed since digital photographs emerged in the 1990s and raised the question of whether and how they were still indexical or not, is that we are moving away from calling on an original image as a reference when discussing matters of visual representation.

The original image has effectively been replaced by raw data as the primary trace left by reality once it has entered a camera. Raw data—as problematic as the term itself may be—in its inaccessibility, however, has structural similarities to photo negatives and latent images of analogue photography. So, when Daniel Rubinstein and Katrina Sluis (2013) point out that digital images are always just one out of many possible visual representations of the underlying data, we can say the same with regard to the latent images of photochemical exposures. The fragile connection between data and image was already a point of interest in the discussion of the 1990s. Artist (and publisher) Andreas Müller-Pohle, for example, translated a digital scan of Nicéphore Niépce's famous first photograph into a variety of decorative data prints.[10] What at first comes across as being in awe of large amounts of data, even today, still articulates our inability to establish a meaningful connection between the two ontological domains. Müller-Pohle's title *Digital Scores* is possibly more revealing than the panels themselves as it suggests that data is both a trace or outcome and something that needs to be performed or retranslated into an aesthetic form. And again, all this likewise applies to the latent images and negatives of analogue photography, which were widely ignored by traditional photo theories. The technological change that we are witnessing might change our view of photography and the questions we are asking to a higher degree than the medium of photography itself.

Computational photography makes us aware of a paradoxical situation: There is an indexical (in the sense of causal) relationship between the photographed subject and the raw data a camera collects. But this raw data—the noise that Steyerl describes—is of limited to no value (significance) for the beholder. Unlike the indexes that we find in Charles Sanders Peirce—the smoke, the weathercock, etc.—camera data can no longer be read by a human interpretant and thus its indexical character (as effect and sign) remains unaccomplished because of an opaque wall of numeric abstraction. The representational function of photography only becomes possible with a subsequent step of interpretation, combination, and other non-indexical procedures. This second step then also becomes the subject of scholarly critique and artistic inquiry. Such is the case with recent works by Trevor Paglen where he used machine learning

7   A computer that remixes our visual memories to provide us with new ones that are likely in a statistical sense; the sci-fi feeling that Steyerl's anecdote comes with possibly also has to do with our inability to evaluate the effectiveness of the algorithms she refers to. Overall, it remains difficult for humanities scholars to assess how photography actually is changing here. This caused not only by the technical nature of these changes but also by the fact that a lot of what is going on is hidden inside the black boxes of proprietary soft- and hardware. We are left with the resulting images and the user activities that bring them forth but both are only a part of the entire system.

8   J. Whitehill, G. Littlewort, I. Fasel, M. Bartlett, and J. Movellan, "Toward Practical Smile Detection," *IEEE Transactions on Pattern Analysis and Machine Intelligence* 31, no. 11 (2009): 2106–11; a demonstration of the feature in Sony's Alpha 6300 camera: https://www.youtube.com/watch?v=Godpu72R2c4.

9   One version can be found here: https://anthology.rhizome.org/versions.

10 See artist's website, http: http://muellerpohle.net/projects/digital-scores/.

techniques to reveal how computers translate data into rendered photographs. Paglen trained a neural network with images of the post-colonial philosopher Frantz Fanon and then asked the computer to render a portrait based on the features that the machine identified as distinguishing Fanon. In a similar way, he trained his systems to classify images associated with terms such as omens and portents, monsters, and dreams.[11] The final synthetic images are created by using actual digital noise as raw data and increasing the trained model's sensitivity until it sees something where there is nothing. Paglen thus produces artifacts that unveil the usually invisible algorithms. He speaks of invisible images here as they do not address anybody but represent a closed-circuit of images made by machines for machines.

Loss of Perspective

The translation of images into interpretable data is but one aspect of computational photography. Another less discussed one is the fact that many methods not only resolve the concept of a primary image but also overcome the singularity of such an image. Image data usually derives not from a single but from several exposures. HDR extends the dynamic range of luminosity by combining several exposures with different stops. Panorama stitching requires the photographer to point her camera in different directions to capture a wider field of view in a sequence of images. With single lens systems different exposures necessarily represent different moments in time. This has changed with more recent camera designs with multiple lenses that, owing to their different positions and perspectives, make it possible to extract more precise spatial information, as is also the case in the INTRA SPACE setup. We can speak of a collected or aggregated indexicality—but indexicality after all—that tries to overcome shortcomings of cameras in comparison to human perception. The fact that several images are combined into one does not yet distinguish current computational photography from the digital photography of the 1990s. But the notion of digital photography, as conceived then, refers to procedures applied to visible and identifiable images with image processing software such as Photoshop. Computational photography, on the other hand, develops its own dynamics as it is applied automatically by the apparatus itself—an apparatus whose hard- and software is, of course, designed by humans.

A software that possibly marks the threshold between both paradigms is Microsoft's meanwhile discontinued Photosynth. It was most notably used for CNN's online project "The Moment," which depicts the inauguration of Barack Obama as US president in 2009. In the wake of citizen journalism, CNN asked people who attended the ceremony and took photos of it to contribute them to a single, collective photomontage. The submitted images were then combined and presented with the Photosynth software, which allowed website visitors to navigate between different viewpoints. The result is a hybrid form of testimony which at the same time affirms the documentary quality of photography in the accumulation of 628 witnessing photos and photographers but also creates glitches and tensions between these photos simply because, and in contradiction to the project title, it does not represent a single moment. William Uricchio, in his analysis of the project, has found that "there is no correct or authorized viewing position, no 'master shot' within which everything else is a recomposition. Instead, there is simply a three-dimensional space made up of many textures and granularities, and the means to move within it."[12] "The Moment" thus is also symptomatic of the loss of authority that single images in the context of traditional media have had.

Taking Photosynth as a forerunner of computational photography inside cameras, we can say that one difference to earlier modes of photography is the dissolution of temporal and spatial singularities that find their way into an image. An image of computational photography no longer refers to a specific view of the camera, it aggregates points in time and space and thus overcomes the central perspective of the Renaissance. This not only affects the anthropomorphic viewpoint but also the virtual plane placed between the eye and the scene, as the raw data often preserves three-dimensional information. This is the case with the Kinect camera, which Microsoft introduced in 2010, and in Apple's iPhone X, which uses 3D data for (among other things) post hoc lighting changes, where virtual illumination hits the spatial representation of a situation before it is rendered as an image. Another technique is light field photography, where the light from a situation is captured in a way that does not yet predetermine its rendering on an image plane. Other camera designs foresee the replacement of the single lens with multiple optics of lower quality, which in combination nonetheless can provide images of higher quality once their raw data has been merged. In all of these techniques, it is not primarily the image itself that becomes subject to interpretation but the situation and the point of view that finally transforms it into an image. In a laboratory setup with an object, a camera, and a single light source at the Max Planck Institute for Informatics in Saarbrücken it was possible to use the data provided by the camera to render an image from the perspective of the light source.[13] "You can't have a point of view in the Electronic Age," as Marshall McLuhan said.[14] Perspective has turned into an option, a convention, and it is interesting to see how, for example, Paglen's renderings try to bypass the question of perspective. While technically they use a virtual camera for rendering, this camera however does not produce a situation that can be seen as specific. The specificity of these images is that of a typology.

11 See Paglen's exhibition, http://
    metropictures.com/exhibitions
    /trevor-paglen4.
12 William Uricchio, "The Algorithmic Turn:
    Photosynth, Augmented Reality and the
    Changing Implications of the Image,"
    Visual Studies 26, no. 1 (2011): 30.

13 Hayes, "Computational Photography," 98.
14 "Marshall McLuhan: The World is Show
    Business," YouTube video, 6:31, posted by
    globalbeehive, April, 27, 2010, https://
    www.youtube.com/watch?v=9P8gUNAVSt8.

Coming back to the notion of a probabilistic realism, computational photography in many ways works against an understanding of realism that has to be conceived as subjective in the sense that it requires a point of view that somebody or something has to take and that can be called to name. A probabilistic realism, on the other hand, is the result of echoes and feedbacks in a distributed network or, as Rubinstein writes, a "rhizomatic assemblage of interconnected fragments."[15]

Embracing Entanglements

For INTRA SPACE a plurality of images is provided by the small cameras dotted around the room. It is them that define a stage-like zone of computational visibility rather than the elements of physical architecture. Unlike regular video cameras that would require a power cable to receive electricity and a video cable to send images, the IP cameras of the INTRA SPACE system are merely connected via Ethernet cables, which provide electricity and transmit image data. The cameras are no longer connected apparatuses but extensions of a computer network.[16] The multiplicity of cameras becomes necessary because of the insufficiency of the camera as a measuring device for representing comprehensive spatial information. Within the application of photography, the ability of the technique to make the world flat and portable is a vital feature. However, if one is no longer interested in the photographs themselves but in the data that can be extracted from them, this compression feature turns into a shortcoming, which has to be compensated for by adding to the now insufficient devices. What remains is the camera's ability to capture/measure things from a distance.

A technical challenge of the setup lies in unifying the various measurements. This is also the starting point of Karen Barad's exploration of the "philosophy-physics" of Niels Bohr and his writings on quantum physics. She is interested in how Bohr's careful analysis of measurement in science, a practice that I want to compare to that of photography, leads him to reject representationalism.[17] A central question of quantum physics derives from the fact that the usage of different experimental systems results in different and even conflicting measurement results. Bohr's colleague Werner Heisenberg saw this as a problem of epistemology, an uncertainty that we have when it comes to recognizing the features of electrons in a specific situation. Bohr, on the other hand, drew a more radical conclusion, saying that there is an indeterminacy of such features, that electrons may not even have a position or a momentum until they are measured.[18] Barad's take on this is not to fall into the unproductive trap of social constructivism, where signs ultimately win over matter, but rather to understand Bohr, his instruments, and the subjects of his research as entities that constitute each other. In Barad's terminology they do not *in-*

teract as self-sufficient entities, they *intra-act* and thereby (re)define each other. And it is this assumption that subject and object have no stable identities that allows us to develop a different understanding of photographic practices. In INTRA SPACE, we can witness this in the merging of the distinct photographic measurements, mapping them onto a single ideal skeleton, when the avatar's movements deviate from that of the visitor, when limbs are bent in unnatural ways. This is when the resulting CGI image no longer remains an image but becomes physical as we tend to identify and feel with the twisted body.

Explaining Bohr's position on the dynamism of matter, Barad writes: "Moving away from the representationalist trap of geometrical optics, I shift the focus to physical optics, to questions of diffraction rather than reflection."[19] The necessity to find alternatives to geometrical optics as the basis of photography shows in critical, apparatus-orientated photographic practices which likewise often deal with geometry as a contingent property of cameras. Such practices that shift their focus from the image to the apparatus have existed for a long time but have gained a new momentum since the digitization of photography in the 1990s. Well-known examples of such surveys of photographic geometry are the camera obscura installations by Zoe Leonard. In 2011, the artist began a series of such installations that confront the geometry of optics with the specific geometry of the different spaces she used. On the one hand, she brings the visitor back to the very beginning of photography when images could not yet be preserved. On the other, these installations have a very post-photographic character being produced after Leonard herself had temporally abandoned the production of photographic images.[20] The images one encounters inside her camera obscuras are ephemeral, fragile, and also function as a light source for the room itself and thus question widespread photographic concepts.

More explicitly, the Israeli artist and theoretician Aïm Deüelle Lüski has constructed cameras as a critique of visual representations in the context of the political

15 Daniel Rubinstein, "Posthuman Photography," in *The Evolution of the Image: Political Action and Digital Self*, ed. Marco Bohr and Basia Sliwinska (New York: Routledge, 2018).

16 In the science fiction movie *Colossus: The Forbin Project* (1970) it is the network itself (consisting of a US and a USSR supercomputer) that calls for camera extensions to accomplish total surveillance of its operators and world domination.

17 Light in physics can be either understood as continuous waves or as discrete particles.

Both models contradict each other and require distinct methods of measurement.

18 Karen Barad, *Meeting the Universe Halfway: Quantum Physics and the Entanglement of Matter and Meaning* (Durham, NC: Duke University Press, 2007), 115ff.

19 Barad, 135.

20 Courtney Fiske, "In-Camera: Q+A with Zoe Leonard," Art in America, November 2012, http://www.artinamericamagazine.com /news-features/interviews/zoe-leonard -murray-guy/.

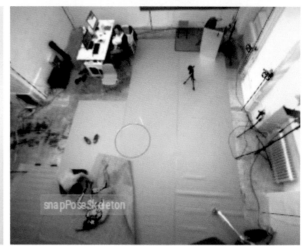

Fig. 54 (previous spread)
TheCaptury, screenshot motion-tracking software interface, 2016

situation in the Middle East. His viewfinder-less cameras document the convergence of various entities in a shared space while evading any purposeful and thus hegemonic visual representation. With his somewhat kaleidoscopic images Deüelle Lüski literally replaces reflections with diffractions as suggested not only by Barad[21] but also by Donna Haraway,[22] from whom she adopts this notion. Deüelle Lüski describes his practice as "distracted concentration,"[23] a mode of perception that is still understood in relation to human consciousness where for Haraway and Barad neither the origin nor the target of light is fixed.

What makes Deüelle Lüski, who works only with traditional, analog techniques, interesting with regard to computational photography is that he conceives the body of the camera as a threshold, a place where light turns into matter. What he strives for is delaying, nearly preventing the materialization of an image in what he calls "the 'struggle' inside the camera obscura and upon the emulsion surface."[24] The camera itself has turned into a discursive device, a phenomenon that also became more relevant with computational photography but remains difficult to grasp. The images of computational photography are figurative but can only be regarded as representational with a very open understanding of what they represent—subjects, expectations, norms, the technology itself, or the threshold Deüelle Lüski addresses. Between reality and an image, we now find raw data that is as inaccessible or even undetermined as the atoms of Niels Bohr.

This threshold cannot be understood with the simplified model of analogies and brings Barad to her proposition of a shift from reflection to diffraction, which she at first derives from specific devices used in scientific practices: "In contrast to reflecting apparatuses, like mirrors, which produce images—more or less faithful—of objects placed a distance from the mirror, diffraction gratings are instruments that produce patterns that mark differences in the relative characters (i.e., amplitude and phase) of individual waves as they combine."[25] So while a reflection produces an analogon, a representation by means of similarity, diffraction creates complex patterns that are jointly caused by an instrument and its subject. This becomes evident when we look at the flutter shutter technique to reduce motion blur caused by relative movement between a camera and one or more of its subjects. In analogue photography there are basically two options to avoid this usually unwanted effect: we can reduce either the relative movement or the duration of exposure. Computational photography, however, provides an option that seems counter-intuitive at first sight: the camera collects several images at random intervals with different exposure times and then infers relatively sharp images from them[26]. The fact that the images feature different degrees of motion blur means that those that are less sharp are deliberately out of focus. But the comparison between the images allows the software to ascertain the relative movement that caused the problem. It can compensate for the shortcomings of the hardware because it "knows" something about what the camera sees. Such a technical awareness of a situation was originally conceived by the inventors of cybernetics in the 1940s to improve the ability of missiles to hit moving targets. In the case of IN-TRA SPACE the closed circuit starts with the visitor's body and its capture through a dozen IP cameras. It is then transformed into data and brought back into the space as a CGI image of the avatar's body, to be seen by the visitor and an audience of spectators and technicians. Seen as a contemplation on representation by means of technical images this structure is not even necessarily computational but can also be traced back to the beginnings of video art with the installations of Peter Campus and the TV Buddha of Nam June Paik. In any case, such loops, just like cybernetic feedback structures, partially suspend the distinction between machinic and human agency. They constantly oscillate between software and hardware, between signs and matter, and thus circumvent any determination of primary agency on either side. The programmed camera is a device that persistently measures but is also measured in order to adjust its measurement values. Digitization was initially understood as a translation of matter into signs but meanwhile we have started to understand that the digital has its own material constraints and cannot be seen as a purely semantic but also as a material domain. The camera itself has lost its former stability with regard to its configurations and its position in the process of documenting the world as it can also be observed during the development of INTRA SPACE. There, the virtual CGI camera more and more lost its stable position that created a mirror-like image when it was attached to the body of the avatar to show how, for instance, the hand would see the rest of the virtual body if it only had eyes.[27]

21 Barad, *Meeting the Universe Halfway*, 29.
22 Donna Haraway, "The Promises of Monsters: A Regenerative Politics for Inappropriate/d Others" (1992), in *The Haraway Reader* (New York: Routledge, 2004), 70.
23 Ariella Azoulay, *Aïm Deüelle Lüski and Horizontal Photography* (Leuven: Leuven University Press, 2014), 235.
24 Azoulay, 238.
25 Barad, *Meeting the Universe Halfway*, 81.

26 Amit Agrawal, "Motion Deblurring Using Fluttered Shutter," in *Motion Deblurring: Algorithms and Systems*, ed. A. N. Rajagopalan and Rama Chellappa, (Cambridge: Cambridge University Press, 2014), 141–60.
27 Regarding identifications of the camera with persons and objects, see Birk Weiberg, "Maschinenbilder: Zur postsubjektiven Kamera," in *Archäologie der Zukunft*, ed. Heiko Schmid, Frank-Thorsten Moll, Ursula Zeller, and Mateusz Cwik (Friedrichshafen: Zeppelin Museum, 2014), 23–44.

Steyerl, when writing about computational photography, has suggested viewing its intermediary processes as proxies. These proxies for Steyerl are considered the subject matter of critical inquiries because they might be informed by economic or political interests. Such a critical discourse, however, necessarily perpetuates the very idea of representation and of a proper closure of the gap between matter and sign. Barad and other critics of modernism, on the other hand, simply claim that originally there is no distance to be bridged. Identities are thus not recognized and represented but are the result of repetitions and variations. "A performative understanding of scientific practices"—and as stated before, I identify these with photographic ones—"takes account of the fact that knowing does not come from standing at a distance and representing but rather from a *direct material engagement with the world*."[28] As photography has been a vital contributor of constructing such distances, one question to be answered is what practices and studies of cameras as non-distancing devices might look like.

A conclusion, I wish to propose, is not limited to computational photography but rather takes this most recent development as a starting point to read photography in a different way. From this perspective, photography has first been chemical, then optical, and now computational. The changing identities of photography herein are not simply ontological transformations by means of technical progress but also different modes of perceiving the medium. The optical has dominated our understanding of photography with metaphors such as mirror or window borrowed from the fine arts. It is analogue not only in a technical but also in a conceptual sense. The diffractive methodology that Barad has suggested, "a way of attending to entanglements in reading important insights and approaches through one another"[29], provides a different approach to photography if we consider it as a practice that is a diffractive entanglement itself. Can we understand the camera as a diffractor and what do we win with it? Distortion would be an integral part of photography and not a defect of an otherwise ideal mirror. Different results from different apparatuses do not lead to uncertainty but complementarity. Any kind of translation, the proxies Steyerl writes about, does not estrange us from a situation but brings all its relata closer together: "Images or representations are not snapshots or depictions of what awaits us but rather condensations or traces of multiple practices of engagement."[30]

Fig. 55
INTRA SPACE, virtual figure in the Unity scene, with supporting guides placed by Christan Freude
to trace head movements in relation to virtual cameras, still from video, 2017

28 Barad, *Meeting the Universe Halfway*, 49.
29 Barad, 30.
30 Barad, 53.

Literature

Agrawal, Amit. "Motion Deblurring Using Fluttered Shutter." in *Motion Deblurring: Algorithms and Systems*, edited by A. N. Rajagopalan and Rama Chellappa, 141–60. Cambridge: Cambridge University Press, 2014.

Ameluxen, Hubertus von, Stefan Iglhaut, and Florian Rötzer, eds. *Fotografie nach der Fotografie*. Dresden: Verlag der Kunst, 1996.

Azoulay, Ariella. *Aïm Deüelle Lüski and Horizontal Photography*. Leuven: Leuven University Press, 2014.

Barad, Karen. *Meeting the Universe Halfway: Quantum Physics and the Entanglement of Matter and Meaning*. Durham, NC: Duke University Press, 2007. doi:10.1215/9780822388128.

Batchen, Geoffrey. "On Post-photography." *Afterimage* 20, no. 3 (1992).

Callon, Michel. "Some Elements of a Sociology of Translation: Domestication of the Scallops and the Fishermen of St. Brieuc Bay." In *Power, Action, and Belief: A New Sociology of Knowledge?*, edited by John Law, 196–233. London: Routledge & Kegan Paul, 1986.

Farocki, Harun. "Phantom Images." *Public* 29 (2004): 12–22.

Fiske, Courtney. "In-Camera: Q+A with Zoe Leonard." *Art in America*, November 2012, http://www.artinamericamagazine.com/news-features/interviews/zoe-leonard-murray-guy/.

Flusser, Vilém. *Into the Universe of Technical Images*. Translated by Nancy Ann Roth. Minneapolis: University of Minnesota Press, 2011. Originally published in German in 1985.

Haraway, Donna. "The Promises of Monsters: A Regenerative Politics for Inappropriate/d Others" (1992). In *The Haraway Reader*, 63–124. New York: Routledge, 2004.

Hayes, Brian. "Computational Photography." *American Scientist* 96, no. 2 (2008): 94–99.

Hoel, Aud Sissel. "Operative Images: Inroads to a New Paradigm of Media Theory." In *Image—Action—Space*, edited by Luisa Feiersinger, Kathrin Friedrich, and Moritz Queisner, 11–27. Berlin: De Gruyter, 2018.

Latour, Bruno. "Drawing Things Together." In *Representation in Scientific Practice*, edited by Michael Lynch and Steve Woolgar, 19–68. Cambridge, MA: MIT Press, 1990.

———. "Technology Is Society Made Durable." in *A Sociology of Monsters: Essays on Power, Technology and Domination*, edited by John Law, 103–31. London: Routledge, 1991.

———. *Pandora's Hope: Essays on the Reality of Science Studies*. Cambridge, MA: Harvard University Press, 1999.

Mitchell, William J. *The Reconfigured Eye: Visual Truth in the Post-photographic Era*. Cambridge, MA: MIT Press, 1992.

Pantenburg, Volker. "Working Images: Harun Farocki and the Operational Image." In *Image Operations: Visual Media and Political Conflict*, edited by Jens Eder and Charlotte Klonk. Manchester: Manchester University Press, 2017. doi:10.7228/manchester/9781526107213.003.0004.

Rubinstein, Daniel. "Posthuman Photography." In *The Evolution of the Image: Political Action and Digital Self*, edited by Marco Bohr and Basia Sliwinska. New York: Routledge, 2018.

Rubinstein, Daniel, and Katrina Sluis. "The Digital Image in Photographic Culture: Algorithmic Photography and the Crisis of Representation." In *The Photographic Image in Digital Culture*, edited by Martin Lister, 22–40. 2nd ed. London: Routledge, 2013.

Steyerl, Hito. "Proxy Politics: Signal and Noise." *e-flux Journal* 60 (December 2014). http://www.e-flux.com/journal/proxy-politics/.

Uricchio, William. "The Algorithmic Turn: Photosynth, Augmented Reality and the Changing Implications of the Image." *Visual Studies* 26, no. 1 (2011): 25–35. doi:10.1080/1472586x.2011.548486.

Weiberg, Birk. "Maschinenbilder: Zur postsubjektiven Kamera." In *Archäologie der Zukunft*, edited by Heiko Schmid, Frank-Thorsten Moll, Ursula Zeller, and Mateusz Cwik, 23–44. Friedrichshafen: Zeppelin Museum, 2014. doi:10.17613 /yegs-2625.

Whitehill, J., G. Littlewort, I. Fasel, M. Bartlett, and J. Movellan. "Toward Practical Smile Detection." *IEEE Transactions on Pattern Analysis and Machine Intelligence* 31, no. 11 (2009): 2106–11. doi:10.1109/tpami.2009.42.

Artificial Intelligence as a Conduit for a New Dialogical Commons?

Dennis Del Favero, Ursula Frohne, and Susanne Thurow

The introduction of intelligent interfaces into interactive artworks is triggering a seismic shift in the way artists and audiences are being positioned in the field, significantly impacting on the aesthetics and nature of artistic spaces and their communicative as well as affective qualities. Rather than representing merely a new, powerful tool at the artists' disposal, artificial intelligence (AI) can both refine the focus of conventional creative practice whilst also radically propelling it beyond its present coordinates.[1] The progression of digital technology from a passive tool to independently responding agent[2] (as outlined in our text on pp. 200–15) is an evolutionary cultural turning point that expands the terms on which art has pivoted up into the present day, namely solely mediating and reflecting human experience.[3] AI amplifies technology's role as an active, intervening agent, reformulating dominant aesthetics, and revolutionizing the nature and focus of the artistic process.[4] The human ontological quest, which expresses itself in our attempt to create a world of objects and to form relations to them,[5] here becomes decentered through the introduction of an autonomous nonhuman agency that radically focuses artistic enquiry on the process of establishing and maintaining a fundamentally new relation.[6] Since the machine and the human user enter into a co-agential relation, the artwork no longer solidifies into a stable human-driven expression but continually shifts and morphs in response to the machine agent's unpredictable response, forestalling closure while extending interaction into a calculated infinitude. If the machine turns from a tool into an equal interlocutor, the question arises of what this means for general human subjectivity, creative practice, and the process of art reception, since intelligent machine interfaces affect human thinking, experiencing, expression, and intersubjective negotiation in manifold ways. As scholars like N. Katherine Hayles point out in critical investigations of cybernetic theories and contemporary culture, it is useful in the context of the Digital Age to conceive the body itself as a machine with a set of organic interfaces that can freely connect with machinic ones to afford new kinds of experiences and knowledges.[7] Such coupling of interfaces nec-

1   Ary Fagundes Bressane Neto and Flavio Soares Correa da Silva, "A Computer Architecture for Intelligent Agents with Personality and Emotions," in *Human-Computer-Interaction: The Agency Perspective*, ed. M. Zacarias and J.V. Oliveira (Berlin: Springer, 2012), 264.

2   Maurice Pagnucco et al., "Implementing Belief Change in the Situation Calculus," in *Logic Programming and Nonmonotonic Reasoning*, ed. P. Cabalar and T. C. Son, Lecture Notes in Computer Science 8148 (Heidelberg: Springer, 2011), 439–51.

3   N. Katherine Hayles, "Speculative Aesthetics and Object-Oriented Enquiry (OOI)," in *Speculations V: Aesthetics in the 21st*

Century, ed. Ridvan Askin et al. (Brooklyn: Punctum, 2013), 164.

4   Neil Brown et al., "Performing Digital Aesthetics: The Framework for a Theory of the Formation of Interactive Narratives," *Leonardo* 44, no. 3 (2011): 217.

5   Hayles, "Speculative Aesthetics and Object-Oriented Enquiry (OOI)," 158.

6   Manuel de Landa and Graham Harman, *The Rise of Realism* (New York: Polity Press, 2017), 11.

7   N. Katherine Hayles, *How We Became Posthuman: Virtual Bodies in Cybernetics, Literature, and Informatics* (Chicago: University of Chicago Press, 1999), 247ff.

essarily favors or backgrounds certain communicative channels (e.g., INTRA SPACE foregoes reliance on verbal language and instead investigates the expressive capabilities of the human motor-sensory apparatus), activating human users in particular ways to prime, and hence mold them to interact with the machine interface. While it may be possible to achieve a seamless coupling of the human and machine in the future, for example through incorporation, the current technological standard still requires a palpable interface that limits such co-articulation. This still-present, productive friction between human and machine at this point in time invites us to critically reflect on the implications of such merging, allowing on the one hand to affectively explore the scope of such abstract concepts like Karen Barad's theory of "intra-action,"[8] yet on the other hand also to contemplate AI's potential for creating new intersubjective spaces that may give rise to a new space for interaction and sharing of data, a new commons. As technological progress proposes to emancipate us from our organic physical and cognitive limitations, it is imperative to explore the question of what the new opportunities and limitations are that human-machine co-agency affords and how these developments may lead to new forms of sociality in the future. Interactive artworks like INTRA SPACE provide an opportunity to study the qualities of an emergent human-machine coupling, affording tangible experiences of concepts that no longer consider artistic and social space as fully separate from the machine.

Implications of Human-Machine Coupling

The advent of pervasive intelligent computer interfaces heralds a shift in the aesthetic conceptualization of subjectivity and creativity because these notions have been conventionally modeled on the grounds of human-driven cognition, perception, and action, where technology has been simply a framing and implementation tool. As indicated, AI offers more than simply an evolution in the usage of tools, representing a step-change in the development of communication by introducing an enhanced intelligence into the processing of information.[9] With general problem solving being one of the strongest drivers of human action in the artistic as well as in the broader social context,[10] powerful AI programming (such as neural networks, search algorithms, or fuzzy logic) can productively assist in formulating problems and articulating innovative solutions. Setting aside the important question of the limitations that computer technology imposes on what can be specified as a problem (on the grounds of available and quantifiable data and experience) and hence become accessible for exploration; our key focus of investigation here shall rest on the possibilities opening up for artistic investigation that result from advanced human-machine co-agency, considering how computers can augment human problem-solving approaches and offer new kinds of input that open new pathways for cognition, perception, and action into the future. Presently, there are two options for computer-based problem solving: the computer can either autonomously solve problems for us, or we can jointly solve problems in close collaboration with it. In the context of art making, the former option reconfigures or almost replaces the role of the human artist,[11] with the machine assuming sole control of the creative process, made possible by deploying a form of AI decision making known as "serial autonomy." The latter option configures human-machine interaction on the grounds of a form of AI decision making known as "parallel autonomy"—defined by both agencies working in collaboration with one another to formulate and address a problem in novel and effective ways.[12] INTRA SPACE is an experimental exploration of the latter.

In light of the fast-progressing advances in AI technologies, a consideration of digitally augmented artistic processes has to take into account the implication for concepts of creativity arising in this context. Creativity can be defined as a practice comprising the identification of a constellation of cognitive and motor-sensory objects as well as their constitutive relations and their processing into a new set of objects that allows thinking and shaping their relations along new vectors. With such reconfiguration achieved, it becomes possible to transpose and apply the gained insight into new contexts that open capacity for novel solutions to either known or previously unreflected problems.[13] Conventionally, creativity has comprised a form of innovative problem solving that represents a socially constituted act, premised on communication between human individuals and their surrounds, be it their biological, cultural, and/or historical environments.[14] Hence, the dominant problem-solving approach has been determined by human relation to the world, premised on the human's biological embodiment and socialization within the world. As such, it has yielded varied and diverse (in terms of cultural, socioeconomic, or geopolitical perspectives) yet is also a specifically species-bound form of problem solving. This underlying particularity announces itself in the comparison to

8   Karen Barad, "Posthumanist Performativity: Toward an Understanding of How Matter Comes to Matter," *Signs* 28, no. 3 (2003): 801–31.

9   Manuel de Landa, "Virtual Environments and the Emergence of Synthetic Reason," in "Flame Wars," ed. Mark Dery, special issue, *South Atlantic Quarterly* 92, no. 4 (1993): 794.

10 Conceived here in the widest sense as working through experiences of emplacement within a set of relations to an externally experienced world of objects while acting to effect a status-change conducive to one's own goals.

11 Mark D'Inverno and Jon McCormack, "Heroic vs Collaborative AI," in *Proceedings of the 24th International Joint Conference on Artificial Intelligence*, ed. Qiang Yang and Michael Wooldridge (Palo Alto, CA: AAAI, 2015), 2439ff.

12 John Markoff, "Toyota to Finance $50 Mission 'Intelligent' Car Project," *New York Times*, September 4, 2015, https://www.nytimes.com/2015/09/05/science/toyota-artificial-intelligence-car-stanford-mit.html.

13 Phillip McIntyre, "Creativity as a System in Action," in *Handbook on Research and Creativity*, ed. Kerry Thomas and Janet Chan (Cheltenham: Edward Elgar, 2013), 88–89.

14 Csikszentmihalyi, quoted in McIntyre, 88–89.

nonhuman problem solving and information processing, which in comparison to animal kingdom practices has frequently been used to validate arguments for humanity's evolutionary dominance (persuasively laid out by popular writers like Yuval Noah Harari).[15] However, with the advent of an autonomous AI, this age-old validation mechanism is unsettled because AI—through its capacity for data storage, rapid interpretation, and dynamic algorithmic evolution—can match and, in many fields, surpass human capabilities for information processing.[16] Advanced AI changes the available scale of communication because machines can rapidly and effectively communicate with each other and confront the human user with new constellations and interpretations of data that reveal and amplify the underlying, previously concealed patterns, and offer additional solutions to defined problems. In the artistic domain, such advances are finding fruitful application in various fields, such as in AI-assisted theatrical set design platforms that support ideation and iterative modeling through intelligent simulation and automated risk-evaluation.[17] The introduction of an autonomous machine agent into the creative process adds a significant layer of complexity into the ideation and production process, previously solely controlled by the human user, and changes its nature to involve fundamentally different kinds of agencies. One human, the other machinic. This new process of decision making between autonomous agencies enables exploration of a wider range of information in rapidly shifting contexts, giving rise to unpredict-able and hence new and imaginative results. Hence, rather than primarily addressing—as Harari does—the important implications of advances in AI that may challenge our species' dominance,[18] it is worth considering what they may offer to the enrichment of creativity in the artistic field and how they may become instrumental in laying the groundwork for a new cultural commons.

A New Form of Sociality?

In AI-driven creative processes, the scope of creativity no longer simply results from dialogue between human actors and their organic, social, and cultural environments but is significantly shaped by the agency exerted by autonomous AI. Such expansion of agent categories consequently also impacts on the forms of sociality brought forth in artistic spaces, with intersubjectivity now involving both human and nonhuman agents negotiating a shared under-standing of a situation, each affecting each other's reasoning and experience of reality through social interaction in a shared space.[19] Since we cannot gauge the "experience" of machines from a subjective position, except for analyzing their sensing and mathematical processing of data, the focus of interactive art will necessarily have to revolve around human experiences and engagements with this new form of sociality and its consequences for the constitution of artistic spaces. While new genres of AI-driven interactive art situated in tech-nologically saturated environments have been continually emerging,[20] there has been little analysis of their qualities and consequences for overall spatial conceptualizations of art in the Digital Age. INTRA SPACE provides an opportunity to examine such qualities, previewing and incubating novel forms of creative expression and reception. Representing more than merely a new type of mediation, technologically saturated environments like the one deployed in INTRA SPACE are different from bare performance spaces as they activate unforeseen aspects affecting creative scope. They tangibly introduce the concept of a nonhuman agency which responds to human interaction from a radically different ontological position, enabling interplay between a new physical and virtual space, carrying a "magical" quality that affords immersion in spaces in which the individual finds dialogical response and immediate spontaneous reciprocation. The machine agent's response manifests in ways that enable an appreciation of this new space as malleable, responsive and non-fixed—traits of our surroundings that we often do not become aware of because of our everyday perceptive habits.[21] It enables plying these open through novel input that surprises and calls for an adjustment of reactive patterns through estranging conventional interactive parameters. The compelling interaction thus replaces the hermetically closed and aesthetically honed output as a key value of the artistic process, with INTRA SPACE not first and foremost seeking to deliver a carefully crafted choreographic work but a research apparatus to explore human motor-sensory behavior at the interstice to the machine interface. Through the digital realm's deconstructive nature that results from resequencing, reassembling, and remodeling of data, environments can be transformed and constituted at will. For example, by doubling, distorting, or recording, sampling, and playing back movement sequences that allow human users to investigate the full capacities of their motor-sensory apparatus, and to conjure alternative subjectivities that such experimentation can inspire. The apparently infinite interactive loop that results can thereby indirectly challenge human ontological certainty, by affording capability to explore "a vision of Nature's forces that bind the world, all its seeds and sources and innermost life," as famously summed up by Goethe's Heinrich Faust (1808).[22]

15 Yuval Noah Harari, *Sapiens: A Brief History of Humankind* (New York: Harper, 2015).

16 DeepMind, "AlphaZero: Shedding New Light on the Grand Games of Chess, Shogi and Go," https://deepmind.com/blog/alphazero-shedding-new-light-grand-games-chess-shogi-and-go/.

17 Susanne Thurow, "Response to the Metamaterial Turn: Performative Digital Methodologies for Creative Practice and Analytical Documentation in the Arts," *Australian and New Zealand Journal of Art* 17, no. 2 (2017): 245ff.

18 Yuval Noah Harari, *21 Lessons for the 21st Century* (New York: Spiegel & Grau, 2018).

19 Ullrich Melle, in *Husserliana: Edmund Husserl — Gesammelte Werke*, vol. 7 (The Hague: Nijhoff/Kluwer, 1950), 435.

20 Exemplified, for example, in works like Wayne McGregor's choreographic exploration *Living Archive* (2019) or Lauren Lee McCarthy's *The Changing Room* (2017).

21 Barad, "Posthumanist Performativity," 801–31.

22 Johann Wolfgang von Goethe, *Faust, Part One*, trans. David Luke (Oxford: Oxford University Press, 1987), lines 382–85.

The question then begs what the consequences are of the users' behavior in spaces that are shaped by intelligently moving figures and images. In his discussion of contemporary art, Sven Lütticken provides an insightful engagement with Augusto Boal's notion of the "spect-actor,"[23] demonstrating how the distribution of roles between acting and looking have become substantially transformed in much contemporary practice. In opposition to traditional audiences that are shackled to their position vis-à-vis an artwork or a movie screen, actuating a Platonic cave scenario directed by the human artist; the users in interactive works such as INTRA SPACE are invited to enact an explicitly performative regime of viewing that radically reconfigures traditional receptive modes by challenging the users' emotional, psychological, and physical capacities. The users are hence emancipated from the traditional passive mode of reception, instead called on to position themselves through interaction within the immersive spatial setting that simultaneously activates them as viewer and performer.[24] These roles momentarily intermingle like a defocused image within which established aesthetic orders are blurred, while visions of a possible public screen space emerge as temporal crystallizations. It is the spectator who acts, rather than contemplates, to the extent that no one "owns" the performance and the user is cast in an active role of interpretation, dialogue, and exchange. Space here becomes a frame for relational ensembles that ties the users, machine agent, and onlookers (performers-in-waiting) into transformational dialogical assemblage. Instead of the one-way, or monological, exchange encoded in the traditional onlooker-performer constellation, this dialogue constitutes a strategy enabling vital participation that Boal conceives as the most common and healthy dynamic between agents, capable of channeling into the constitution of a living community rather than a mute mass public.[25] Interacting with the apparatus enables the users to experience themselves as distinct individuals as well as integrated parts of a collective based on and furthered through collaborative action. As such, works like INTRA SPACE redefine the artistic space as a site of collective viewing in the way they centralize the notion of intersubjectivity and stimulate forms of mutuality which are no longer based in the first place on the relation between the spectator and the work of art, but also on the perceptual experience and the psycho-social relations among users and machine agents within the space.

INTRA SPACE here functions as a laboratory in which new concepts of sociality can be investigated through calibration of the dividing lines between human and nonhuman self and other. Through sampling of motion-tracked data, the machine agent in INTRA SPACE uncannily doubles the user's choreography, adopting and elaborating on particularities of the users' expression that become renewed input for their dialogical response. The users are thus invited to recognize part of themselves within the machine agent, cut off from their personal self and reconstituted in a radical other, which intensifies the reciprocal relation. Recognizing such reflection validates the users' input as significant building blocks for shared creation of reality in the artistic space, affirming their agency in growing a commons through emergent and tentative interaction. It creates a mutuality where previously singular, one-way communication dominated, replacing it with a communicative feedback loop in which the machine turns into a constant respondent and interlocutor that forestalls a clear divide between human and nonhuman agencies. Such new performative spaces transform artistic practice from a solely human expressive and sense-making exercise into an intersubjective negotiation between different types of agencies who radically differ in their interpretative reasoning and processing of information. Interacting in such spaces may thus expand our capacity to recognize and engage with other human and nonhuman agents by immersing us in novel communicative settings and ontological frameworks. Rather than art pivoting on a *mise-en-scène* approach, focused on establishing a human-centered audience-screen constellation, it comes to advance a *mise-en-commune* aesthetic that is based on transformative multi-agent transactions.

Consequently, AI-driven interactive art can disrupt established orders of visibility and incubate new orders of social gathering and processes of cultural exchange that call into being a public sphere along the lines conceptualized by Michael Warner in his path-defining work *Publics and Counterpublics*.[26] Reflecting on the pervasive decline we have been witnessing of the centralized, nation- or city-related public, Warner positions art and activism as key spheres in which groups of individuals may be able to generate publicness from their socio-economic patterns of coexistence, communication, collaboration, and conviviality. For communication between a few or between many to assume such public character, the scene of staged encounter must lead them to acknowledge their having-something-to-do-with-each-other as people who are not relatives and yet whose fate is unequivocally interlinked. Such a public would be a time-space inhabited by a collective of people who are enjoying the freedom of their non-belonging—a collective engaged in what Deleuze and Guattari called "unnatural participation."[27] In such a moral community,[28] thinkers like Jean-Luc Nancy propose that such coexistence—a being-together without a genetically or socio-economically warranted belonging, a solicitous being-with—may possibly give rise to alternative models of interaction that are not premised on leveling out one's own sense of strangeness and uniqueness.[29] While Hito Steyerl cautions that a

23 Augusto Boal, *Theatre of the Oppressed* (London: Routledge, 2006), 118.
24 Sven Lütticken, "Performance Art after TV," *New Left Review* 80 (March–April 2013): 117.
25 Boal, Theatre *of the Oppressed*, 110.
26 Michael Warner, "Publics and Counterpublics," *Public Culture* 14, no. 1 (Winter 2002): 55–56.
27 Gilles Deleuze and Félix Guattari, *A Thousand Plateaus* (Minneapolis: University of Minnesota Press, 1987), 345.
28 Andrew Mason, *Community, Solidarity, and Belonging: Levels of Community and their Normative Significance* (Cambridge: Cambridge University Press, 2000), 27.
29 Jean-Luc Nancy, *Being Singular Plural* (Stanford, CA: Stanford University Press, 2000).

multitude of spect-actors may never congeal into any cohesive commons, this very lack may also be translated into positive terms as an aspirational presentiment of a people-yet-to-come.[30] A new dialogical commons conceived through the coupling of human and machine agencies necessarily would not only feature humans but also consolidate the machine's ontological status as part of this future community. However, techno-logic itself will not automatically prompt democratic evolution. Strategic intelligence is needed to wrest a democratic collectivity from what new technologies and media regimes have to offer. Key to such strategic reflection has to be a deep-seated appreciation of non-belonging. Neoliberal socioeconomic theories, often misconstrued in a trope of atomist isolation inherited from an early-twentieth-century cultural critique, are in fact obsessed with affiliation through nativist identities. If their maxim of capitalizing on relations has been in the process of steadily undermining communal solidarity, then this is because solidarity is an affectionate form of organizing, collectively derived from not having access to established extended bourgeois networks. Solidarity, which has informed communal formations outside of the dominant power arrangements, can redress a sense of social isolation and instead congeal a new collective political subject. Instead of reproducing the conventional socioeconomic bonds produced by the traditional establishment, the consistency of organized groups and communities verifies a different form of "togetherness," which—without hopes of yielding a utopian universal community—might give us confidence to act in accord without the constant motivation of socio-economic trade-offs. AI-driven interactive artistic spaces, through their configuration of agencies and uncontrollable escalation, can afford experiences of an extended and flexible intersubjective network. They can also oppose the dominant trend on digital platforms towards carefully curated realities that predominantly function as echo chambers for polarizing discourses that prevent the formation of a commons, making us less resilient and capable of dealing with difference. For example, social media platforms have provided us with capabilities to infinitely mold and expand our personal identities, splicing physical and virtual realities in ways that interconnect individuals across the world into ever shifting communities that defy traditional dividing lines. However, these new social communities are constituted on opaque grounds, operating as privately controlled assemblies that are designed to organize user data according to monadic self-interests and capture it to sell to third parties. They pivot on the provision of a precarious mixture of division and homogeneity that thrives on friction and othering, rather than exploration of mutuality and solicitousness. AI-driven interactive installation art may provide a compelling arena in which alternative models of intersubjective aesthetics can be modeled and explored, prefiguring a commons that is defined by its openness to uncertainty and evolution rather than one scripted to insular recurrence and division.

*

30 Hito Steyerl, "Is a Museum a Factory?"
e-flux Journal 7 (June 2009), https://
www.e-flux.com/journal/07/61390/is-a
-museum-a-factory/.

Literature

"AlphaZero: Shedding New Light on the Grand Games of Chess, Shogi and Go." https://deepmind.com/blog/alphazero -shedding-new-light-grand-games-chess -shogi-and-go/.

Barad, Karen. "Posthumanist Performativity: Toward an Understanding of How Matter Comes to Matter." *Signs* 28, no. 3 (2003): 801–31.

Boal, Augusto. *Theatre of the Oppressed*. London: Routledge, 2006.

Bressane Neto, Ary Fagundes, and Flavio Soares Correa da Silva. "A Computer Architecture for Intelligent Agents with Personality and Emotions." In *Human-Computer-Interaction: The Agency Perspective*. Edited by M. Zacarias and J. V. Oliveira, 263–85. Berlin: Springer, 2012.

Brown, Neil, Timothy S. Barker, and Dennis Del Favero. "Performing Digital Aesthetics: The Framework for a Theory of the Formation of Interactive Narratives." *Leonardo* 44, no. 3 (2011): 212–19.

De Landa, Manuel, and Graham Harman. *The Rise of Realism*. New York: Polity Press, 2017.

De Landa, Manuel. "Virtual Environments and the Emergence of Synthetic Reason." In "Flame Wars: The Discourse of Cyberculture." Edited by Mark Dery. Special issue, *South Atlantic Quarterly* 92, no. 4 (1993): 793–815.

Deleuze, Gilles, and Félix Guattari. *A Thousand Plateaus*. Minneapolis: University of Minnesota Press, 1987.

D'Inverno, Mark, and Jon McCormack. "Heroic vs Collaborative AI." In *Proceedings of the 24th International Joint Conference on Artificial Intelligence*, edited by Qiang Yang and Michael Wooldridge, 2438–44. Palo Alto, CA: AAAI, 2015.

Goethe, Johann Wolfgang von. *Faust, Part One*. Translated by David Luke. Oxford: Oxford University Press, 1987.

Harari, Yuval Noah. *21 Lessons for the 21st Century*. New York: Spiegel & Grau, 2018.

———. *Sapiens: A Brief History of Humankind*. New York: Harper, 2015.

Hayles, N. Katherine. "Speculative Aesthetics and Object-Oriented Enquiry (OOI)." In *Speculations V: Aesthetics in the 21st Century,* edited by Ridvan Askin, Paul J. Ennis, Andreas Hägler, and Philipp Schweighauser, 158–79. Brooklyn: Punctum, 2013.

———. *How We Became Posthuman: Virtual Bodies in Cybernetics, Literature, and Informatics*. Chicago: University of Chicago Press, 1999.

Lütticken, Sven. "Performance Art after TV." *New Left Review* 80 (March 2013): 109–30.

Markoff, John. "Toyota to Finance $50 Mission 'Intelligent' Car Project." *New York Times*, September 4, 2015, https://www.nytimes.com/2015/09/05/science /toyota-artificial-intelligence-car-stanford -mit.html.

Mason, Andrew. *Community, Solidarity, and Belonging: Levels of Community and Their Normative Significance*. Cambridge: Cambridge University Press, 2000.

McIntyre, Phillip. "Creativity as a System in Action." In *Handbook on Research and Creativity*, edited by Kerry Thomas and Janet Chan, 84–97. Cheltenham: Edward Elgar, 2013.

Melle, Ullrich. In *Husserliana: Edmund Husserl–Gesammelte Werke*. Vol. 7. The Hague: Nijhoff/Kluwer, 1950.

Nancy, Jean-Luc. *Being Singular Plural*. Stanford, CA: Stanford University Press, 2000.

Pagnucco, Maurice, David Rajaratnam, Hannes Strass, and Michael Thielscher. "Implementing Belief Change in the Situation Calculus." In *Logic Programming and Nonmonotonic Reasoning*, edited by P. Cabalar and T. C. Son, 439–51. Lecture Notes in Computer Science 8148. Heidelberg: Springer, 2011.

Steyerl, Hito. "Is a Museum a Factory?" *e-flux Journal* 7 (June 2009). https://www.e-flux.com/journal/07/61390/is-a-museum-a-factory/.

Thurow, Susanne. "Response to the Metamaterial Turn: Performative Digital Methodologies for Creative Practice and Analytical Documentation in the Arts." *Australian and New Zealand Journal of Art* 17, no. 2 (2017): 238–50.

Warner, Michael. "Publics and Counterpublics." *Public Culture* 14, no. 1 (Winter 2002): 49–90.

Epilogue

What Beings Are We?

Christina Jauernik and Wolfgang Tschapeller

In the third of the *Ten Books on Architecture*, dedicated to the design of temples, in the second chapter, "On Symmetry: In Temples and in the Human Body," Vitruvius incorporates a small, niche-like cavity wherein huddles a being about which we know no more than the proportions of its body parts to one another. The being cannot simply be; it is planned, engineered, "so designed by nature that the face, from the chin to the top of the forehead and the lowest roots of the hair, is a tenth part of the whole height; the open hand from the wrist to the tip of the middle finger is just the same; the head from the chin to the crown is an eighth, and with the neck and shoulder from the top of the breast to the lowest roots of the hair is a sixth; from the middle of the breast to the summit of the crown is a fourth." And so on, until all the proportions have been defined, but no size as yet.

Thus begins the cycle, some 2000 years before our time—the cycle of human bodies quantified, designed, constructed, and planned: in Bosch's *Garden of Earthly Delights*, circa 1500, the phantasmagorical precursors of Constant's *New Babylon*; in 1924, Vertov's "I am kino-eye, I am a mechanical eye. I, a machine, show you the world as only I can see it"; in 1951, Corbusier's Modulor; in 1961, Lem's *Solaris*, an intelligent being that breaks the human mold, shapeless and boundless, a swaying mass, an ocean capable of materializing deceptively real-seeming reflections of people from human beings' traces of memory; in 1968, a woman and a man set on a blanket by Ray and Charles Eames; in 1984, "A Cyborg Manifesto" by Haraway; in 1993, Kwinter's *Figure in Time*; in 1999, *MAKEHUMAN*—a software; in 2000 *L'Intrus* by Nancy; in 2003, *From Cyborgs to Companion Species*, Haraway again; in 2012, *The Building of Bodies* by Alex Schweder La.

"WHAT BEINGS ARE WE?" is a lecture series that chronicles the nature of our bodies circa 2018. After "WORLD, VERSION 1 + 2" (2004), "HANDS HAVE NO TEARS TO FLOW" (2012) and "INTRA SPACE" (2014/2017), "WHAT BEINGS ARE WE" is the fourth project that experiments with the substances, constructions, and manifestations of our bodies in a near future.

Heirs of Vitruvius
Lichens, Lapdogs & Cyborg Cows

Fahim Amir

Not only religions are made, but trouble, too, says Donna Haraway.[1] As a committed compostist of intellectual estates, and a queer-leaning heir of historical
materialism, feminist standpoint theory, indigenous multiverses, and disarmament
campaigns, this biologist and science philosopher does not gaze upwards,
to a god in the sky and his ostensible "gaze from nowhere."[2] Haraway pokes her
nose into the hind gut of a South Australian termite, where she goes looking
for the contours of non-innocent coexistence.[3] Her readings lead to the idiolectal
pamphlets of female former slaves such as Sojourner Truth, who had not
mastered the sovereign language of power, but did not let that stop them from
making trouble.[4]

No solitary sun shines down to bathe the world in the searchlight of a school-
masterly god, or colonial enlightener; instead, in Haraway's world, the biolu-
minescent bodies of marine creatures become disco balls for the cruel and kind
party called evolution. And there is blood on this dance floor.

Tasting, Touching, Thinking

Donna Haraway is concerned with making wild kin, instead of remaining
caught up in the subdivisions of taxonomic regulation and heteronormative
reproduction. That is why she calls to us: We are all lichens!

Lichens are symbiotic communities of a fungus (or several fungi) and an alga
(or several algae) practicing photosynthesis. This life form, collectively called
lichen, exhibits traits that none of its component parts possesses by itself.
And nor are the members of this idiosyncratic patchwork entity subsumed in
a greater whole (an organism, Mother Earth, etc.). Lichens were probably
the stuff the Israelites ate when they wandered in the desert for 40 years. It was
called *manna* or *bread from heaven*, for, like a gift from God, it could be
found each day anew on the ground. The English word *lichen* is derived from
a Greek term that means both "tree moss" and "licking." More than just flirting
with sexual politics, this is an attempt to politicize the concepts we use to
think other concepts by engaging all senses. So what would result, asks Donna

1   Donna Haraway, *Staying with the Trouble:
    Making Kin in the Chthulucene* (Durham,
    NC: Duke University Press, 2016).
2   Donna Haraway, "Situated Knowledges:
    The Science Question in Feminism and the
    Privilege of Partial Perspective," *Feminist
    Studies* 14, no. 3 (1988): 575–99.
3   Donna Haraway, "Otherworldly
    Conversations; Terran Topics; Local Terms,"
    Science as Culture 3, no. 1 (1992): 64–98.
4   Donna Haraway, "Ecce Homo, Ain't (Ar'n't)
    I a Woman, and Inappropriate/d Others:
    The Human in a Post-humanist Landscape,"
    in *Feminists Theorize the Political*, ed.
    Judith Butler and Joan W. Scott (New York:
    Routledge, 1992), 86–100.

Haraway—and with her, an entire tradition of science critics and philosophers—
if we understood the production of knowledge not as cracking and exploring
bodies, or as shining a light into the darkness, but instead as tasting and touching, like octopus and jellyfish tentacles do, or a constantly vibrating spider's
prosthesis-like net of slimy, sticky threads?

Humanity, a Must?

The interlacings formed by these non-plants are not the well-ordered lines of
the Vitruvian Man, which posited man as the measure of all things in a reinter-
pretation of classical antiquity, and became an emblematic image in Leonardo
da Vinci's depiction of well-formed proportionality and perfection (and the
possibility to achieve perfection). A belief in the unique, self-regulating, and
intrinsic moral force of human reason is part of the humanistic legacy linked
to this figure. The Vitruvian Man was interrogated in various ways in the course
of the lecture series "What Beings Are We?" As the heraldic animal of the
sort of humanism that combined biological, moral, and discursive notions of
seemingly genuinely human abilities to form the idea of rational progress, it
has in fact become questionable.[5]

Historically, humanism—as criticized by Haraway (and many others)—developed
to become a civilizational model. The *vision* associated with this model implied
Europe as more than an arbitrary, geopolitical space, instead framing European
civilization as a universal attribute of the human intellect, capable of lending
a special quality to any object, any place. This form of humanism accompanied
almost all colonial enterprises as the image of the ideal and destiny of civilization. The humanistic idea of Europe as the point of origin of critical reasoning
and self-reflection can also be clearly heard in contemporary attempts to
rhetorically defend Europe against the threat of fascism. It goes beyond a more
or less problematic attitude that might be corrected with some goodwill:
Eurocentric humanism is a structural element of our cultural practice, embedded
in institutional and educational practices that produce reality.

Medusa or Tesla

In Fabrizio Terranova's film *Donna Haraway: Story Telling for Earthy* Survival
(2016), Haraway discusses two *National Geographic* cover photos. In both
cases, the model gracing the cover is Koko, the famous lowland gorilla (who
knew one thousand hand signs of sign language and recognized two thousand
words of spoken English). On one cover, she is pictured with her pet cat, and
on the other, she is holding a Japanese camera and taking a picture of her reflection in the mirror. Koko is framed as almost human—she has another animal

as a companion and pet, and she has control of her own image, she recognizes herself in the mirror—thus becoming a proxy for universal humanity.

The many jellyfish and octopus tentacles that wobble across the screen in Terranova's film can be interpreted as an ironic nod to Medusa, the mortal goddess at whose mere sight bio-men instantly turned to stone, who died when she saw herself in a mirror. Instead of the omniscient, distant gaze of Enlightenment and the pitfalls of the male gaze, Haraway advocates a politics of touching and being touched. However, this enterprise is anything but free of danger—as anyone who has ever touched a tentacle or been touched by one can testify.

Haraway's insistence on jellyfish and octopuses, dogs and cyborgs emphatically underlines that nobody can exist everywhere. It is the opposite of the image of universal man in a spacesuit, soon on his way to Mars, powered by Tesla batteries, capable of founding a colony anywhere. No—there are certain places and habitats that can enable and sustain certain forms of life. That is why the film repeatedly poses the question of how the habitat that produced the Haraway animal is constituted, and how that animal acted in the habitat, forming and changing it.

Lacking a Spine, yet on an Even Course

Haraway's animals are cyborgs, and thus politically non-innocent, hybrid beings of different worlds, or vectors of posthumanistic relationality. In this context, Haraway seeks to keep materiality and relationality at the same level and the same volume. No one is connected to everyone, but everyone is connected to someone or something.

In Haraway's interpretation, the human figure—like all other biological and inorganic entities—is a figure in a game of cat's cradle, the children's game played with a loop of string where you produce different, new figures depending on how you move your hands (a game that served as a knowledge archive and accounting tool in older cultures). The OncoMouse, the first living organism to be patented, but also regular lapdogs are figures that connect us to one another and to other worlds. What Haraway attempts to do is sketch experimental futures. She is concerned with tentacular thinking, with the octopus and the spider: touching and sticking, coming loose and entangling,

5   Cf. Christopher Hight, *Architectural Principles in the Age of Cybernetics* (New York: Routledge, 2008); and Beatriz Colomina and Mark Wigley, *Are We Human? Notes on an Archaeology of Design* (Zurich: Lars Müller Publishers, 2016).

lacking a spine yet charting an even course—a course that enables continued existence, instead of lines that begin in the emptiness of self-exegesis and end in the nothingness of outer space.

Architects on the Brink

The more we focus the optical apparatus of insight on politics, the more we blur all other distinctions of modernism.

Haraway's *When Species Meet* (2008) includes a drawing of a cartoon dog in the place of Vitruvius. Can a dog be the representation of, if not everyone, at least of some? Her book *Staying with the Trouble* (2016) includes a drawing that shows an ancient species of orchid with blossoms formed in such a way as to attract a specific species of wasp. The wasp has since become extinct, while the orchid persists as a sort of botanical negative image of the disappeared body of the wasp. Perhaps the Vitruvian Man is similar to the orchid's blossom, conserving as an image something that has long since ceased to exist.

And just when the tides of history seemed ready to wash humanity clean, the universal body as a model is uncertain like never before.

Architects are standing on the brink of the future, in the midst of a rampant crowd of cyborg bodies, holocaust bodies, prosthetic bodies, animal bodies, pornographic and mutated bodies, disabled, migrated, and colonized bodies. However, instead of making reactionary reference to the dubious idyll of an imaginary premodern era (as is the case with the line "when tomatoes still tasted like tomatoes"), Donna Haraway's ideas enable us to grasp dairy cows, with their feeding, monitoring, and milking machinery, as proletarian cyborgs. There is a cow with a gun. To liberate us all.

Literature

Colomina, Beatriz, and Mark Wigley. *Are We Human? Notes on an Archaeology of Design*. Zurich: Lars Müller Publishers, 2016.

Haraway, Donna. *Staying with the Trouble. Making Kin in the Chthulucene*. Durham, NC: Duke University Press, 2016.

Haraway, Donna. "Ecce Homo, Ain't (Ar'n't) I a Woman, and Inappropriate/d Others: The Human in a Post-humanist Landscape." In *Feminists Theorize the Politica*, edited by Judith Butler and Joan W. Scott, 86–100. New York: Routledge, 1992.

———. "Otherworldly Conversations; Terran Topics; Local Terms," *Science as Culture* 3, no. 1 (1992): 64–98.

———. "Situated Knowledges: The Science Question in Feminism and the Privilege of Partial Perspective." *Feminist Studies* 14, no. 3 (Fall 1988): 575–99.

Hight, Christopher. *Architectural Principles in the Age of Cybernetics*. New York: Routledge, 2008.

Terranova, Fabrizio, dir. *Donna Haraway: Story Telling for Earthly Survival* (2016) Film, BE/82'/16:9

Vitruvius, *De Architectura Libri Decem*, 22 BC. In *Vitruvius on Architecture* (Two Volumes), edited by Frank Granger from the Harleian Manuscript 2767. Cambridge, MA: Harvard University Press, 1931.

Constant's Call
The Architecture of Kitsune

Hannes Mayer

Changing identities, shapeshifting, and metamorphosis have fascinated cultures from their early beginnings. A world of beliefs, imagination, animation, and superstition sought explanations for the extraordinary in the ascribed characters of other bodies, animals, and creatures. In Japan, kitsune—the foxes associated with the god Inari—would sometimes enter the body of a young woman from under her fingernails and subsequently alter her features as well as her behavior. The rational world of scientific knowledge has suppressed many of the once common narratives, yet digital technologies have helped to create a new world of animation and imagination—addressing the fascination with being someone else.

In INTRA SPACE, a digital character is mapped onto someone else with great ease. With no need to wear any markers or suits—the person in the real world remains apparently unchanged, yet is joined by a digital twin of silver appearance that follows movements after a brief static pose that match the virtual with the physical body.

How should one describe such a setup? Is it a projection, an animation, an operation, a theater of digital puppets, a choreography? Does it have to be described as one world or two worlds, and most importantly, can it be described as architecture? Would this include the whole scenario or only parts thereof: the bodies, the space, and the hardware or software setup?

Descriptions of the world become possible through relations. In spring 2015, in parallel to the start of INTRA SPACE, Wolfgang Tschapeller conceived a design studio based on Constant Nieuwenhuys's New Babylon at the Academy of Fine Arts. It is not a coincidence. Both INTRA SPACE and New Babylon hover in abstract space, their "constructions"—bodies and structures—cannot deny their technical origins. Nevertheless, their reason for existence is not the newness of any particular technology itself and therefore neither project is linked to any particular point in time. In both cases, a possible translation to architecture remains vague, yet they describe a strong and memorable vision. Notwithstanding the striking absence of details, they employ a suggestive power, which call for fundamental questions about our existence, society, and built environment. Mark Wigley thus reads Constant's vision not as a city, but as a provocation.[1] With his own words, he writes the agenda for the inhabitants of New Babylon: "Nature has been replaced. Technology has long been the new nature that must now be creatively transformed to support a new culture. The increasingly traumatized inhabitants have to take over the shaping of their own spaces to recover the pleasure of living."[2]

1   Mark Wigley, *Constant's New Babylon: The Hyper-architecture of Desire* (Rotterdam: 010 Publishers, 1998), 71.

2   Wigley, 9.

Does this call extend to INTRA SPACE? Is INTRA SPACE catalyzing a new culture based on new technologies aimed at the pleasure of living? Does it follow that INTRA SPACE has to be read as a habitat—real and/or virtual—despite its procedural dominance of bodies and identities? With no nature left but no superstructure either—is INTRA SPACE a new Eden whose inhabitants are only known by their innocent first names?

In 1960, almost a decade before the moon landing, the two researchers Manfred E. Clynes and Nathan S. Kline suggested adapting the human organism to the hostile conditions of outer space rather than building expansive space stations.[3] Unfit for outer space, they asked what it needed "to allow man to live adequately in the space environment" and proposed "self-regulating man-machine systems" which freed man to explore.[4] It was in this publication that they coined the term cyborg.

Centering everything on the human body, their approach was deeply anti-architectural, questioning altogether the need for (space) architecture, hitherto considered a pre-condition for life in outer space. If at all, architecture was to be found in the body itself and its "instrumental control systems."[5] Does INTRA SPACE follow a similar agenda?

Is INTRA SPACE against architecture?

INTRA SPACE is against architecture in its conventional sense. It challenges the idea and concept of building and the built environment. It does not aim at incrementally advancing construction by integrating technologies from other fields—nor does it look at technologies itself in an act of pseudo-engineering. It defines the non-building as architecture. In that sense, INTRA SPACE is candidly utopian and employs cunning methods of dystopia in the Orwellian tradition. Shift the focus away from the projected abstract bodies and a system of cameras connected to control systems give testimony to the rapidly expanding array of sensory extensions that break with the modernist idea of (empty) space as a binary opposite to matter. Today, space is dense and densified in the virtual realm from where it can be exported back into the real. Far from Eden, the opposing narrative reads INTRA SPACE as a comment on surveillance and tracking, on the control of other bodies and identities. It can be interpreted as a playful take on identity theft—one that goes beyond personal details and includes whole body descriptions, does not stop with faces but even includes movements. For the pessimist amongst us, it is a tale on pervasive technologies that monitor, profile, categorize, and ultimately monetize us.

In New Babylon they play. In INTRA SPACE they dance.

As Mark Wigley suggests, New Babylon has to be understood as a cultural project. A way out of a technocratic nightmare that saw nature disappear long ago, New Babylon is an emergency exit in the linear tunnel of progress that leads onto a playground. Is INTRA SPACE the stage behind another exit door? What are the relationships between dance and architecture if one excludes the conventional act of building? At the Bauhaus, Oskar Schlemmer directed the Bauhausbühne and often extended the body with three-dimensional costumes—spatial sculptures—into space. Schlemmer was masking the body with costume-sculpture-architecture, thereby restricting its movements and formulating a systematic, modernist counter-position of abstraction to the expressionist body-focused and body-revealing work of Rudolf von Laban, Mary Wigman, and others.[6]

INTRA SPACE discretizes and encapsulates the systematic within a system of tracking and mapping—allowing the expression of movements of the physical body to be unrestricted. It is a parallel duality of the real physical body and the virtual avatar. The costume-sculpture-architecture now appears in the virtual realm—not as something we recognize as an object, but as a dynamic object in the shape of a virtual identity and person. Here, INTRA SPACE is a study of three-dimensional space in reality and in the virtual, of controlled physical and virtual bodies in motion and their mutual dependencies out of which a choreography emerges. The choreography mirrors the character and feelings of those who dance and their respect towards their virtual identities governed by the digital control setup. Sometimes weird artifacts appear or the virtual camera attached to a body penetrates and allows for the painless introspections of digital body-hulls—eyeballs hovering in space surrounded by the tessellated inside of empty digital bodies. Dance as a means of digital anatomy. Do these bodies long to be filled? Intimate relations are to be found right in front of it.

3 Manfred E. Clynes and Nathan S. Kline, "Cyborgs and Space," *Astronautics*, September 1960, 26.
4 Clynes and Kline, 26.
5 Clynes and Kline, 27.

6 Hannes Mayer, "Dance," in *The Bauhaus: It's All Design*, ed. Matteo Cris et al. (Weil am Rhein: Vitra Design Museum, 2015), 37.

They dance.

Speaking about morphology, the architecture and computer graphics pioneer John Frazer differentiated between the sciences, which seek to find a theory of explanation, and architecture with its quest for a theory of generation.[7] INTRA SPACE, despite being a research project, does not explain, it generates. It generates doubt towards conventional constructions grounded in the realm of feasibility. INTRA SPACE is firmly ungrounded, yet based on the competence of an interdisciplinary research team. If one considers and examines INTRA SPACE as a scientific research project—it sits comfortably within the realm of representations. It is a digitally constructed description of the world based on real (time) input in a renaissance tradition where a systematic understanding of seeing leads to a completely new way of designing and, ultimately, a new way of building. This then constitutes a theory of explanation employed as a theory of generation.

How will INTRA SPACE eventually materialize? Is it "realized in its effect on others," as Wigley evaluates the legacy of New Babylon? Or, is it already completed and this text is a part of its documentation and archiving? What does INTRA SPACE make us look for? Will the architectural drive to physically build and materialize eventually challenge the powerful neo-Babylonian abstraction—or, are we satisfied with a stimulation of the imagination that has not only projected animals into human bodies, but propelled the discipline of architecture? How do we like architecture? Do you like architecture to be a box? Or, more like a Japanese fox?

In "Demain la poésie logera la vie," Constant did not only see the rectangle "losing its meaning," he also warned the architects "against becoming dispersed between the science of the engineer and the inventiveness of the sculptor" and "encourage[d] them rather to face the new conditions head on, eyes open."[8] Situated within an arts school at the Institute of Art and Architecture, INTRA SPACE follows Constant's call and proposes a rare position on how artistic and artificial intelligence can complement each other in a time of no less "profound transformations."[9]

Architecture becomes an intimate affair.

7   John Frazer, *An Evolutionary Architecture*, (London: Architectural Association, 1995), 20.

8   Constant Niewenhuys, "Demain la poésie logera la vie," in Wigley, *Constant's New Babylon*, 78.

9   Constant, in Wigley, 78.

Literature

Clynes, Manfred E., and Nathan S. Kline. "Cyborgs and Space." *Astronautics*, September 1960, 26–27.

Frazer, John. *An Evolutionary Architecture*. London: Architectural Association, 1995.

Mayer, Hannes. "Dance." In *The Bauhaus: It's All Design*, edited by Matteo Cris, Mateo Kries, Jolanthe Kugler. Weil am Rhein: Vitra Design Museum, 2015.

Nieuwenhuys, Constant. "Demain la poésie logera la vie," translated as "Tomorrow Life Will Reside in Poetry." In Wigley, *Constant's New Babylon*.

Wigley, Mark. *Constant's New Babylon: The Hyper-architecture of Desire*. Rotterdam: 010 Publishers, 1998.

Image Credits

Towards an INTRA SPACE
Christina Jauernik and Wolfgang Tschapeller
In collaboration with Christina Ehrmann, *Drawings for INTRA SPACE*, 2019.
© INTRA SPACE
Fig. 1
Cartography of Neighborhoods, INTRA SPACE, 2019
Fig. 2
INTRA SPACE
Fig. 3
View of the project space with Projection Screen C
Fig. 4
Biography of project space including all technical, virtual, engineered, and human contributors, their positions, specifications, and collaborative engagements
Fig. 5
Zoom into project space
Fig. 5a
Body model, skeleton, and spheres; drawn based on the concept developed by Nils Hasler, 2017
Fig. 6
Detail (zoom-in): Overlapping field of views, 12 cameras J
Fig. 6a Industry camera installed in the tracking area, 2017
Fig. 6b Virtual camera, INTRA SPACE
Fig. 6c Figure shown with virtually placed camera positions, experiments, 2017
Fig. 7
Detail (zoom-in): Figures
Fig. 7a
Photograph, reenacting Venus Cupid Folly Time, Esther and Christina. Photo: Christian Freude
Fig. 7b
View from the tracking camera, screenshot of software interface. Esther and Christina with two skeletons (unknown-2; snapPoseSkeleton-6). Screenshot: Christian Freude
Fig. 8
Detail (zoom-in): Skeleton
Fig. 8a Four of the twelve cameras, motion tracking screen (monitor H), 2017
Fig. 9
The Virtual Camera
Fig. 10
Jason, screenshot excerpt of programming language for the virtual figures' behavior
Fig. 10a
Jason

Figs. 11–12
Experiment 1: Orthogonal camera as mirror with Carla and Esther, January 2016. Photo: Wolfgang Tschapeller; image editing: Markus Wörgotter
Fig. 13
Experiment 2: Perspective camera attached to Christina's right hand, working with Carla, April 2016. Camera: INTRA SPACE; image editing: Markus Wörgötter
Figs. 14–18
Experiment 2: Perspective camera attached to Christina's right hand, working with Old Man, May 2017. Camera: INTRA SPACE; image editing: Markus Wörgötter
Fig. 19
Experiment 2: Rehearsal Esther, Christina, and two figures, Bob and Bob, perspective camera attached to Esther's inner right wrist, May 2017 Camera: Ludwig Löckinger
Fig. 20
Experiment 2: Rehearsal Esther and Bob, perspective camera attached to Esther's inner right wrist, May 2017 Camera: Ludwig Löckinger; image editing: Markus Wörgötter

Vital Technologies: The Involvements of "the Intra"
Vicky Kirby
Fig. 21
Jean-Martin Charcot, *Autographic Skin*, 1877

Dancing with Machines: On the Relationship of Aesthetics and the Uncanny
Clemens Apprich
Fig. 22
Stuart Patience, *Spin Round Wooden Doll – Nathaniel dancing with Olympia at the ball*. 2018. Courtesy of Heart Agency © Stuart Patience/heartagency.com
Fig. 23
INTRA SPACE working situation, Dominikanerbastei, Vienna, 2017. Photo: Günter Richard Wett

Body of Landscape
Esther Balfe
Figs. 24–41
Practicing Virtual Conditions. Rehearsal: Esther Balfe, Christina Jauernik. Video stills, 2017. Camera: Ludwig Löckinger

INTIMACY LOSS SKINNING
Christina Jauernik
Figs. 42–46
Christina Jauernik, *working with skeletons*,
October 2018, Sitterwerk artist residency,
Switzerland

Skin Dreams
John Zissovici
Figs. 47, 48, 53
John Zissovici, *head shapes*, 2017, Vienna.
Video stills
Fig. 49
Still from recording, experiments with
hand camera. INTRA SPACE 2017
Fig. 50
Francesco Morone, *Stimmate di San
Francesco*, 14th century. Tempera on
canvas, 84.5 × 56.5 cm. Museo di
Castelvecchio, Verona. © Photographic
Archive, Museo di Castelvecchio, Verona
Fig. 51
Philippe Lapierre, *Untitled #155*, 2020.
Drawing
Fig. 52
John Zissovici, *The Door,* 2017. Photo: John
Zissovici

**The Entangled Apparatus: Cameras as Non-
distancing Devices**
Birk Weiberg
Fig. 54
TheCaptury, screenshot motion-tracking
software interface, 2016
Fig. 55
INTRA SPACE, virtual figure in the Unity
scene, with supporting guides placed by
Christan Freude to trace head movements
in relation to virtual cameras. Video still,
2017

Biographies

Fahim Amir is an author, curator, philosopher, and artist. He studied art and philosophy with influential thinkers like Jacques Derrida and Judith Butler, and has held guest professorships at the Academy of Fine Arts Vienna, University Campinas São Paulo, and University of Art and Design Linz. He works at the intersection of nature-culture, colonial historicity, and urbanism. Amir curated the Live Art Festival 2013 "Zoo 3000: Occupy Species" (Kampnagel, Hamburg) and "Salon Klimbim: Von vegetarischen Tigern und utopischen Unterhandlungen" (Secession, Wien). He is coeditor of *Transcultural Modernisms* (Sternberg Press, 2013) and most recently wrote the epilogue to the German edition of Donna Haraway's *The Companion Species Manifesto (Das Manifest für Gefährten: Wenn Spezies sich begegnen*, Merve Verlag, 2016). He is currently working on the book project *Schwein und Zeit: Tiere, Politik und Verbrechen* (Nautilus, 2018).

Clemens Apprich is visiting research fellow at the Mel Hoppenheim School of Cinema at Concordia University in Montreal. He is a member of the Global Emergent Media Lab at Concordia and a member of the Centre for Digital Cultures (CDC) at Leuphana University of Lüneburg. Apprich studied philosophy, political science, and cultural history and theory in Vienna, Bordeaux, and Berlin, and was a junior research fellow at the Ludwig Boltzmann Institute for Media.Art.Research in Linz as well as at the Institute for Human Sciences in Vienna. During his studies he was actively engaged in the media art initiative Public Netbase. Apprich cofounded the Post-media Lab (PML) at the CDC and was Principal Investigator of Making Change, a joint research project between the CDC and the Hivos Knowledge Programme. He is one of the founders and editors of *spheres*, an open peer-reviewed journal for digital cultures and works as a curatorial advisor of transmediale, a festival for art and digital culture in Berlin. Apprich's current research focuses on the epistemological, social, and technical analysis of filtering algorithms, asking how they are organizing digital cultures, what role they play in the transformation of democratic societies, and to what extent they can be explained by the latest push in computation, in particular in automated data analysis and machine learning. Together with Wendy Chun, Hito Steyerl, and Florian Cramer he co-authored *Pattern Discrimination* (University of Minnesota Press/meson press, 2019), which investigates the centrality of race, class, gender, and sexuality to big data network analytics and bridges research fields in the arts, humanities, and data sciences. He is also the author of *Technotopia: A Media Genealogy of Net Cultures* (Rowman & Littlefield, 2017).

Esther Balfe began her professional dance studies and training at the Rambert School for Contemporary Dance and Ballet, in West London, under the direction of Ross McKim. There she performed works by McKim, Sir Fredrick Ashton, and Mark Bruce. Upon leaving Rambert she was offered a position in Saarbrücken under the direction of Philip Landsdale, thereafter she joined Liz King's ensemble in Heidelberg and later in Vienna with the newly founded Tanz Theater Wien, working with Catherine Guerin, Emmanuel Obeya, Georg Reischl, Nigel Charnock, and Benoît Lachambre. Prior to this she also worked with choreographer Jai Gonzales at Unterwegs Theater and Philip Talard at the National Theater Mannheim. Esther Balfe was invited to Albuquerque as Artist in Residence at the University of New Mexico. Between 2005 and 2006 Esther Balfe worked with Michael Keegan Dolan in his former company Fabulous Beast Dance Theatre. In 2005, Esther Balfe first appeared as a Guest Artist for Ballett Frankfurt, joining the newly formed Forsythe Company as a full member in 2006. Esther Balfe worked at TFC for the next decade, immersed in the collaborative, creative process with William Forsythe, touring and performing his works internationally up until 2015. She was instrumental in the creation of Forsythe's works during this period, including *Yes We Can't, I Don't Believe in Outer Space, Defenders*, and *The Returns*. Other repertoire works included: *WoolfPhrase, Three Atmospheric Studies*, and *Decreation*. In 2012 Esther Balfe became a professor of contemporary dance and currently works and teaches at the Music and Arts University Vienna, MUK. Her recent positions and collaborations include: artistic collaborator and workshop leader for Scott DeLahunta, MotionBank, Frankfurt am Main, 2012; workshop leader, with Mani Obeya,"The

Imaginative Body," ImPulsTanz, Vienna, 2014; "Ganymed" at the Kunsthistorisches Museum, Vienna, directed by Jacqueline Kornmüller 2015–17; artistic collaborator and performer for INTRA SPACE, directed by Wolfgang Tschapeller 2015–17; movement analyst and dancer for John Gerrard from 2014 to the present, including *Exercise (Dunhuang) and X.Laevis (Spacelab) 2017*; guest teacher for Rambert School & Rambert Summer Academy, Ballet Preljocaj; workshop leader, with Christina Jauernik, "Otherness: Attentional Forms," ImPulsTanz, Vienna, 2018; performer for Alex Gottfarb in *NEGOTIATIONS*, 2018–19; performer for Schauspielhaus, Vienna production Sommer, director Elsa-Sophie Jach, 2019.

Gabrielle Cram lives and works as dramaturge, researcher, and publisher for contemporary dance and performance in Vienna. Her research focuses on transpersonal agency within transmedia alliances and her applied movement research on mixed abled strategies. The engagement in transdisciplinary fields and practices of translation—between genres, spaces, times, locations, languages—takes an important role in her work. Her practice is marked by diverse forms of mediation such as the creation of spaces for negotiation and contact zones for still open processes.

Dennis Del Favero is a Scientia Professor and world-renowned research artist. He is currently Chair Professor of Digital Innovation, Director of the University of New South Wales (UNSW)'s iCinema Research Centre and Expanded Perception & Interaction Centre (Sydney, Australia), as well as Visiting Professorial Fellow at ZKM Center for Art & Media (Karlsruhe, Germany), at IUAV – University of Venice (Italy), and at Academy of Fine Arts (Vienna, Austria), and Visiting Research Fellow at the University of California, Santa Barbara (USA). His expertise lies in interdisciplinary art projects that explore the relationship between human and nonhuman systems through the experimental reformulation of immersive aesthetics using digital media.

Christina Ehrmann studies in the master program architecture at the Institute for Art and Architecture of the Academy of Fine Arts Vienna. With exchanges at the Bartlett School of Architecture London and the Universidade do Porto. Her works are at the interface of art and architecture, and these are characterized by process-oriented approaches and interdisciplinarity—with a focus on the interaction of society and space. In 2018 she worked on several short film projects together with Christopher Gruber, which were exhibited during the art festival in Ravensburg.

Ursula Frohne is a professor of art history at the Westfälische Wilhelms-Universität Münster (Germany). Over the past two decades, she held the same position at the University of Cologne as well as at International University Bremen (both Germany) and was a visiting professor at the Department of Modern Culture & Media at Brown University (USA). Prior to embarking on her academic career, she worked as Chief Curator at the ZKM Center for Art & Media (Karlsruhe, Germany). She has published widely on the sociology of the artist, contemporary art practice, and technological media (photography, film, video, installation), political dimensions, and socioeconomic conditions of art and visual culture.

Christina Jauernik studied art and architecture at the Academy of Fine Arts Vienna and the University of Arts Berlin, contemporary dance at the MTD Hogeschool voor de Kunsten Amsterdam, and choreography and visual arts practices at Dartington College of Arts, UK. From 2012 she has worked with Wolfgang Tschapeller ZT GmbH and since 2014 as artistic researcher with the INTRA SPACE team under the direction of Wolfgang Tschapeller. She has received the Start Scholarship for Architecture and Design from BKA 2016, the Margarete Schütte Lihotzky Scholarship 2015, IMPACT13 Scholarship PACT Zollverein Essen, Danceweb Scholarship 2006, and was nominated on the shortlist of the MAK Schindler Scholarship in 2017. Among others, Christina Jauernik has participated in the exhibition and publication project by Wolfgang Tschapeller, "Hands have no tears to flow: reports from | without architecture" commissioned for the Austrian Pavilion, Venice Biennale of Architecture, 2012.

Biographies

Vicki Kirby is Professor of Sociology in the
School of Social Sciences, University of
New South Wales, Sydney. The motivating
question behind her research is the puzzle
of the nature/culture, body/mind, body/
technology division, because so many political and ethical decisions are configured
in terms of its developmental assumptions
and asymmetries. Vicki Kirby is also interested in "the language question"—what is
language and how does the way we answer
that question define the human and inau-
gurate the political? Vicki brings feminism
and deconstruction into conversation in
innovative ways in order to contest and
reconfigure these taken-for-granted
structures of thought. Her books include:
What If Culture Was Nature All Along?
(2017); *Quantum Anthropologies: Life at
Large* (2011), *Judith Butler: Live Theory*
(2006); and *Telling Flesh: The Substance
of the Corporeal* (1997). She has held many
research positions, including Erasmus
Mundus Professor Utrecht University; visiting
professor, Institute of Advanced Study in
the Humanities and Social Sciences, University of Bern; Visiting Human Sciences
Professor, George Washington University;
Humanities Research Centre Visiting
Fellow, Australian National University; and
Auckland University Foundation Fellow.
Brown University is documenting her research
in their Feminist Theory Papers at Pembroke
Center's Christine Dunlap Farham Archives,
John Hay Library. Kirby is also a founding
member, Advisory Board Digital Semiotics
Encyclopedia; a member of Terra Critica;
international editorial advisory Board
Borderlands journal; editorial board, *New
Materialisms Series*, Edinburgh University
Press; editorial associate, *Critical Post-
humanisms*; advisory board, *Itineration:
Cross-Disciplinary Studies in Rhetoric,
Media, and Culture* journal; Science
Advisory Committee, Semiotica, filosofi,
arte, letteratura, Athanor Book Series,
Milan; Editorial Board Member: *New Critical
Humanities*; Editorial Board Member:
Experimental Practices Series, Brill; Inter-
national Advisory Board, *Catalyst:
Feminism, Theory, and Technoscience*
journal.

Ludwig Löckinger studied cinematography at
University of Music and Performing Arts
Vienna (Filmakademie Wien). He works as
a cinematographer and realizes his own film
projects. He also works as senior lecturer
at the Academy of Fine Arts Vienna.
Filmography: *180 – Hundertachtzig* (2000,
50 min., 35 mm); *Die Freisetzung* (2007,
11 min., 35 mm); *Jeannette* (2009, 13 min.,
HDCAM); *Daschka* (2011, 17 min., HDCAM);
Oxytocin (2016, 11 min., DCP).

Hannes Mayer is an architect and Senior
Researcher at Gramazio Kohler Research,
Chair for Architecture and Digital Fabrication at ETH Zurich, where he oversees
all research and teaching and directs the
master's program in Architecture and
Digital Fabrication (MAS DFAB). Prior to
joining ETH Zurich, Hannes Mayer was the
Roland Rainer Chair 2014/15 – Professor
for Architectural Design and Research at
the Academy of Fine Arts in Vienna and
taught design studios and postgraduate
design research at the Bartlett School of
Architecture (UCL) as well as University of
Westminster, London. In parallel, he was
the director and editor-in-chief of the
thematic review for architecture archithese
until he started publishing his own magazine
manege für architektur in 2016. The same
year he was artist in residence at Villa
Kamogawa, Goethe Institut, Kyoto. Hannes
Mayer is a frequent lecturer and visiting
critic and a prolific initiator as well as
experienced chair of public events. His
more than seventy articles on architecture
and related fields have been published in
AD, ARCH+, archithese, *a+u, Baumeister,
trans, Werk, Bauen + Wohnen,* as well as in
various edited books.

Diane Shooman received her PhD in comparative literature from Brown University in
1987, and taught at Oberlin College, Clark
University, and Skidmore College before
moving to Vienna in 1990. She teaches
"Comparative Forms of Art" (Vergleiche
künstlerischer Disziplinen) in the Department
of Painting & Graphic Art of the Institute
of Fine Arts and Cultural Studies at the University of Art in Linz, and Humanities at the
UAS Technikum-Wien. Diane Shooman was
a Core Adjunct Faculty member of the
Hollins University/American Dance Festival
MFA program in dance from Summer
2008–Summer 2010. She authored a Q&A
dance column called "Ask Dr Shooman"
(Fragen Sie Dr Shooman) for the Viennese
cultural weekly *Falter*, where she has also
published guest essays on dance. Diane

gave a keynote lecture called "Dance in the Circular City" at the Austrian Studies Association Conference in March 2015. She held a talk at the INTRA SPACE research project symposium in April 2016, and was the guest speaker for the EU project "Dancing Museums" in May 2016. Shooman received the "Oswald" Prize for Best Actress in a Leading Role for the Sparverein die Unzertrennlichen in 1999, has moderated a variety of art and music events, and was a vocalist/harmonizer/dancer for the band Chrono Popp und die Sorry Babies for five years. While cultivating her own musical oeuvre, and perpetually pondering how to counter a politics of art that paradoxically excludes the perceptual needs and potential of the body in a critical discourse on the manipulation and exploitation of the body, Shooman is currently pursuing research on the choreographies of George Balanchine and William Forsythe, the corporeality of music, literature, architecture, and art, and—always! —moving in and loving the mercurial city.

Susanne Thurow is a post-doctoral research fellow at UNSW's iCinema Centre, where her research focuses on performative aesthetics as opened up by new digital technologies. She holds a PhD from Christian-Albrechts-Universität zu Kiel (CAU, Germany), which explored the hybrid aesthetics of contemporary Australian Indigenous theater (Routledge, 2019). Her professional background in the past ten years has been further consolidated by work for companies such as Thalia Theater (Hamburg), Big hART Inc., the Universities of Melbourne and Sydney, Goethe Institut, as well as CAU.

Wolfgang Tschapeller is an architect working in Vienna. He initially trained as a carpenter, and studied architecture at the University of Applied Arts in Vienna and at Cornell University in Ithaca, NY. Wolfgang Tschapeller has taught as a visiting professor at Cornell University; the University of Art and Design in Linz, Austria; and the State University of New York in Buffalo, as well as other academic institutions. In 2004/05, he was the McHale Fellow at the State University of New York in Buffalo. Since 2005, Wolfgang Tschapeller has been a professor of architecture at the Academy of Fine Arts in Vienna and as of 2012 has been the head of the Institute of Art and Architecture. Since 2013, he has been visiting professorial fellow at the iCinema Research Center at the University of New South Wales, Australia. Wolfgang Tschapeller lectures internationally, recently at the SAC Städelschule Architecture Class, Frankfurt am Main, in May 2019. His major projects include the BVA 1, 2, and 3 series for the Vienna headquarters of the Austrian Insurance Fund for Public Employees, the design for the construction of a hotel in the Schwarzenberg Palace Garden in Vienna, and the European Cultural Centre between the Palatine Chapel and the city hall in Aachen, Germany. In 1998 and 2006, he worked on projects for Linz Opera House, in 2010 on the project for the Centre for Promotion of Science in Belgrade, in 2012 on a project for the University of Applied Arts Vienna and since 2014 the Fine Arts Library for Cornell University, Ithaca NY. The administrative building of the municipal authority in Murau, Austria, completed in 2002, and the St. Joseph House (2007) embody some of his quintessential ideas. Wolfgang Tschapeller ZT GmbH was founded in 2007 in Vienna, with Wolfgang Tschapeller as its managing director.

Birk Weiberg is research associate at the Zurich University of the Arts and the Lucerne University of Applied Sciences and Arts, where is he is currently involved in research projects on the digitization of behavioral biology and post-photography. He studied art history, media theory, philosophy, and media arts in Karlsruhe and Berlin. Birk Weiberg gained his PhD in art history from the University of Zurich with a thesis on the development of optical effects in Hollywood cinema. He was a visiting scholar at the California Institute of the Arts and a junior fellow at the Internationales Kolleg für Kulturtechnikforschung und Medienphilosophie (IKKM) in Weimar. His current research focuses are histories and aesthetics of photographic images, post-digital culture, artistic practices and research, and the digital transformation of research practices.

John Zissovici teaches architectural design and courses that deal with the impact of digital media on architectural thinking. His current research centers on imagescape urbanism. His architectural work includes built projects, installations, competitions, and speculative work. He has been published in Japan, Austria, Germany, Ireland, and the US. His large-scale installations involving digital media, robotics, and videos have been exhibited at the Phoenix Museum of Art, the Burchfeld-Penney Art Center, Tsing Ha University in Beijing, and the Herbert F. Johnson Museum of Art in Ithaca, NY. John Zissovici received his bachelor's and master's of architecture from Cornell University.

This book emerges from the artistic research project "INTRA SPACE, the reformulation of architectural space as a dialogical aesthetic" (2015–17) directed by Wolfgang Tschapeller, Institute for Art and Architecture, Academy of Fine Arts Vienna in collaboration with Michael Wimmer, Institute for Computer Graphics and Algorithms, Technical University Vienna. A project funded by FWF Der Wissenschaftsfonds/Austrian Science Fund, PEEK AR299-G21.

Project Team: Esther Balfe, Gabrielle Cram, Dennis Del Favero, Dmytro Fedorenko, Christian Freude, Ursula Frohne, Nils Hasler, Christina Jauernik, Ludwig Löckinger, Mohammad Obaid, Simon Oberhammer, Martin Perktold, Franz Pomassl, Diane Shooman, Michael Thielscher, Tom Tucek, Birk Weiberg, Michael Wimmer

Advisory Board: Karen Barad, Marcos Cruz, Bojana Kunst, Sanford Kwinter, Maria Palazzi, Jürgen Sandkühler

] a [academy of fine arts vienna

Sternberg Press